T0329487

PANIC IN THE SENATE

PANIC IN THE SENATE

THE FIGHT OVER THE SECOND BANK OF THE UNITED STATES AND THE AMERICAN PRESIDENCY

By Michael J. Trapani

Algora Publishing
New York

Library of Congress Cataloging-in-Publication Data

Names: Trapani, Michael, 1982- author.
Title: Panic in the Senate: the fight over the Second Bank of the United
    States and the American presidency / Michael Trapani.
Other titles: Fight over the Second Bank of the United States and the
    American presidency
Description: New York: Algora Publishing, 2021. | Includes bibliographical
    references and index. | Summary: "President Andrew Jackson campaigned
    passionately to limit the power of the federal government and that of
    the central bank. In a story that resonates today, this book analyzes
    the heated debates over the role of the President, and how much power
    the central bank (now called "the Fed") could exercise in controlling
    the nation's economy"— Provided by publisher.
Identifiers: LCCN 2020057076 (print) | LCCN 2020057077 (ebook) | ISBN
    9781628944556 (trade paperback) | ISBN 9781628944563 (hardcover) | ISBN
    9781628944570 (pdf)
Subjects: LCSH: Bank of the United States (1816-1836)—History. | Jackson,
    Andrew, 1767-1845. | United States. Congress (23rd, 1st session:
    1833-1834). Senate. | Executive power—United States. | Banks and
    banking, Central—United States—History—19th century. | Banks and
    banking—United States—History—19th century. | United States—Politics
    and government—1829-1837.
Classification: LCC HG2525 .T73 2021 (print) | LCC HG2525 (ebook) | DDC
    332.1/1097309034—dc23
LC record available at https://lccn.loc.gov/2020057076
LC ebook record available at https://lccn.loc.gov/2020057077

For Kelly, Addison, and Everly

Table of Contents

Introduction   1

Chapter 1: The Commencement of Hostilities   7

Chapter 2: A Question of All Time   17

Chapter 3: As the Legislature Commands   35

Chapter 4: And This is Republicanism!!!   51

Chapter 5: A New and Detestable Feature   71

Chapter 6: At Any Time Otherwise Order and Direct   89

Chapter 7: The Bank Has Fallen   107

Chapter 8: Sentinels in this Institution   123

Chapter 9: We Are All Political Electioneers   143

Chapter 10: An Army of Retainers   159

Chapter 11: Efficient and Immediate Relief   171

Chapter 12: The Vote and the Aftermath   179

Final Thoughts   191

Acknowledgements   193

BIBLIOGRAPHY   197
    Government Documents   197
    Books, Articles, and Dissertations   197
    Published Correspondence, Public Papers, Letters and Memoirs   199
    Newspapers   200

INDEX   201

INTRODUCTION

On a particularly tense March day in the United States Senate, Henry Clay, who commanded the floor, speaking on behalf of Philadelphia mechanics who had been crushed by Andrew Jackson's war with the Second Bank of the United States, turned his attention to Vice President Martin Van Buren, who was presiding over the session. The Kentuckian, with the eyes and ears of a packed gallery fixed upon him, implored the vice president to:

> "Go to him and tell [Jackson], without exaggeration, but in the language of truth and sincerity, the actual condition of his bleeding country. Tell him it is nearly ruined and undone by the measures which he has been induced to put in operation...Depict to him, if you can find language to portray, the heart-rending wretchedness of thousands of the working classes cast out of employment. Tell him of the tears of helpless widows, no longer able to earn their bread, and of unclad and unfed orphans who been driven, by his policy, out of the busy pursuits in which but yesterday they were gaining an honest livelihood...Entreat him to pause, and to reflect that there is a point beyond which human endurance cannot go, and let him not drive this brave generous, and patriotic people to madness and despair."[1]

Clay's impassioned plea to the vice president brought women in the gallery to tears. At that point, Van Buren ordered another senator to take his chair so he could descend to the floor and perhaps confront Clay on his direct challenge. The gallery held its collective breath at the possibility of a brawl on the Senate floor as Van Buren approached his challenger. Instead, the vice president calmly asked the Kentuckian "for another pinch of [his]

---

[1] *Register of Debates*, 23rd Cong., 1st sess. (Mar. 7, 1834), 831-832 (Senate).

1

aromatic Maccoboy." Clay obliged, Van Buren took a pinch from Clay's gold-plated snuff box, and the tension thus eased.[1]

Such was the story of one of the more dramatic moments of what became known as the Panic Session of 1833–1834. The Panic Session was the latest battlefield of Andrew Jackson's crusade against the Second Bank of the United States, what would be dubbed, the Bank War. The Bank War was the single most important political battle fought in the antebellum period outside of the slavery issue. Its outcome forced a shift in the basic structure of the nation's economy, a structure that, save for a brief five year interlude, governed its finances since the time of Washington. Central banking, according to fair observers, had created a stable financial structure for the nation, providing capital for Americans that allowed them to keep up with a world that was fast modernizing and industrializing. By destroying the BUS and railing so emphatically against paper money in general, Jackson and his supporters committed themselves to an alternate financial system that would have serious implications for the country moving forward.

Perhaps more importantly, the Bank War brought forth political changes that would shape the country's future as it tumbled undaunted down the path to civil war. The remnants of the two-party system that had coalesced into a jumbled political mess following the War of 1812 had begun restoring itself under two new banners with only loose ties to the old parties as Andrew Jackson rose to power. The Bank War would solidify the pro and anti-Jackson forces into two cohesive parties that would vie for control of the nation for the next two decades.

Finally, from the ashes of the Bank War emerged an office of the president far different than the one that existed at the war's onset. Prior to the Bank War, presidents watched over the nation with a somewhat detached eye, careful to let the country run itself through Congress and intervening when national interest required them to do so. Andrew Jackson's prosecution of the Bank War changed the presidency forever, leaving the office with greater authority and a more intimate connection to the people than had been previously conceived.

For these reasons, the Bank War has become a fixture in any history of the period. Scores of able historians have tackled the issue, whether within a survey of the Jackson era (or however an individual historian may choose to label the period), within a history of banking in the United States, or in works specifically devoted to the Bank War. Considering the voluminous literature already available, I do not condescend to believe I can offer any

---

[1] Pierre-Marie Loizeau, *Martin Van Buren: The Little Magician* (New York: Nova Science Publishers, Inc., 2008), 112.

grand revelation that will compel a fundamental change in how the Bank War is viewed. This book serves a different, but equally important function.

Writing surveys of the Jacksonian era is a daunting task. The sheer volume of crucial events that must be covered in order to paint a full picture of the time forces those brave enough to take on the task to choose moments to analyze in-depth and others at which to make only brief stops. Banking and economic histories of the period are abundant as well, but many focus on the complex particulars of banking and economic policy. While the Bank War figures prominently in these works, the focus often remains on its economic impacts. Specific books and articles on the Bank War are also widely available, but the topic is so complex, much like the era it occurred within, that historians are forced to write either a general history to provide readers with a digestible and accessible account, or focus on one specific aspect of the war and illustrate its impact on the overall outcome. This last piece is where this book fits into the historiography of the Bank War.

This book is an examination of the debates that occurred in the Senate during the 23rd Congress, specifically between December, 1833 and April, 1834. The Panic Session, as it came to be known, is one of those specific aspects of the Bank War that has received much attention from historians, but none have ventured deeply into the details of what individual senators argued and how they drew upon the Constitution and the earliest debates that built the country's structure of government to support and refute one another. These arguments laid bare before the nation the competing views on two of the most pressing political questions that consumed the country at that time: In what direction would the country move economically and what was the government's role in that movement? And, perhaps more importantly, would Andrew Jackson be permitted seize for himself and future presidents power many at the time felt the office was never meant to have? The overwhelming majority of coverage on the Panic Session in the Senate focuses on the resolutions put forth by Henry Clay, how prominent senators such as Daniel Webster and John C. Calhoun argued on their behalf, and how the Jacksonian opposition, generally condensed down into the words of Thomas Hart Benton, pushed back against them. Trimming down the three month debate to the words of just these men fails to capture the complexity of the constitutional arguments and debates over the merits of central banking that consumed the session. Contributions of men such as Samuel Southard, Theodore Frelinghuysen, Peleg Sprague, and Thomas Ewing on the anti-Jacksonian side, and Ether Shepley, William Wilkins, Felix Grundy, and Nathaniel Tallmadge, on the Jacksonian side, are critical to achieving a full understanding of how the Bank War took the country down the political path it did.

The Panic Session in the Senate is of utmost importance to outcome the Bank War, as the upper chamber was home to the most vocal and influential Jackson opponents. Indeed, if Jackson was to be defeated it would be the anti-Jacksonian majority in the Senate that would deliver the fatal blow. Likewise, if Old Hickory could emerge from the session alive if not bloodied, it would be unlikely that a stronger, more able force could emerge to muster any true threat to his designs. In short, the Panic Session was the climax of the Bank War and while the conflict would continue after the session's end, its outcome was decided. Such a crucial event requires a much deeper analysis than is presently available.

I do not say this to disparage any of those who have written on the Bank War in the past. Their works are comprehensive and necessary pieces of history, without which our understanding of the Jacksonian era would be severely limited. I wrote this book to fill in a gap in the story. To add a piece of the puzzle that is there, but needs to be pushed in fully in order to see the whole picture. The book begins with a brief overview of the origins of the Bank War and its state at the time the Senate convened in December, 1833. It continues with a look at the first month of the session and how the actions the Jackson administration took while the Senate was out of session planted the seeds of the panic which was to follow. The core of the book revolves around the two resolutions proposed by Henry Clay censuring the president and the Treasury secretary for their actions in regards to the Bank. This part of the book dives deep into the Senate *Register of Debates* to provide the reader with the senators' own words and to create a conversation between them as if it were happening in real time when in reality, the conversation spanned over three months. Framing the discussion by theme allows for the formulation of a constant, cohesive dialogue between multiple senators when days or weeks separated their individual comments. Creating this cohesive dialog was by far the most challenging aspect in writing this book. Finally, the book concludes with a look at the aftermath of the session and its impact on the political and economic future of the country.

History is, first and foremost, a story. A story to inform, a story to entertain. For far too long, too many people's stories had been ignored, left untold. The twenty-first century historian has done a fantastic job bringing those untold stories to life by committing them to paper for the world to enjoy. The ignored have largely been marginalized groups who had to struggle for recognition and respect in a world that did not view them as equals. But one does not necessarily need to be part of a marginalized group to be ignored by history. Even those who had risen to the lofty status of a United States senator could be forgotten by history, drowned out by larger than life personalities who have captivated the minds of generations of Americans. This book is meant to illuminate their contributions to a most crucial debate in American history and allow them to join their more well-known colleagues in this fight for America's future.

Anytime richness can be added to an already robust story is exciting to all who share a love and passion for history. This particular story begins in Washington D.C. on pleasant fall day in 1833.

CHAPTER 1: THE COMMENCEMENT OF HOSTILITIES

On the afternoon of September 23, 1833, Roger B. Taney sat down at his desk and attended to his work for the day. Among his daily chores was keeping up with his correspondence and included with his letters on the pleasant early fall day was one from Andrew Jackson, President of the United States. For Taney, receiving a letter from the president was nothing out of the ordinary. Taney was Jackson's attorney general and had become one of his closest political allies, working his way into the not-so-secret group of the president's confidants known as the Kitchen Cabinet. This missive though was of greater importance than anything the president had previously sent him. The message within was short and direct:

> Sir, Having informed William J. Duane Esqr, this morning that I have no further use for his services as Secretary of the Treasury of the United States, I hereby appoint you Secretary of the Treasury in his stead, and hope you will accept the same and enter upon the duties of said office forthwith, so that no injury may accrue to the public service.[1]

The information came as no surprise to Taney; he himself had penned the order relieving Duane of his duties as Treasury secretary delivered earlier that morning.[2] The nomination of the 56-year-old Maryland attorney to take charge of nation's treasury served as the Old General's latest strike in his

---

[1] John Spencer Bassett and David Maydole Matteson, eds., *Correspondence of Andrew Jackson: Volume V 1833-1838* (Washington D.C.: Carnegie Institution of Washington, 1931), 206, Hathitrust.org.

[2] *Correspondence of Andrew Jackson,* 206.

ongoing war with the Second Bank of the United States (BUS), a war he had been waging since his first days in office. Just three days later, the new secretary of the Treasury ordered the removal of the public deposits from the BUS and halted the deposit of all future public moneys as well.[1]

Some years earlier, the Second Bank of the United States had joined Jackson's impressive and lengthy list of opponents. Fighting was almost as reflexive as breathing for the old war hero; he had spent the majority of his life fighting, both literally and figuratively, against personal enemies. These enemies took many forms; individual people such as John C. Calhoun, John Quincy Adams, Henry Clay, and Nicholas Biddle were the highest profile on the long list of Jackson's adversaries. Jackson was not shy about picking fights with groups either. He fought Seminole Indians on the field of battle while Cherokee Indians fought him in the court of law. Institutions were no safer from Old Hickory's wrath; he snatched victory from the jaws of defeat in his battle with the Cherokee by openly defying a ruling from the Supreme Court allowing them to remain on their land rather than forcibly move west of the Mississippi like other tribes in the area. The response to the court's decision attributed to Jackson — "Marshall has made his decision, now let him enforce it" — is likely apocryphal but reveals Jackson's flippant attitude towards the court and his willingness to defy decisions opposed to his views. The BUS was an opponent akin to the latter type — a war against an American institution. Jackson never found a fight he would not engage in and rarely found one he could not win. The Second Bank of the United States, however, would serve as perhaps Jackson's most formidable opponent.

The heir to Alexander Hamilton's First Bank of the United States, the Second Bank of the United States commenced operations in 1816 and, like its predecessor, was granted a twenty year charter. Hamilton's bank met with considerable opposition from Jefferson and his Republican allies, opposition deriving from questions regarding its constitutionality, from the Bank's potential to wield tremendous political influence on the fledgling government, and from the strong likelihood that the Bank would create a moneyed aristocracy centered in the North. Despite these objections, Hamilton was able to convince Washington of the Bank's necessity to create a stable economic foundation for the young nation. By most standards, the Bank succeeded and the country's economy remained relatively stable throughout its twenty year lifespan.

---

[1] Despite the order, the deposits were not actually removed from the Bank. Instead, the government would deposit no future moneys with the Bank and allow the deposits already there drain out through regular expenditures. See, Ralph Catterall, *The Second Bank of the United States* (Chicago: University of Chicago Press, 1902), 295.

In 1811, as the sun was about to set on the First Bank's charter, the Republican-led Senate mustered enough anti-Bank sentiment to defeat a bill of renewal. Its defeat required the tie-breaking vote of Vice President George Clinton; this remains one of the most consequential tie-breaking votes a vice president has ever cast. In a turn of irony fit for a Shakespearean play, it was Henry Clay, twenty years later one of the Bank's strongest allies, who wrote the message Clinton submitted along with his negative vote. The bill's defeat came at a terrible time as by the following year, the United States would be at war with Great Britain but with no central financial institution to manage its economic activities. By war's end, the need for another national bank was obvious to provide a uniform national currency, provide credit for a rapidly growing economy, and market government securities.[1] Additionally, the influx of state banks in operation since the War of 1812 created a need for a central banking authority to corral their behavior.[2] Lastly, the desire for a national bank was also a part of a general plan to strengthen the national government, a plan many of the new stable of young Republicans, basking in the glory of an ambiguous victory, strongly advocated in the wake of the War of 1812.

The Second Bank of the United States did not get off to a good start. Just three years into its existence, the country plunged into a depression, the first of its kind during peacetime. Foreign goods flooded American markets following the resumption of trade with Europe after the War of 1812, creating a large trade deficit and necessitating the need for a protective tariff. At the same time, a sharp increase in European demand for American crops in 1816 stimulated a rise in demand for land to produce for the suddenly expanded market. These developments of course had little to do with the BUS and alone would be unlikely to create an economic crash, but the BUS added the necessary ingredients. The BUS fueled the land grab by the unregulated expansion of notes, especially among its western branches, which allowed for rampant speculation, creating a speculative bubble.[3] When the bubble burst, the western branches engaged in sharp curtailment of their loans which placed immense pressure on state banks to call in their own loans to remain solvent, leading to widespread foreclosures on western farms. Additionally, an abundant European harvest in 1818 reduced the demand for American grain and sent prices downward, an uptick in the cotton trade between Britain and India forced American cotton export prices down 50 percent, and political

---

[1] Daniel Walker Howe, *What Hath God Wrought: The Transformation of America, 1815-1848* (New York: Oxford University Press, 2007), 81.

[2] Arthur M. Schlesinger, Jr. *The Age of Jackson* (Boston: Little, Brown and Company, 1953), 9.

[3] Paul Kahan, *The Bank War: Andrew Jackson, Nicholas Biddle, and the Fight for American Finance* (Yardley, PA: Westholme Publishing, 2016), 24-25.

troubles in South America impeded the crucial acquisition of specie from Mexico. The coalescing of these factors created a depression that became known as the Panic of 1819, and although its causes were not entirely the fault of the BUS, many people, especially those who harbored ill-feelings towards the Bank to begin with, placed blame solely at its feet. Indeed, the Panic reawakened Old Jeffersonian Republicans' opposition to banking and paper money in general, thereby laying the foundation upon which Jackson would build his anti-Bank army.[1]

The BUS would recover though under the leadership of Nicholas Biddle. The 37-year-old Philadelphian inherited the mess left behind by the Panic of 1819 when he took over as president of the BUS for the departed Langdon Cheves in 1822. Although riddled with personal foibles, Biddle was, according to Robert Remini, "the best thing that ever happened to the Bank. He was a brilliant administrator, the prototype of the modern business executive, who had a genuine comprehension of the subtleties of banking...[and] he transformed...a nationwide branch-banking system...into a bona-fide central bank."[2]

Biddle took various steps to put the Bank on sound footing but the most important was his ability to provide a safe and uniform currency for the country. By issuing bank drafts in small amounts, Biddle circumvented the requirement that all BUS bank notes be signed by the president and cashier — a requirement making it virtually impossible for the Bank to issue notes in small denominations, leaving the task of circulating widely used small notes to the state banks and thus perpetuating their usefulness. These small denomination drafts, that were made to look indistinguishable from BUS notes, could be issued by any BUS branch with the signature of the branch president. Receivable for tax payments to the government, the branch drafts passed as money. In a corresponding move, Biddle called on state banks to redeem, in specie, notes held by the BUS. These dual actions worked to drive the state currencies out of circulation, leaving BUS notes and drafts as the only sound and stable currency. Although a bit cutthroat, Biddle's policy moves allowed the BUS to prosper and by the time Jackson took over as president, it had achieved widespread popularity and support among the people.[3]

Jackson's ill feelings toward the Bank can be at least partially explained by the financial losses he sustained during the Panic of 1819 and his constitu-

---

[1] Cathy Matson, "Matthew Carey's Learning Experience: Commerce, Manufacturing, and the Panic of 1819," *Early American Studies: An Interdisciplinary Journal* 11, no. 3 (Fall 2013): 473.

[2] Robert V. Remini, *Andrew Jackson and the Bank War: A Study in the Growth of Presidential Power* (New York: W.W Norton & Company Inc., 1967), 35.

[3] Remini, *Jackson and the Bank War*, 37-39.

tional scruples regarding Congress's authority to create a national bank. The Bank also bestowed unfair privileges on a select and undeserving few which posed a direct threat to the simple, egalitarian republican society Jackson sought to restore where all white men had equal opportunity to succeed on the strength of their own labor.[1] Lastly, the president despised the preponderance of British investors in BUS stock. Jackson feared that British influence over the Bank, and by extension the nation's economic system, would restore British authority over its former colonies, thereby reversing the hard fought American victory in their war for independence.[2]

Despite these misgivings, it does not appear that Jackson entered the White House with the intention of destroying the Bank.[3] His animosity towards the BUS heightened, though, when he learned that it supported John Quincy Adams and anti-Jackson congressional candidates in the election of 1828. Jackson's hostility to the Bank thus took the form of a dangerous concoction of practical opposition and personal animus. Despite investigations of electioneering launched by the administration, Biddle seems to have remained confident about the safety of his bank during Jackson's first year. Even the president's annual message to Congress, delivered in December, 1829, did not shake Biddle's confidence, although it probably should have. The president talked of the importance of considering at that time the question of recharter with the Bank's expiration just a few years away and then added a damning assessment: "Both the constitutionality and the expediency of the law creating this Bank are well questioned by a large portion of our fellow citizens; and it must be admitted by all that it has failed in the great end of establishing a uniform and sound currency."[4] The wild inaccuracy of the statement aside, Jackson made clear his position on the Bank; he did not approve of it as presently constituted and wanted to see changes.[5]

Although not overly concerned about the Bank's future after Jackson's address, Biddle took steps to ensure the public was aware of its usefulness. In early 1830, Biddle worked with pro-BUS Jacksonian, Samuel Smith, who chaired the Senate Finance Committee, to launch an investigation into the

---

[1] Strictly speaking, such a society had never existed in America, and therefore it could not be truly "restored." However, in Jackson's mind, this society had once existed and one at least resembling it still did; and the BUS was inimical to its full restoration. See, Harry L. Watson, *Liberty and Power: The Politics of Jacksonian America* (New York: Hill and Wang, 2006 [first edition 1990]), 148.

[2] Watson, *Liberty and Power*, 144.

[3] Bray Hammond, *Banks and Politics in America: From the Revolution to the Civil War* (Princeton, NJ: Princeton University Press, 1957), 370.

[4] This assessment of the Bank was written by Colonel James Hamilton, son of Alexander Hamilton. A succinct explanation for how Hamilton came to write that passage can be found in, Remini, *Jackson and the Bank War*, 61-63.

[5] Remini, *Jackson and the Bank War*, 65.

---

claims made by the president in his address. The final report, written by Biddle himself (although his authorship was not revealed), maintained that the BUS was constitutional and had provided the country with a stable and sound currency. The House conducted their own investigation and developed a report that reached the same conclusions. The reports so lauded the Bank and its benefits to the country that Biddle seemed concerned the President would take offense from being so roundly contradicted. If Biddle was concerned, he certainly had an odd way of showing it — using BUS funds, Biddle had the committee reports printed and distributed widely. This move irritated Jackson more than the reports themselves.[1]

Throughout 1830, Biddle sought to ingratiate himself to Jackson by forming bonds with the pro-Bank members of his inner circle, William Lewis most extensively. These efforts seemed to further agitate Jackson, who believed his news organs were doing a poor job of espousing his more critical views of the Bank and that perhaps Biddle's meddling was working to affect pro-Bank sentiment within his circle. Nevertheless, Lewis still wrote confidently to Biddle in May that Jackson would not oppose a National Bank with such modifications as to ease the Old General's stated concerns. Biddle received a letter of similar sanguinity regarding the Bank's chances for recharter in July from Josiah Nichol, a friend of Jackson's. The president dashed hopes for a simple compromise with Biddle to recharter the bank, however, in his second annual address to Congress given in December. Jackson announced that nothing had changed since the previous year's address to ease his reservations about the Bank and he went on to suggest a new shell of a bank in place of the BUS, stripped of all power besides serving as an arm of the Treasury Department with its sole function being that of a depository for public funds and state notes.[2]

Although disappointed with Jackson's address, Biddle shrugged it off as mere bluster, and after the Peggy Eaton affair forced a reshuffling of Jackson's cabinet early in 1831 — a reshuffling that brought several friends of the Bank into the administration — Biddle had more reason to be optimistic.[3]

With Jackson's reelection bid approaching, the question now emerged as to whether or not the Bank's recharter would play a role in its outcome. The Bank should not have been an issue at all had it not been for what turned

---

[1] Stephen W. Campbell, *The Bank War and the Partisan Press: Newspapers, Financial Institutions, and the Post Office in Jacksonian America* (Lawrence, KS: University of Kansas Press, 2019), 50-51; Hammond, *Banks and Politics*, 378.

[2] Remini, *Jackson and the Bank War*, 67-70; Hammond, *Banks and Politics*, 378-382.

[3] The Peggy Eaton affair is a fixture in all Jacksonian era histories. A particularly nuanced and intriguing account is found in, Kirsten E. Wood, "'One Woman So Dangerous to Public Morals,' Gender and Power in the Eaton Affair," *Journal of the Early Republic* vol. 17 no. 2 (Summer 1997): 237-275.

out to be a horrible political miscalculation by Biddle with an assist from some prominent National Republicans.[1] Jackson knew the Bank was a polarizing issue and one that could cut deeply into his electoral advantage or even cost him the election. The latter did not concern Jackson much — he was supremely confident that he would win regardless of the status of the Bank — but it was extremely important to him that his margin of victory exceeded his 1828 triumph. With a Bank-friendly majority in Congress, a recharter bill would surely pass and force Jackson to either sign it, thus alienating supporters in New York who opposed the monster bank, or veto the bill at the risk of losing pro-bank men in Pennsylvania. To avoid such a dilemma, Biddle and Jackson reached a tentative agreement, with new Secretary of Treasury Louis McLane serving as the intermediary. Jackson would allow the rechartering of the BUS as long as Biddle waited until after the election to apply for it.[2]

The president seemed to hold up his end of the bargain by announcing on December 6, 1831, in his third annual address to Congress, that although he still harbored his old misgivings about the Bank, he would leave the question of its recharter to the people and Congress. But Biddle was not satisfied; he had been led to believe by McLane that Jackson would abandon the reservations he had voiced in his previous two annual addresses.[3] Jackson had at least considered this but Taney, at that point his attorney general, convinced him that such a statement would amount to a surrender to Biddle. Jackson followed Taney's advice and reaffirmed his displeasure with the BUS "as at present organized."[4] Perhaps convinced that the tentative agreement with Jackson would not bear fruit, Biddle fell in line with the urging of prominent National Republicans and influential directors who served on the Bank's board to submit the recharter bill to Congress before the election.[5] Already chosen as the party nominee, Henry Clay wanted to put the bank on the ballot hoping to ride its popularity to victory. On January 9, 1832, both houses were a presented a bill rechartering the Second Bank of the United States. After months of wrangling, the bill passed in the Senate on June 11 by a 28-20 vote and in the House of Representatives on July 3 by a vote of 107-85.[6] Jackson

---

[1] Catterall, *The Second Bank*, 215-218. Catterall downplays Clay's influence over Biddle in pushing for early recharter, claiming that Biddle ultimately made the decision on his own. He does concede though that prominent National Republicans such as John Sargeant, Daniel Webster, and Clay to a lesser extent may have helped push Biddle to his final decision.

[2] Hammond, *Banks and Politics*, 383.

[3] Remini, *Jackson and the Bank War*, 73-74; Catterall, *The Second Bank*, 212-213.

[4] Hammond, *Banks and Politics*, 384; Catterall, *The Second Bank*, 213.

[5] Hammond, *Banks and Politics*, 385.

[6] Catterall, *The Second Bank*, 235.

promptly vetoed the bill, and on July 10, sent to Congress perhaps the most consequential veto message issued by a United States president, thus staging the election as a contest between the anti-Bank Jackson and the pro-Bank Clay, precisely as Clay hoped. Clay, though, misjudged the Bank's appeal, Jackson's popularity, or both; Jackson won by a crushing electoral margin (although his share of the popular vote shrank slightly from 1828). Biddle and the National Republicans gambled that the Bank's popularity would trump that of Old Hickory, but it was not to be. The gamble accomplished nothing more than drawing out the fullest extent of Jackson's wrath toward the BUS. By putting the Bank on the ballot against the enormously popular and equally vengeful Jackson, Biddle had all but signed its death warrant.[1]

To Jackson, his victory signaled a mandate from the people to kill the Bank now rather than wait for it to die naturally on March 3, 1836, when its charter expired. Besides, as far as the vindictive Jackson was concerned, a natural death was too kind a fate for the Bank that had tried to destroy him, to embarrass him. The Bank needed to die now, and Jackson would deliver the death sentence. Removal of the public deposits would be the chosen method of execution. The only remaining obstacle for Jackson was finding a willing executioner.[2]

According to the Bank's charter, only the secretary of the Treasury could order the removal of the public deposits from the BUS, and Jackson found it difficult to find an obliging officer to carry out his sentence. There was little expectation that Secretary McLane, a friend of the Bank, would dole out Jackson's punishment, so the president needed to seek out a replacement more amenable to his wishes. Jackson decided on a Pennsylvanian and known opponent of the Bank, William J. Duane, to take charge of the Treasury Department. Duane, whose father was a devoted Old School Jeffersonian Republican who abhorred both commercial banks and paper money,

---

[1] Remini and Catterall both advance the view that the early recharter was a terrible miscalculation by Biddle and Clay and led to the Bank's ultimate destruction. Hammond recognizes the foolishness of engaging in combat with Jackson but feels he was going to kill the Bank regardless and so the decision to force its recharter did not play as large a role in its demise as others contend. For this view, see, Hammond, *Bank and Politics*, 386. Others have argued that putting the Bank on the ballot when he had maximum leverage over Jackson was Biddle's best chance to win the Bank War. For this view, see, Kahan, *The Bank War*, 92.

[2] It is generally believed that Jackson arrived at his decision to remove the deposits following his reelection. However, a letter from William Bradley to Henry Clay dated October 16, 1832 suggests the plan may have been hatched earlier. Bradley warned Clay that "a most nefarious scheme" was in the works; that if Jackson were reelected, the deposits would be removed from the BUS and deposited in certain state banks. See, William Bradley to Henry Clay, October 16, 1832, in *Papers of Henry Clay Volume 8: Candidate, Compromiser, Whig, March 5, 1829 — December 31, 1836*, eds. Robert Seager II and Melba Porter Hay (Lexington, Kentucky: University of Kentucky Press, 1984), 583.

seemed an obvious choice. As a Pennsylvania state legislator, the younger Duane led a movement against the governor's plan to relieve distress caused by the Panic of 1819 by expanding loans backed by paper. In 1829, he signed much publicized Philadelphia memorial in opposition to the BUS. These anti-Bank credentials gave Jackson confidence that he had found the right man to carry out his wishes, but the Old General would find his confidence misplaced.[1]

Duane, reluctant to take the position in the first place, accepted the position only after much cajoling from his predecessor and told Jackson of his decision on January 31, 1833.[2] McLane was reassigned to head the state department and Duane assumed his duties on June 1, 1833. Beginning on his first night as secretary, Duane was bombarded frequently by Jackson's closest advisors with questions about his desire to have the deposits removed and, much to the president's chagrin, Duane expressed strong objections. Although anxious to see the Bank close its doors, in a letter to Jackson he characterized the deposit scheme which would replace the BUS as "arbitrary and needless."[3] Duane so opposed the idea that he promised to resign if he could not move Jackson from his position.[4] Jackson, though, would not be swayed and on September 18, he had Taney read to his cabinet a paper enumerating his reasons for removing the deposits and, perhaps to assuage Duane's fears, the president expressed his insistence upon taking full responsibility for the decision. Removing the burden of responsibility did nothing to change the principled secretary's mind, and to make matters worse for Jackson, Duane now refused to resign his post as he had previously indicated. The two men exchanged letters and met personally over the next few days. Duane pushed to postpone the decision on removal until Congress reconvened in December, but the president refused the request. Jackson had finally had enough of his recalcitrant officer — Duane's dismissal soon followed, and so it goes how Taney got hold of the axe with which he would execute the BUS whose head lay precariously on the chopping block.[5]

---

[1] Sean Wilentz, *The Rise of American Democracy: Jefferson to Lincoln* (New York: W.W. Norton & Company, 2005), 212, 395.

[2] William J. Duane, *Narrative and Correspondence Concerning the Removal of the Deposites and Occurrences Connected Therewith* (Philadelphia, 1838), 3-5.

[3] For Duane's full letter explaining to Jackson his reasons for opposing his plans, see, Duane, *Narrative*, 38-55.

[4] Duane, *Narrative*, 90.

[5] As the focus of this book is on the debate in the Senate over the removal of the deposits and not the entire Bank War, the treatment of the period between Jackson's rise to the presidency and the Taney's appointment as Secretary of Treasury is admittedly abbreviated. For more in-depth coverage of the period, see, Catterall, *Second Bank*, 186-305; Hammond, *Banks and Politics*, 326-423; Remini, *Jackson and the Bank War*, 49-125

Taney was a logical choice to carry out Jackson's order. By 1833, the attorney general had "so won upon the regard of General Jackson that he had become his most trusted and his most confidential advisor."[1] Taney aided the president in crafting his annual addresses to Congress that first hinted at Jackson's eventual course of ordering the deposits removed, he co-wrote Jackson's famous recharter veto message, and he expressed his positive views on removal in his official communications. When Jackson put the question of moving on from the BUS to his cabinet in March, 1833, Taney was only one who endorsed the president's proposal.[2] If the General needed any convincing to initiate the removal (it is likely that he did not), he got it in an August, 1833 letter from his loyal attorney general. Taney wrote that "the step [removal] should be taken before the meeting of Congress, because it is desirable that the members should be among their constituents when the measure is announced, and should bring with them, when they come here, the feelings and sentiments of the people."[3] He continued by voicing his adamant position that the Bank be stripped of its power through the removal of the deposits, but asserted his unwavering loyalty by assuring Jackson, "if you determine against [removal], I shall most cheerfully acquiesce, and shall cordially support any other course of proceeding which you think may be preferable." But the most important passage of the letter came at the end, where Taney assured Jackson that if he "find it necessary to call for my services, to aid in carrying [removal] into execution, they will be promptly and willingly rendered."[4] Jackson welcomed such assurances, knowing the intransigent Duane would be unlikely to carry out his wishes.

With the loyal Taney installed as head of the Treasury Department, Jackson's sentence against the BUS was carried out swiftly. When the 23rd Congress reconvened two months later, it would find itself locked in a heated debate over the ramifications of Jackson's and Taney's actions that would forever alter the role of the American president, the country's understanding of the Constitution, and its relationship with centralized banking.

---

[1] Samuel Tyler, *Memoir of Roger Brooke Taney, L.L.D.: Chief Justice of the Supreme Court of the United States* (Baltimore: John Murphy & Co., 1872), 190-191.

[2] Remini, *Jackson and the Bank War*, 113.

[3] Taney to Jackson, August 5, 1833, quoted in Remini, *Jackson and the Bank War*, 195-196.

[4] Taney to Jackson, August 5, 1833, quoted in Remini, *Jackson and the Bank War* 197.

Chapter 2: A Question of All Time

The first session of the 23rd Congress convened on December 2, 1833, just sixty days after Taney's order to remove the deposits from the BUS went into effect. The men who comprised the Senate at the start of the 23rd Congress are among the most talented and highly regarded to ever serve the country. Headlining the group were three of the greatest senators in the history of the institution: Henry Clay, John C. Calhoun, and Daniel Webster. While these three deserve the historical accolades that posterity has heaped upon them (as well as the criticism for their views on slavery), it would be a grave disservice to overlook the contributions to the grand debate of their colleagues — contributions in some ways exceeding even those of the Great Triumvirate. Among the forty-eight men who convened in December, 1833 sat thirteen former or future governors, five secretaries of State, seven other cabinet level secretaries, a Speaker of the House, and three vice presidents, one of whom out of necessity would become president of the United States. It is altogether fitting that such a distinguished Senate would tackle questions of such momentous proportion.

The immense popularity Jackson enjoyed throughout the country did not carry over to the Senate. Only twenty of the forty-eight members were Jackson men and before the end of the session, the president would lose another ally when William C. Rives of Virginia resigned his seat and was replaced by anti-Jacksonian, Benjamin W. Leigh.[1] An important source of

---

[1] Rives resigned after learning the Virginia state legislature directed its senators to vote in favor of restoring the deposits to the BUS. Unwilling to violate the wishes of his state and equally unwilling to compromise his own principles, Rives chose to resign.

Jackson's lack of support in the Senate stemmed from defections within his own party. No fewer than four members of the Senate were at one point Jackson men but had since abandoned the Old General, and one, Alabama's Gabriel Moore, could be counted as only a loose ally. Moore's trouble with the administration centered on his opposition to the appointment of Martin Van Buren as minister to Great Britain. Although Moore stuck by Jackson in his war against the BUS, his trust as a loyal Jacksonian eroded enough that the Alabama legislature requested he resign his seat. To this he refused, but was promptly defeated in his bid for reelection in 1837.[1]

One key defection was future president, John Tyler of Virginia. Tyler had only reluctantly supported Jackson in 1828. The Old General entered the White House touting majority rule and reduced federal power in favor of increased autonomy for the states, a model for government Tyler could get behind.[2] But the young Virginian was also a strict constructionist and he did not fully trust the new president, worrying that Jackson's rhetoric, while sincere, could become a vehicle to seize unprecedented, unconstitutional power. Despite these worries, Tyler eventually fell in line with the party in support of Old Hickory. Upon Jackson taking office, the reluctant Virginian's fears were soon realized. The appointment of a relatively uninspiring collection of cabinet members that Jackson could dominate if he chose to and the bestowing of patronage positions on loyalists regardless of their qualifications — a practice soon to be dubbed the spoils system — horrified Tyler and convinced him that Jackson was building a government machine entirely beholden to him.[3] The Nullification Crisis in 1832 brought Tyler to his breaking point; Jackson's support of the Force Bill revealed that his support of states' rights extended only to where the views of a state aligned with his own. Tyler's vote against the Force Bill served as his official break with Jackson. The authoritarian measures Jackson took in his war against the BUS further infuriated Tyler, and despite his own misgivings regarding the Bank, those concerns paled in comparison to concerns over the president's flagrant disregard for the Constitution and compelled Tyler to join Clay and his allies in denouncing him.[4]

---

[1] Thomas M. Owen, *History of Alabama and Dictionary of Alabama Biography, Volume IV* (Chicago: S.J. Clarke Publishing Company, 1921), 1224.

[2] Watson, *Liberty and Power*, 98.

[3] Rewarding political friends with patronage positions had become a somewhat accepted aspect of American government, but Jackson's use of patronage juxtaposed to the previous president, John Quincy Adams — who shunned patronage to the point of political disadvantage — alarmed men like Tyler. See, Watson, *Liberty and Power*, 85-86, 103-104.

[4] Oliver Perry Chitwood, *John Tyler: Champion of the Old South* (Newtown, CT: American Political Biography Press, 1939), 83-123.

At least one senator seems to have broken with Jackson over the Bank issue. In 1832, John Black of Mississippi was appointed as a Jacksonian Democrat to fill the Senate seat vacated by Powhatan Ellis. By the following November, when his seat came up for reelection, Black ran as an anti-Jacksonian. Little exists in the historical record to explain Black's change of heart, but a late 19th century study on the history of the Magnolia State hints quite strongly at the reason. In his chapter on future Jacksonian senator and Secretary of State Robert J. Walker, John Francis Claiborne discusses Walker's brief dabbling with the anti-Jacksonians over pecuniary losses he sustained due to the removal of the deposits. Walker wrote a letter to Black who had previously voiced his support of Walker's break from Jackson as Black, in Claiborne's words, "had gone over to the bank party."[1] The characterization of Black's political loyalties as "the bank party" strongly implicates Jackson's stance towards the bank as the source of the senator's defection.

Another key defection came from Willie P. Mangum of North Carolina. Mangum joined the Senate in 1831 as a Jacksonian and had in fact been one of the electors who cast a ballot for the Old General in 1828. Initially loyal to Jackson, Mangum voted in favor of Van Buren's nomination as minister to Great Britain, a nomination ultimately rejected thanks to the maneuverings of John C. Calhoun. He also voted against the bill to recharter the National Bank and supported Jackson's reelection bid. The battle over the tariff and nullification, though, would soon test his loyalty to Jackson and ultimately push him to the opposition. Like Tyler, Mangum supported states' rights and disapproved of nullification, but abhorred Jackson's threat of force against South Carolina. The Nullification Crisis, by pushing the North Carolinian to work with Clay and Calhoun against Jackson, weakened the bonds of Mangum's loyalty to the president, but the Bank War dissolved them completely. Although he had voted against the recharter bill in 1832, it was due more to his dislike of the bill itself rather than a disdain for central banking in general. Home state support for the BUS pushed Mangum further toward the pro-Bank side. The removal of the deposits cemented Mangum's break from the administration and he became one of the leading anti-Jackson voices in the Senate.[2] So important did Mangum become to the anti-Jackson (later Whig) movement that he would pick up a smattering of electoral votes in their unsuccessful attempt in 1836 to wrest the presidency away from Jackson's successor, Martin Van Buren.

[1] John Francis Hamtramck Claiborne, *Mississippi as a Province, Territory, and State: With Biographical Notices of Eminent Citizens Volume I* (Jackson, Mississippi: Power & Barksdale, 1880), 415.

[2] Henry Thomas Shanks, ed., *The Papers of Willie Person Mangum* (Raleigh: NC State Department of Archives and History, 1950), xxii-xxx.

Perhaps no break from Jackson was messier than that of Mississippi's George Poindexter, however. Poindexter had been instrumental in the creation of Mississippi's state constitution in 1817 — a document that while holding to some true Jeffersonian liberal principles, established strong safeguards for the growing cotton planter aristocracy. Jackson, as a fellow westerner and Indian fighter, had long since been a friend to Mississippians, and when he ran for president, the Magnolia State, Poindexter included, supported him. However, it soon became clear that Jacksonian democracy threatened the cotton aristocracy Poindexter had worked so hard to protect. Indian treaties forged by Jackson opened up the northern part of the state to be flooded by common folk looking for new opportunities. As one Poindexter biographer put it, "[c]otton conservatism was swept away in the wave of Jacksonian democracy." In 1832, the Mississippi legislature did away with Poindexter's state constitution and replaced it with one modeled after the new democracy of which Jackson had been anointed leader. For Poindexter, who had been elected to the Senate two years prior, the destruction of the constitution he had poured his heart and soul into creating compelled him to break with the president.[1] The break put the Mississippian on Jackson's list of enemies, and so bitter was the Old General at his former ally that when a deranged house painter named Richard Lawrence botched the first assassination attempt on a United States president in 1835, Poindexter was among those the paranoid Jackson accused of orchestrating it. Even though Poindexter denied any involvement and no evidence emerged to prove otherwise, Jackson's accusation was enough to cost him his bid for reelection.[2]

The Jacksonians certainly had their work cut out for them, facing, in the words of Thomas Benton, "the prodigious, scathing invective of American statesmen the most talented and powerful who ever united in opposition."[3] Clay, Webster, and Calhoun headlined the anti-Jacksonian contingent but they were joined by an impressive cast of able statesmen including Samuel Southard and Theodore Frelinghuysen from New Jersey, Thomas Ewing from Ohio, Peleg Sprague from Maine, and William Preston from South Carolina. On the other side, Benton headed an equally impressive stable of Jackson supporters headlined by Silas Wright and Nathaniel Tallmadge

---

[1] Mack Buckley Swearingen, *"The Early Life of George Poindexter: A Story of the First Southwest"* (PhD diss., University of Chicago, 1932), 158-159.

[2] Mel Ayton, *Plotting to Kill the President: Assassination Attempts from Washington to Hoover* (Potomac Books: Sterling, VA, 2017), 35; Though Lawrence was insane, the motive for the attack stemmed from Jackson's opposition to the BUS, which Lawrence felt would jeopardize the payment of a considerable sum of money he believed the government owed him.

[3] Thomas Hart Benton, quoted in, William Meigs Montgomery, *The Life of Thomas Hart Benton* (J.B Lippincott Company: Philadelphia, 1904), 228.

from New York, Felix Grundy from Tennessee, John Forsyth from Georgia, William Wilkins from Pennsylvania, Ether Shepley from Maine, and Isaac Hill from New Hampshire. Presiding over the session was Vice President Martin Van Buren whose political acumen elevated him to the top of Jackson's list of confidantes and would eventually secure for himself the designation as the Old General's handpicked successor. A somewhat humorous depiction of the Senate comprised during the 23rd Congress appeared in a February edition of the *Lancaster Examiner*:

> Mr. Van Buren and Mr. Forsyth would make a capital span; they look so much alike...Mr. Van Buren don't speak loud enough in the Senate; he talks like a mouse in a cheese. Mr. Clay speaks too loud when he whispers; all his neighbors overhear what he says...People say Mr. Preston wears a wig and that he almost gesticulated it off the other day. It is a pity Mr. Calhoun won't learn of him to pronounce correctly, for he clips off and chews up the tails of his words most cruelly...Isaac Hill is eternally writing letters. It costs the People dear to pay for his stationary...Grundy has a fine amiable countenance...Calhoun is rather too dogmatic in his manner...Wilkins looks as Lord Wellington looked in 1828. He is a good dancer in the bargain; Lord Wellington don't dance. The Senate Chamber presents a more dignified appearance than the House of Lords, but the Lords, never put their feet upon the desks.

Questionable desk etiquette certainly did not stop the members of the upper chamber from engaging in some of the fiercest debate in the history of the Senate.

***

On the second day of the session, the president, as stipulated by the Constitution, submitted a report on the current state of the Union. Towards the end of the report, Jackson wrote, "[s]ince the last adjournment of Congress, the Secretary of the Treasury has directed the money of the United States to be deposited in certain State banks designated by him, and he will immediately lay before you his reasons for this direction."[1] (Jackson curiously left out any mention of replacing Duane with Taney, although the members surely were already abreast of the change.) The Senate, undoubtedly anxious to hear an official explanation for the actions of the administration, would not have to wait long for further explanation — Taney's reasons for removal of the deposits arrived in the chamber and were read aloud the following day.[2]

Over the next few days, late-coming senators took their seats and the Panic Session of the winter of 1833–1834 began in earnest. On December

---

[1] *Senate Journal.* 23rd Cong., 1st sess., (Dec. 3, 1833), 15.
[2] Full examination of Taney's report can be found in chapters 8-9.

10, Henry Clay took to the Senate floor. Once the youngest man to serve in the United States Senate, by 1833, Clay had ascended to the top of the very impressive mountain of distinguished statesmen currently seated in the Senate chamber.[1] He addressed his colleagues with a sense of urgency, introducing a subject "perhaps exceeding in importance any other question likely to come before the present Congress."[2] The subject, of course, was the removal of the deposits. Having received Taney's reasons for the decision six days earlier, Clay reminded the Senate of their duty according to the charter, "to decide or not they were sufficient to justify the act."[3] Considering the weight of the question at hand — the state of the public treasury was of utmost importance — Clay proposed a motion that the full Senate begin considering the measure the following week rather than passing it on to a committee for examination.

This proposition was met with protest from one of Jackson's strongest defenders in the Senate, Thomas Hart Benton of Missouri. Benton and Jackson had a long history; the former served under Jackson in the War of 1812. Of greater interest, Benton and Jackson once came to blows over a dispute involving Benton's brother, Jesse. Jackson and his friend, General John Coffee, crossed paths with the Benton brothers near the City Hotel in Nashville on September 4, 1813. The combative Jackson threw some fighting words in their direction to which, the brothers did not react kindly. The ensuing brouhaha left Jackson with a gunshot wound in the left arm compliments of Jesse's pistol while Thomas narrowly avoided taking a bullet from Jackson's gun. Thomas did not escape unscathed, however — he tumbled down a flight of stairs and was then pistol-whipped by Coffee.[4] In the twenty years since the near fatal encounter, the two had put their past behind them and Benton became one of the president's staunchest anti-BUS allies, having proposed a resolution to the Senate in 1831 against the renewal of the Bank's charter that came within three votes of passing.[5]

While recognizing the Senate's authority to examine Taney's report, Benton implied that he would prefer to have it examined first by a committee,

---

[1] Clay replaced John Adair as a Senator from Kentucky after his resignation in November, 1806. At the time, Clay was only 29 years old and therefore constitutionally barred from serving in the Senate. There is no record, however, of his age having been an issue. See, James Klotter, *The Man Who Would Be President* (New York: Oxford University Press, 2016), 25-26.

[2] *Register of Debates*, 23rd Cong., 1st sess., (Dec. 10, 1833), 25 (Senate).

[3] *Register of Debates*, 23rd Cong., 1st sess., (Dec. 10, 1833), 25 (Senate).

[4] This story can be found in almost any Jackson biography. This particular version comes from, Jon Meacham, *American Lion: Andrew Jackson in the White House* (New York: Random House, 2009), 29-30.

[5] Wilentz, *The Rise of American Democracy*, 363.

considering the economic complexity of its contents and graveness of the charges against the Bank. He asked if his fellow senators "were now about to proceed to the consideration of this document as it stood, and, without receiving any evidence of the charges, or taking any course to establish their truth, to give back the money to this institution?" Without having a committee first investigate the report, Benton feared the Senate would be acting as both "witness and juror" and worried that taking up Clay's motion amounted to "an admission of the truth of every charge which had been made in the report, and as a flight from investigation." Benton also made clear his belief that the issue was more fitting to be first examined in the House, as that body initiates all revenue bills — an argument Benton would return to at a later date.[1] Despite his pleas to the contrary, Clay's motion passed and consideration of Taney's report was made the special order for the following Monday.

Clay rose once more to offer a resolution requesting that Jackson confirm the authenticity of the now famous cabinet paper read on September 18, 1833, and if genuine, submit a copy of it to the Senate. The resolution was then laid on the table until the following day when upon resumption of the discussion, John Forsyth voiced some confusion over the resolution. Specifically, he wondered what purpose bringing the paper before the Senate would serve and questioned why anyone would doubt its authenticity. Clay responded to the future secretary of State with stinging condescension, calling the reasons for the resolution "obvious" and saying that therefore "he had not thought it necessary to suggest them."[2] To appease the Georgian, Clay explained his reasoning. First, the paper was read to the cabinet and then circulated out to the public as the president's words. However, Jackson offered no official statement to the Senate confirming the authenticity of the paper. Had the paper remained a private communication between the president and his cabinet, Clay pointed out, there would be no need to call for its authenticity, as it would be privileged executive business. But having been released to the public, Clay felt it right to afford Jackson the opportunity to vouch for its authenticity by requesting he submit a copy. Compliance with the request would leave no doubt that paper was genuine.[3]

This was not the only reason behind Clay's resolution, however. Of greater importance to him was the unprecedented nature of the paper. To Clay's knowledge, this was first instance in which a presidential paper read to the cabinet was published for public consumption. This tactic was char-

---

[1] *Register of Debates*, 23rd Cong., 1st sess., (Dec. 10, 1833), 26 (Senate).
[2] *Register of Debates*, 23rd Cong., 1st sess., (Dec. 11, 1833), 30 (Senate).
[3] *Register of Debates*, 23rd Cong., 1st sess., (Dec. 11, 1833), 30 (Senate).

acteristic of the way Jackson ran his administration. The populist president had a talent for skillfully making his thoughts known to his cabinet and the people, and only after expressing his desires, he worked to enlist support for what he wanted done. The nature of the paper was also troubling. Clay acknowledged the president's constitutional authority to call on his cabinet for their opinion on certain matters but found that "this document was a reversal of that constitutional rule; for, instead of going to the heads of departments for their opinions, the President had, by this paper, communicated the reasons which ought to influence their judgement."[1] If this paper was an official act of the president, Clay merely wanted it put before the Senate.

Forsyth shot back that he could not understand why Clay so desired to have this paper on official record in the Senate unless he had some specific use for it in mind. Forsyth then speculated on the reason by bringing up for the first time an argument that many other Jacksonian senators would return to throughout the debate — the Senate did not have the authority to investigate the president for wrongdoing that could be construed as criminal. Forsyth quipped that he "could imagine that one branch of the Legislature might, under certain circumstances, have a right to call for [the paper], and, if it were refused when called for, to obtain it by the use of means within its power. But this was not that branch of the Legislature."[2] Forsyth was claiming that the use Clay seemed to have for this paper was to investigate if Jackson had committed a high crime or misdemeanor, which would be grounds for impeachment and therefore under the jurisdiction of the House, as that body was responsible for charging the president with such crimes. Benton then chimed in that requiring from the president a paper communicated to his cabinet would create a slippery slope; could the Senate then request any communication, written or spoken, with even a single member of his administration? The paper could be found in the newspaper, Benton added. Any senator wishing to refer to it could have readily accessed it; the Senate need not trouble the president to produce it himself.

George Poindexter of Mississippi next took the floor and introduced another point of debate that would soon consume the Senate. After first voicing his support for Clay's resolution, Poindexter put forth a critical question to his colleagues — the question of "whether the broad line which the constitution has drawn between the President of the United States and the control of the national chest shall be effaced, and whether, by the virtue of the power of appointment, the President of the United States shall not only

---

[1] *Register of Debates*, 23rd Cong., 1st sess., (Dec. 11, 1833), 30 (Senate).
[2] *Register of Debates*, 23rd Cong., 1st sess., (Dec. 11, 1833), 31 (Senate).

take command of the army and navy, but shall also assume the unlimited control of the public purse?"[1] Poindexter viewed Jackson's paper as a direct instruction to Treasury Secretary William Duane to remove the deposits. The secretary refused, and was summarily fired and replaced with one who would carry out the instructions. If the president could use his power of removal and appointment to carry out his own will, there would be no limit to his authority.

The esteemed Daniel Webster soon spoke and, in a somewhat conciliatory tone, proposed that Clay adjust the wording of the resolution. In Webster's view, the testimony of Forsyth and Benton had sustained the "genuineness of the paper," and so, that piece of the resolution could be safely removed. As to the request to produce the cabinet paper, Webster stated that at the moment it might be premature, but at some point during the session, the Senate would be looking into why the deposits were removed and that paper would be essential to that discussion. Therefore, Webster voiced support for an amended resolution with the call to vouch for the genuineness of the paper removed.[2]

Clay, perhaps piqued by Webster's words, defended his timing for offering the resolution. He observed, "[i]t was clearly the duty of Congress, as early as possible after their meeting, to look into the state of the treasury, and, in this case, to see if the transfers had been made, in conformity with the provisions of law...and understand how, why, and on what authority it had been done." The resolution requesting the paper was part of the Senate's constitutional duty to investigate. Nevertheless, as the true aim of the resolution was to obtain the paper, Clay agreed to the new wording.[3]

The debate continued in this fashion for a bit longer, with Jacksonians repeating the charge that the only plausible explanation for calling for the paper was in the pursuit of charging the president with a crime and therefore within the purview of the House rather than the Senate, and the anti-Jacksonians echoing Clay that it was their duty to investigate all the particulars surrounding the removal of the deposits. When the vote was taken, the resolution passed 23–18; an official request was put in for Jackson to submit a copy of the cabinet paper.[4]

Jackson responded the next day, and unsurprisingly he chose not to comply. "I have yet to learn under what constitutional authority that branch of the Legislature has a right to require of me an account of any communica-

---

[1] *Register of Debates*, 23rd Cong., 1st sess., (Dec. 11, 1833), 32 (Senate).
[2] *Register of Debates*, 23rd Cong., 1st sess., (Dec. 11, 1833), 34 (Senate).
[3] *Register of Debates*, 23rd Cong., 1st sess., (Dec. 11, 1833), 35 (Senate).
[4] *Register of Debates*, 23rd Cong., 1st sess., (Dec. 11, 1833), 35-37 (Senate).

tion, either verbally or in writing, made to the heads of departments acting as a cabinet council," the president wrote. The request having been denied, Clay took one final opportunity to explain his resolution. Because the only proof that the president authorized the document in question came from a news-paper editor who chose to print it, out of respect for Jackson, Clay wanted to provide him an opportunity to authenticate it himself. Since the president refused, Clay would simply refer to the copy of the paper submitted to the public if and when its contents became relevant to the discussion. With that, the matter was dropped.[1]

Consuming the Senate's time with a debate over the submission of a paper that any member could easily access through the newspaper may on the surface seem foolish. However, the substance of the debate would serve as a preview for the more significant debates that would follow. What constitutional authority was granted to the Senate to investigate presidential actions? To what extent, if any, did the president have control over the public purse? Could the president use his power of appointment and removal to see his will carried out? These crucial questions were merely broached during this short debate but would be argued heatedly in the coming months.

For the time being, discussion on the removal of the deposits ceased. The following week, on December 18, Clay submitted two more resolu-tions regarding the deposits. The first requested that Taney submit a copy of former Treasury Secretary, William Crawford's letter to the President of the Mechanics' Bank of New York that he referenced in his report as well as other Crawford communications from around the time of the letter's publication. The other resolution called upon Taney to submit a copy of the correspondence between the agent sent to investigate the condition of the state banks chosen to replace the BUS and the government. (The unnamed agent in Taney's report was Amos Kendall.) The following day, after Benton proposed an amendment expanding the scope of the resolution that was adopted, Clay felt it necessary to explain the reasoning behind the resolu-tions. Taney cited the Crawford letter to establish precedent for his own actions but Clay believed Taney had misinterpreted the intent of the letter. The statements Crawford made were in reference to a specific resolution passed in 1816 and that resolution having long since expired, could not serve as precedent for the secretary's present actions. After some obligatory hostility from Forsyth, the resolution was agreed to.[2]

By December 23, Taney had yet to respond to the resolution, compel-ling Clay to express his regret over the secretary's unwillingness to coop-

---

[1] *Register of Debates*, 23rd Cong., 1st sess., (Dec. 12, 1833), 37-38 (Senate).
[2] *Register of Debates*, 23rd Cong., 1st sess., (Dec. 18-19), 44, 51-53 (Senate).

erate.[1] Three days later, now fully prepared to lay out his argument, Clay introduced two more resolutions. The merit of these resolutions became the special order of the day for the next three months — the longest continuous debate to that point in the history of the Senate. Because of the instrumentality of these resolutions to the ensuing debate, they are given here in their entirety:

> Resolved, That, by dismissing the late Secretary of the Treasury, because he would not, contrary to his sense of his own duty, remove the money of the United States in deposite with the Bank of the United States and its branches, in conformity with the President's opinion, and by appointing his successor to effect such removal, which has been done, the President has assumed the exercise of a power over the Treasury of the United States, not granted to him by the constitution and laws, and dangerous to the liberties of the people.

> Resolved, That the reasons assigned by the Secretary of the Treasury for the removal of the money of the United States deposited in the Bank of the United States and its branches, communicated to Congress on the 3d day of December, 1833, are unsatisfactory and insufficient.[2]

The first of the resolutions directly charged the president with assuming power not granted to him in the Constitution. By removing the secretary of Treasury for not submitting to the president's will and then replacing him with one who would, Clay believed Jackson had taken an unconstitutional hold over the Treasury. The second resolution rejected Taney's stated reasons for the removal as insufficient, thus opening the door for the restoration of the deposits by a joint resolution.

After presenting his resolutions, Clay launched into a three-day speech attacking the whole removal scheme that concluded with such raucous applause from the gallery that it had to be cleared.[3] For the next three months, the great minds of the 23rd Congress would engage in a twofold debate on whether to adopt Clay's resolutions; one over the extent of presidential power and the fate of the constitutional principle of separation of powers, the second an alternating rabid attack and defense of the Bank of the United

---

[1] Taney would respond, but not until December 30. Taney refused to produce the Crawford correspondence, claiming it could all be found in the House documents. Taney reiterated his reasoning for citing Crawford and claimed that Crawford exercised more power over the deposits than he did. He also attached, in accordance with the second resolution, a copy of the correspondence between then Secretary Duane and the unnamed agent sent to check on the status of the state banks. See, *Register of Debates*, 23rd Cong., 1st sess., Appendix 98-101.

[2] *Register of Debates*, 23rd Cong., 1st sess., (Dec. 26, 1833), 58-59 (Senate).

[3] As the ensuing chapters will examine various aspects of the Senate debate, the details of Clay's speech are not discussed here. They are found in conversation with other Senators' thoughts on the issues discussed throughout the rest of the book.

States, an American institution whose presence went back to the days of Washington but whose existence now hung precariously in the balance.

***

On December 26, 1833, upon concluding the first part of a speech that would span three days, Henry Clay wrote to a friend, "[y]ou will have seen from my movements that I do not mean to spare this wicked administration."[1] Indeed, the man whose career is marked by compromise gave no such quarter to Jackson and Taney. The speech formed the foundation of the Senate debate that would not conclude until March 28, 1834 — the day Clay's resolutions came to a vote. The first of the resolutions aroused heated dispute over who controlled the public purse and whether or not the Treasury was an executive or a legislative department. Of greater magnitude however, the Senate launched into a debate over separation of power and whether or not Jackson had abused his constitutional authority and usurped powers not granted to him. The second resolution brought the conversation to the very existence of central banking in America, as a parade of senators took to the floor to articulate their positions. Attacks on one another, the president, Taney, and banking were frequent; the decorum of language generally adhered to in the Senate receded throughout the contentious debate that spanned the winter.

One particular breakdown of decorum of language prompted one of the more contentious exchanges of the session. Before launching into his speech refuting Clay's resolutions, William Wilkins of Pennsylvania first regretted the language employed by the anti-Jacksonians, who conjured up images of revolution, "the constitution lying prostrate and bleeding," and that "civil war was fast approaching." He blamed the language employed, not the current state of affairs since the removal of the deposits, for the state of panic sweeping the nation. Daniel Webster then interjected, asking whether the Pennsylvanian had imputed any of the offensive language to anything he himself had said. When Wilkins indicated that he had, Webster denied ever using such language. Wilkins attempted to drop the point but refused to admit his memory of Webster's warm language was in error. Not satisfied, Webster again insisted that Wilkins go on record in insisting that he had used offensive language despite his denial of having done so. When Wilkins tried to ignore the demand and move forward with his remarks, Webster called him to order. Clay, sensing the proceedings were on the verge of a breakdown, attempted to defuse the situation by maintaining that Wilkins meant no ill will towards Webster and that the former would certainly be willing to drop the matter in the wake of Webster's denial. Van Buren then

---

[1] Henry Clay to Peter B. Porter, December 26, 1833, in *Papers of Henry Clay*, 683.

remarked that Wilkins was not out of order, and after a bit more back and forth, the matter dropped and Wilkins continued with his speech.[1]

This exchange reveals that among much of the Senate existed a great sense of purpose and urgency, as some genuinely believed the fate of the American liberty lay in their hands. Clay, for one, referred to the matter as "a question of all time, for posterity as well as us — of constitutional government or monarchy — of liberty or slavery."[2] While hindsight proved this belief somewhat exaggerated, the sense of urgency pervading within the chamber coupled with the sheer talent of the men who composed it produced perhaps the greatest debate in the history of the Senate.

***

Ostensibly a debate on the removal of deposits from the BUS, the anti-Jacksonians, led by Henry Clay, sought to establish the true question before them as one of executive usurpation. Clay threw down the gauntlet immediately, warning of the larger importance of the proceedings before the Senate in his opening line: "We are in the midst of a revolution, hitherto bloodless, but rapidly tending towards a total change of the pure republican character of the Government, and to the concentration of all power in the hands of one man."[3] With that grandiose statement, Clay made clear that his first resolution was of utmost importance to him as he sought to expose the president's abuse and usurpation of power. Even though the Bank would naturally loom large over the proceedings, it was always woven into the issue of greatest significance — Andrew Jackson's attempt to seize all power of the government.

The very nature of Clay's first resolution drew indignation from the Jacksonians. Benton immediately attacked the resolution as unconstitutional. The Jacksonians had expressed concern that the Senate was inching dangerously close to unauthorized territory when Clay proposed the motion to request a copy of Jackson's cabinet paper. Clay's first resolution directed at the president confirmed those fears. Benton lashed out at the resolution as "a direct impeachment of the President of the United States," an action only the House of Representatives could initiate. He explained that "the first resolution charged both a high crime and a misdemeanor upon the President: a high crime, in violating the laws and constitution, to obtain power over the public treasure...and a misdemeanor, in dismissing the late Secretary of the Treasury from office." Benton erupted, "[i]t is a proceeding in which the First

---

[1] For the full exchange, see, *Register of Debates*, 23rd Cong., 1st sess., (Feb. 6, 1834), 484-486 (Senate).

[2] *Register of Debates*, 23rd Cong., 1st sess., (Dec. 26, 1833), 61 (Senate).

[3] *Register of Debates*, 23rd Cong., 1st sess., (Dec. 26, 1833), 59 (Senate).

Magistrate of the republic is to be tried without being heard, and in which his accusers are to act as his judges!"[1]

Benton's outburst was consistent with his usual style when commanding the floor. One observer described the Missourian as "talk[ing] so loud that he hurts a man's ears. He blows forth such a hurricane of breath, that a spectator must be well anchored not to be blown out by the wind." The observer then joked, "I sometimes wonder how the little figure of Judge Robbins (the diminutive, ancient senator from Rhode Island), who is at the windward, can stand such a tempest — but he is anchored to a Senatorial chair, — and the fastnesses of his mahogany desk are strong."[2] Benton spent most of his time attacking the Bank rather than directly defending Jackson, as doing so would legitimate Clay's resolution as a matter the Senate was constitutionally able to discuss.

Clay had anticipated the attacks upon his resolution as a de facto impeachment and took measures to defend against them. The Senate, Clay explained, could at times act in a legislative, executive, or judicial capacity with its legislative functions being most important. Clay maintained that the first resolution was strictly legislative. It "asserts only that the President has assumed the exercise of a power over the public treasury not granted by the constitution and laws. It is silent as to motive; and, without the *quo animo* — the deliberate purpose of usurpation — the President would not be liable to impeachment." Clay further defended his resolution by casting aside any possibility that the president would be impeached thereby forcing the Senate to act as a jury against him even if all the pieces proving a high crime or misdemeanor fell into place. He questioned, "shall we silently sit by, and see ourselves stripped of one of the most essential of our legislative powers... because, against all human probability, he may hereafter be impeached?"[3] New Jersey's Samuel Southard too scoffed at the ridiculous proposition that because Jackson might be impeached, the Senate must therefore sit on its hands. He asked the chamber, "[a]re these suggestions made in a spirit of irony and sarcasm at our supposed impotence...When in our history, was a triumphant President, at the head of a triumphant majority, impeached?"[4] With Jacksonians comprising just over sixty percent of the House, Clay and Southard had every reason to believe impeachment of this president would never happen.[5]

---

[1] *Register of Debates*, 23rd Cong., 1st sess., (Jan. 2, 1834), 98 (Senate).
[2] *Portland Advertiser*, January 3, 1834.
[3] *Register of Debates*, 23rd Cong., 1st sess., (Dec. 30, 1833), 75 (Senate).
[4] *Register of Debates*, 23rd Cong., 1st sess., (Jan. 9, 1834), 197 (Senate).
[5] John L. Moore, ed., *Congressional Quarterly's Guide to U.S. Elections: Third Edition* (Washington D.C.: Congressional Quarterly Inc., 1994), 956-957.

Jacksonians responded to this line of reasoning with considerable indignation. Nathaniel Tallmadge of New York could see no legislative character in Clay's first resolution. The senator pointed out, "the resolution proposes no legislation. It is not a resolution in which principles are settled, for the purpose of referring the subject to a committee to report a bill in conformity of those principles. It proposes no such thing. If it shall pass, it furnishes no foundation for legislative action." Tallmadge's New York counterpart, Silas Wright attacked Clay's argument that without a *quo animo* to explain the president's actions, the resolution cannot be judicial. Wright claimed quite the opposite: "Any action of the Senate upon [the resolution], going to decide this preliminary question of the *quo animo*, is clearly a judicial action, and therefore an assumption of power, in violation of the constitutional powers of the body."[1] Inferring that a *quo animo* on the part of the president would shift the nature of the Senate's inquiry from legislative to judicial, Wright reasoned that acquitting the president of a *quo animo*, as Clay had done, must also confer a judicial character upon the resolution.

The New York contingent reserved their strongest attacks though for what they viewed as the absurd claim that because Jackson would never be impeached, the Senate was free to investigate his actions. Tallmadge reminded his oppositional colleagues that, "[n]o matter whether an impeachment be anticipated or not, it is the duty of the Senate to keep itself uncommitted and impartial in any possible contingency." He then quoted Justice Joseph Story, who in his *Commentaries on the Constitution of the United States*, warned of the impossibility of maintaining impartiality in an impeachment trial if driven by popular opinion, sectionalism, or partisanship. This, Tallmadge followed with a challenge to any "gentlemen [who] vote for this resolution...let them answer me, whether they feel themselves exempt from that influence more dangerous than popular power and passions or sectional prejudice."[2] Wright added a warning to his fellow Senators:

> If any cause can be more sure than another to render the Senate odious to the people of this country, it will be attempts here to assume the duties of immediate representatives of the people; to constitute ourselves the accusers as well as judges; and, having done this, to resist the known and expressed will of the people, by bringing down upon the head of some too popular public servant the tremendous judicial sentence of this body, without the form of a trial, or even the exhibition of a constitutional accusation.

---

[1] *Register of Debates*, 23rd Cong., 1st sess., (Mar. 12, 1834, Mar. 26, 1834), 902, 1158 (Senate).
[2] *Register of Debates*, 23rd Cong., 1st sess., (Mar. 12, 1834), 903 (Senate).

Wright gave his speech after Tallmadge so it is interesting that the former would make this argument. The Story passage Tallmadge quoted a few days earlier meant to condemn those who let things such as popular opinion influence their thoughts on matters of impeachment. Wright, however, was warning the Senate that taking action against Jackson would draw the ire of the public due to the president's immense popularity. These two opinions seemed to be at odds with one another, but both revealed the senators' disapprobation with Clay's defense of his resolution.

One more senator's contribution to this portion of the debate is worth discussing due to its unique take on the matter. Theodore Frelinghuysen of New Jersey, who a decade later would join Clay at the top of the Whig ticket that nearly won the presidency in 1844, argued, like his future running mate, that the resolution imputed no crime upon Jackson at all and therefore, the Senate would not be in violation of the Constitution in discussing it. His rationale for such thinking, however, was quite different than what others put forth. Rather than examining motive or lack thereof, Frelinghuysen questioned the criminality of the accusation made in the resolution. "But does this charge [violating the Constitution]," the Christian Statesman asked, "even imply a crime in the Executive? Far from it...the powers delegated and the powers reserved in our constitution, are, and have been, from the beginning, matters for constant, animated, and I will add honest discussion and collision. If to differ on these great points implied a crime, the atmosphere of both Houses of Congress would be very dangerous."[1] Frelinghuysen astutely pointed out that congressional actions and discussions so often ventured into questions of constitutionality that labeling each charge of a violation as criminal would be paralyzing. Jackson cited constitutional objections when he vetoed the Bank bill — "did the President, therefore," Frelinghuysen continued, "impute to Congress the wicked and corrupt design of violating the constitution, which alone amounts to crime and guilt? I trust and believe not."[2] Frelinghuysen's brilliant line of reasoning left the Jacksonians in an indefensible position; attempting to refute this point would amount to admission that any accusation of a constitutional violation amounted to a charge of a crime. Such charges were not thrown around lightly and it is therefore unsurprising that none of the Jacksonians who spoke after Frelinghuysen addressed the New Jerseyan's specific point.

Bringing up the matter of impeachment was an attempt by the Jacksonians to flip the script on Clay and his cohorts. In the same way the

---

[1] Frelinghuysen earned this nickname for the passionate moral and legal opposition to Indian removal he voiced in front of the Senate in 1828. See, Wilentz, *The Rise of American Democracy*, 324.

[2] *Register of Debates*, 23rd Cong., 1st sess., (Feb. 3, 1834), 449 (Senate).

McConnell-led Senate would defend their beleaguered president nearly two hundred years later, the Jacksonians first and foremost attacked the process that brought the discussion before them. By accusing the anti-Jacksonians of more numerous constitutional violations than the anti-Jacksonians charged Jackson, the president's allies aimed to put their opponents on record as having supported this unconstitutional effort to tear down the immensely popular Commander in Chief. In contrast, by harping on the impossibility of an impeachment in the House, the president's opponents sought to paint Jacksonians as blind partisans, willing to defend their hero no matter the transgression. Despite their constitutional misgivings, the Jacksonians did freely engage in a robust debate with the anti-Jacksonians over Clay's first resolution. The Senate would find themselves immersed in perhaps the deepest examination of the separation of power, the role of the Executive, and the functions of the government branches, since the creation of the Constitution itself.

CHAPTER 3: AS THE LEGISLATURE COMMANDS

Clay's first resolution explicitly named the president as having orches-trated the removal of the deposits. It is therefore entirely fitting that this was the initial point Clay endeavored upon to prove. To his contention that Jackson ordered the removal, Clay appealed to the common sense of his colleagues in asking; "is there any Senator who hears that requires proof on this point? Is there any intelligent man in the Union who does not know who it was that decided the removal of the deposites? Is it not a matter of universal notoriety? Does any one, and who, doubt that it was the act of the President?"[1] All the evidence Clay needed to reach that conclusion came from Jackson's own words, read to his cabinet in the infamous September cabinet paper. Regarding removal of the deposits, Jackson told his cabinet "to consider the proposed measure as *his own*" and that this decision came "after the most mature deliberation and reflection." (Clay's emphasis)[2]

Jackson did not stop, though, at merely expressing his will and assuming responsibility should it be carried forward. In what Clay referred to as, "conciliating language," Jackson made clear his expectations to his cabinet and specifically Secretary Duane by remarking how "[h]appy will he be if the facts now disclosed produce uniformity of opinion and unity of action among the members of the administration." To this, Clay could not hold back his fury and exploded into a sarcastic tirade:

---

[1] *Register of Debates*, 23rd Cong., 1st sess., (Dec. 26, 1833), 62 (Senate).
[2] Clay is quoting here from Jackson's cabinet paper. *Register of Debates*, 23rd Cong., 1st sess., (Dec. 26, 1833), 62 (Senate).

How kind! how gentle! and how very gracious of these civil and loving expressions must have sounded in the gratified ear of Mr. Duane!...Thus the Secretary was told by the President that he had not the slightest wish to dictate — Oh! no; nothing was further from his intention; *that* he would carefully avoid; the President desired only to convince his judgement, but not at all to interfere with his free exercise of an authority exclusively confided to him. (Clay's emphasis)

By firing Duane and replacing him with the loyal Taney just days later, Jackson proved the reading of his paper served a higher purpose than merely making his wishes known to his cabinet; this was an order and Jackson would see his will carried out at any cost.

Clay also sought to establish Jackson as the mastermind of removal by sarcastically attacking Taney for the speed with which he issued his order, coming just three days after taking over the secretaryship. In the condescending tongue so characteristic of Clay when irritated, the Kentuckian chided, "in three days, with intuitive celerity, [Taney] comprehends the whole of the operations of the complex department of the treasury; perceives that the Government, from its origin, had been in uniform error; and denounces the opinions of all his predecessors!"[1] It was clear to Clay that Taney's official order was nothing more than "a clerical act...in form ministerial, in substance the work of another."[2] Removal was without question Jackson's call.

As anti-Jacksonians took to the floor, many echoed their leader's sentiments. Ohio's Thomas Ewing alluded to the September 20 report in the Jacksonian news organ, *The Globe*, which announced the official decision to remove the deposits from the BUS. Since Taney would not replace Duane as Treasury secretary for another three days, it could not have been the new secretary's call to remove the deposits. Taney was "but the instrument in [Jackson's] hands — a mere machine, which was put into motion, and made to execute the will of him who moved it."[3] Frelinghuysen spoke of Jackson's "interference" in getting the deposits removed while future president, John Tyler, attributed the cause of the Bank's death to Jackson's "direct action."[4]

Not all of the anti-Jacksonians chose to harp on Jackson's role as the driver of removal in their speeches and one, Southard, believed the final decision to be Taney's. Southard viewed the questions before them as more critical than pertaining to the actions of one president or one secretary. Instead, the questions "affect the management and control of the whole treasure of

---

[1] *Register of Debates*, 23rd Cong., 1st sess., (Dec. 30, 1833), 81 (Senate).
[2] *Register of Debates*, 23rd Cong., 1st sess., (Dec. 26, 1833), 64 (Senate).
[3] *Register of Debates*, 23rd Cong., 1st sess., (Jan. 20, 1834), 302 (Senate).
[4] *Register of Debates*, 23rd Cong., 1st sess., (Feb 3, 1834, Feb. 22, 1834), 454, 644 (Senate).

the Union" going forward.[1] Likewise, former vice president turned Jackson enemy, John C. Calhoun, shared a similar sentiment. To the question of whether the removal was an act of Jackson or Taney, Calhoun commented that because it was equally unlawful regardless who ordered it, the question was of no concern to him. He did add, however, that he had "no doubt that the President removed the former Secretary, and placed the present in his place, expressly with a view to the removal of the deposites."[2] Southard, though chose to believe "that the reasons offered by the Secretary are sincere, and that he acted upon his own judgement, not by the command of a superior."[3] Regardless of who they believed made the final call, neither senator intended to give Jackson a free pass — in fact quite the opposite. Both felt the removal so egregious that quibbling over who was ultimately responsible interfered with the more pressing matter of revealing how the blatant disregard for the Constitution threatened the future existence of the republican form of government upon which the country was built.

As many anti-Jacksonians attacked Taney as a mere stooge carrying out the bidding of his superior, the Jacksonians flocked to the defense of the beleaguered secretary. Benton, who spoke first following Clay's initial speech, asked the Senate to look into Taney's past writings on the Bank before chastising him as just an instrument of the president. "The fact is," Benton lectured, "he had long since, in his character of legal advisor to the President, advised the removal of these deposites; and, when suddenly and unexpectedly called upon to his own advice, he accepted it from the single sense of honor and duty, and that he might not seem to desert the President in flinching from the performance of what he recommended."[4] Ether Shepley of Maine also pointed out that Taney had long been a supporter of removal and therefore, "[t]he act of removal was performed...by the proper officer — legally performed, and voluntarily performed — in accordance with a preconceived opinion."[5]

For Shepley, his comments defending Taney and Jackson constituted his maiden voyage as a United States senator. He was elected in March, 1833 to replace John Holmes, perhaps best known as the recipient of the Thomas Jefferson letter containing the famous, "to have the wolf by the ear" slavery metaphor.[6] Shepley entered the Senate as a man for whom the Jacksonians had high hopes. His home state paper, the *Portland Advertiser*,

---

[1] *Register of Debates*, 23rd Cong., 1st sess., (Jan. 8, 1834), 143 (Senate).
[2] *Register of Debates*, 23rd Cong., 1st sess., (Jan. 13, 1834), 216 (Senate).
[3] *Register of Debates*, 23rd Cong., 1st sess., (Jan. 8, 1834), 156 (Senate).
[4] *Register of Debates*, 23rd Cong., 1st sess., (Jan. 2, 1834), 100 (Senate).
[5] *Register of Debates*, 23rd Cong., 1st sess., (Jan 14, 1834), 235 (Senate).
[6] Thomas Jefferson to John Holmes, April 22, 1820.

wrote ahead of his speech that he was a superior talent to Benton if, "Shepley is as a Senator, equal to what he was as a lawyer."[1] Unfortunately for the distinguished attorney, his first foray on the Senate floor was not very well-received. The *United States Gazette* was particularly harsh when comparing Shepley to the departed Holmes: "It was the tact of his predecessor to make the Senate laugh by design; Mr. Shepley possesses the rarer accomplishment of producing the same effect contrary to design...Mr. Grundy laughed until he had to lean his head upon a desk, and Mr. Forsyth as heartily as a cold cynic can laugh."[2] The *Baltimore Patriot* said of him that "Shepley has cut the most ridiculous figure any Senator ever cut," while the *Commercial Advertiser* noted, "[h]e is not the 'bull dog' the administration took him to be. They are disappointed in him. They don't care to own it — But you can see it plain enough."[3] Even the pro-Jackson, *Boston Post* admitted him to be a bit tedious, describing Shepley as "not what may be termed an eloquent, but logical orator — therefore, to his credit as a logician, there were but few ladies of his audience."[4] At a time when a senator's effectiveness was often determined by their ability to attract the fairer sex to the chamber, this was quite the backhanded compliment. It is therefore no surprise that the Senate career of the lawyer from Saco was but a brief one. He left the Senate for a seat on the Maine Supreme Court just three years into his term, since, as one biographer put it, "[i]t was apparent, from the studies and habits of Judge Shepley, that the quiet pursuits of professional duties, and especially in their highest forms as an expositor of the law, were more suited to his tastes than the turmoil of politics."[5] Despite the lukewarm reviews, the freshman senator stood firmly behind Jackson throughout the proceedings.

Senator Forsyth took the defense of Taney forged by Benton and Shepley even further by suggesting he should be treated as a patriot for his actions. In accepting the switch from attorney general to Treasury secretary, he "left a place of honor for another not more honorable, a place of great responsibility for one of greater responsibility, a place uniting honor and profit, which the condition of a large family impelled him to regard, for an honorable place, the profits of which are insufficient to defray his necessarily increased expenditures." Forsyth hinted that the move to the Treasury was a step backwards and served as irrefutable proof of Taney's commitment to the country. Taney was awarded the head of the Treasury because for months he advocated

[1] *Portland Advertiser*, January 3, 1834.
[2] The *United States Gazette*, January 17, 1834.
[3] *The Baltimore Patriot*, January 16, 1834; *Commercial Advertiser*, January 15, 1834.
[4] *Boston Post*, January 22, 1834.
[5] Israel Washburn Jr., "Memoir of Hon. Ether Shepley, LL.D." in *Collections of the Maine Historical Society Volume VIII*, (Portland, Hoyt, Fogg, & Donham, 1881), 415.

the very act Jackson had urged and in doing so, had won the confidence of the president that he would carry out that act. Now, Forsyth fumed, "he is accused of having earned [his position] regardless of the feelings and honors of a colleague, by base subserviency to the mandates of a ruthless master."[1]

As the debate unfolded, almost all the Jacksonians undertook a defense of the secretary. Shepley voiced disgust at the assailing of Taney, a man he described as, "distinguished and honorable, and without reproach even from his enemies." Similarly, Felix Grundy of Tennessee was "astonished" by the treatment Taney had received by his colleagues and claimed him a man of "talents and integrity." William Wilkins of Pennsylvania spoke of Taney's "high personal and political character" while Tallmadge lauded his "willingness to discharge every duty which might be imposed upon him," exemplified by his taking a position less suited to his professional tastes.[2] Indeed, the Jacksonians circled the wagons around one of their own who they thought had been unjustly slandered by his partisan enemies.

Despite having defended Taney's talents and record as an anti-Bank Jacksonian, Grundy took a different position than his allies when he called "the removal of the deposits as emphatically the act of the President" and quoted Jackson from his cabinet paper in which he stated, "I take the responsibility."[3] From there, Grundy launched into a discourse on the importance of executive unity to good government in similar fashion to his colleagues, but the reference to Jackson's assumption of responsibility struck some observers as curious. The *National Gazette* commented that the use of the phrase "I take the responsibility" would set an important precedent for the country. The paper observed that "[i]n the time of Tiberius, some courtier said that a word coined by the Master, in one of his speeches, was good Latin; or if it was not, it would soon become legitimate. Thus, Mr. Grundy may think whatever has been said or done by our Caesar, will become sound constitutional law, whatever it may have been at first."[4] A correspondent from another paper remarked that "[i]ndeed, the whole of Grundy's speech has been a peculiar one, and I was often puzzled to know whether he was puffing or satirizing the administration."[5] While this observation might be a bit overblown — viewed in its entirety Grundy's speech firmly upholds the Jacksonian position — his choice here of siding with the anti-Jacksonians as to who made the call to remove the deposits could be considered misguided.

---

[1] *Register of Debates*, 23rd Cong., 1st sess., (Jan. 27, 1834), 350 (Senate).
[2] *Register of Debates*, 23rd Cong., 1st sess., (Jan. 14, 1834, Jan. 30, 1834, Feb. 6, 1834, Mar. 12, 1834), 234, 417, 491, 918 (Senate).
[3] *Register of Debates*, 23rd Cong., 1st sess., (Feb. 6, 1834), 416 (Senate).
[4] *The National Gazette*, Philadelphia, February 1, 1834.
[5] *The Baltimore Patriot*, February 1, 1834.

By heaping responsibility for removing the deposits on the president, the anti-Jacksonians, at times directly and other times indirectly, implicated Taney as nothing more than the blunt instrument Jackson wielded to crush the BUS. On this point, Taney's friends were largely correct in their defense of him. As previously noted, he was a known adversary of the Bank and had long been a proponent of removing the deposits, even when few in the cabinet agreed with him. Taney, along with Jackson's other friends who opposed the BUS such as Francis P. Blair and Amos Kendall, helped the president craft and disseminate many of his anti-Bank messages, including his famous bank veto message, and provided general guidance on how to best wage his war with the monster moneyed corporation. Jackson clearly wanted the deposits removed and it is near certain that Taney would not have unilaterally removed the deposits without the President's blessing, but the argument that he was nothing more than a malleable pawn of Jackson is simply false.

***

Having presented the reasons demonstrating that Jackson was behind the removal of the deposits, Clay next laid before the Senate the evidence to prove that this measure amounted to a usurpation of congressional power over the Treasury not granted to the president by the Constitution or laws. The abundance of evidence Clay presented and the arguments the Senate advanced in both its support and defense illustrated the stark differences Jacksonians and anti-Jacksonians held regarding presidential power and its limits or lack thereof.

Clay first set out to argue that the president had no power over the public deposits and therefore, his orchestration of their removal was a violation of the Constitution and the laws. Part of the rationale he cited to advance this argument was the controversial claim that the Treasury department was not executive in its character and instead under legislative control. Of all the arguments Clay employed to attack the president, this one may have raised the most eyebrows. In holding to this argument, Clay had stepped out onto a very shaky limb. As every other cabinet department was unarguably executive, claiming that the Treasury was not seemed audacious. On that limb though rested irrefutable proof that Jackson had usurped power. If the Treasury was indeed subject to congressional authority and not executive in its character, Jackson's tampering with it to execute his will would undoubtedly constitute an illegal assumption of legislative power. As long as the limb did not come crashing down, Clay's case was airtight.

One issue the Kentuckian introduced in support of his bold argument centered on the seemingly benign matter of how the department was named upon its creation. Clay reasoned that the Treasury was placed "on a different footing from all other departments, which are, in the acts creating them, denominated executive, and placed under the direction of the President. The Treasury Department, on the contrary is organized on totally different principles."[1] Clay's use of the word, "denominated," referred to the actual naming of the department when created by Congress. The Treasury, State (initially called Foreign Affairs), and War departments were all established by the 1st Congress during the summer of 1789. The first created was the State department and when the vote passed the House, the bill was titled, "An act for establishing an Executive Department, to be denominated the Department of Foreign Affairs." Likewise, when the War department was so established, its name too included the label, "Executive Department." The bill establishing the Treasury department though, created last among the three, curiously omitted the executive label and was simply titled, "An act to establish the Treasury Department."[2] Jacksonians and anti-Jacksonians spent considerable time examining whether this omission was purposeful or just an oversight.

The first senator to bring up the naming controversy directly was Ether Shepley. He remarked, "[i]t is said the treasury is organized upon a different principle from the rest of the departments. In what consists the difference? A name? A difference of name is to alter the power given by the constitution to the Executive!" This argument, Shepley held, was ridiculous and misguided, especially when considering that shortly after the department's creation, the same Congress passed another act in which the treasury was properly referred to as an executive department.[3]

Shepley left the naming dispute at that but the next senator to speak, William Rives of Virginia, went into considerably greater detail. Rives called the notion that the Treasury department was not executive an "extraordinary novelty," altogether inconsistent with how the department and its secretary had been viewed throughout the life of the Republic. If the anti-Jacksonians were basing this wild theory on the omission of the word "executive" from the bill's title, they would be guilty of "forget[ting] the most familiar facts which have been passing under our eyes, for nearly half a century..." The omission, Rives contended, was accidental, as "the title was the same as of the other acts, in all the preliminary and intermediate proceedings, down to the very passage of the act."[4] Days later, William Wilkins of Pennsylvania also argued

---

[1] *Register of Debates*, 23rd Cong., 1st sess., (Dec. 30, 1834), 78.
[2] *Annals of Congress*, 1st Cong., 1st sess., (August 4, 1789, July 27, 1789), 57, 53-54 (House).
[3] *Register of Debates*, 23rd Cong., 1st sess., (Jan. 14, 1834), 236 (Senate).
[4] *Register of Debates*, 23rd Cong., 1st sess., (Jan. 17, 1834), 286-287 (Senate).

the omission was accidental and pointed out that the day following the vote, when Congress set the salary of the Treasury secretary, he was referred to as one of the *"Executive officers* of government."[1] (Wilkins' emphasis.) Along the same lines, Tallmadge cited the act of April 24, 1800 which preceded the seat of government's move from Philadelphia to the District of Columbia. The act empowered the "Secretaries of the four Executive Departments" to prepare rooms for the business of government. Again, the Treasury department was lumped in with the others that were unquestionably recognized as executive.[2] Forsyth reasoned the omission was to avoid repetition, as when the bill was brought up for a vote, the department was referred to as executive; it was only after the bill was passed that the name was shortened.[3] From the anti-Jacksonian side, Ewing felt the suggestion absurd that such a glaring omission be in any way accidental and replied, "taking into view the circumstances under which these acts were passed, and the high importance attached to them by the Congress and the people of the day, it could hardly be by accident that the title of these laws, reported by the same committee, and under consideration by the same Congress, at the same time, should differ in so important a feature."[4]

Perhaps recognizing the blowback he would receive for suggesting that such erudite men would make so careless an error, Rives did entertain the possibility that the omission was not accidental. He remarked that the less specific name chosen for the Treasury may have been due to the complex nature of the department compared to the other executive departments. Unlike the State, War, and Navy departments which were organized very simply with the head directing subordinates to perform the various functions required of them, the Treasury was "complex and diversified." Officers of the Treasury, including the comptroller, auditor, register, and treasurer, all derived their duties from the law, and some duties, such as those of the comptroller and auditor, were more judicial in nature. It was therefore possible, the Virginian reasoned, "doubts might have risen as to the propriety of denominating the whole Department an Executive Department." The functions of the secretary, though, Rives pronounced, "are obviously and exclusively executive."[5]

***

---

[1] *Register of Debates*, 23rd Cong., 1st sess., (Feb. 6, 1834), 491 (Senate).

[2] *Register of Debates*, 23rd Cong., 1st sess., (Mar. 12, 1834), 897 (Senate).

[3] *Register of Debates*, 23rd Cong., 1st sess., (Jan. 27, 1834), 347 (Senate). Considering the other two departments were labeled as executive both before and after they were voted on, assigning tautology concerns as the reason for the omission from the Treasury's name seems far-fetched.

[4] *Register of Debates*, 23rd Cong., 1st sess., (Jan. 20, 1834), 305 (Senate).

[5] *Register of Debates*, 23rd Cong., 1st sess., (Jan. 17, 1834), 287 (Senate).

While the naming controversy produced some curious rationalization by both sides, the functions of the department, its secretary, and where the ultimate responsibility for his actions came to rest formed the true crux of the argument over whether the Treasury department was executive or not. Clay referred to the Bank's charter to remind the Senate that it was to Congress, not the president, to whom the secretary was ultimately responsible. After quoting section sixteen which stipulated the secretary as the trigger man for any removal, and Congress as where the secretary must report his reasons for removal, he asked, "[c]an language, as to the officer who is charged with the duty of removing the deposites, be more explicit? The Secretary of the Treasury alone is designated. The President is not, by the remotest allusion referred to." Making the secretary responsible to Congress when a removal occurred, Clay continued, conformed to what the 1st Congress envisioned when it created the Treasury department in 1789 — that the Treasury department carried out the functions of the legislature and therefore its head officer fell under congressional, not executive control.[1] This vision aligned with the constitutional stipulation that only Congress could appropriate money and left how it should be drawn for the law to determine.

Clay added that the president had no role with the department beyond the appointment of officers and the authority to remove them. Instead, "[t]he Secretary is required by the law to report, not to the President, but directly to Congress. Either House may require any report from him, command his personal attendance before it. It is not, therefore, true that the Treasury is one of the executive departments, subject to the supervision of the President." Later in his speech, Clay made sure to clear up any possible misconceptions his statements may have created. While answerable to Congress, Clay explained, "[the Secretary] has no legislative powers," and his functions are "altogether financial and administrative." In fact, he argued, the secretary's whole role was not executive, but administrative.[2] Clay had already maintained that Jackson was behind the order to remove the deposits, a contention that even some Jacksonians admitted to be true. By arguing that the secretary was responsible to the legislature rather than the executive, Clay sought to remove any constitutional or legal influence of Jackson over the secretary's actions.

If Clay had gone out on a limb in voicing this argument, he must have felt relief to look behind him and see some allies venturing out onto the limb with him, although maybe not quite as far. Southard conceded that when the Treasury department was created, "[i]t was necessary...to leave it, in some

---

[1] *Register of Debates*, 23rd Cong., 1st sess., (Dec. 26, 1833), 65 (Senate).
[2] *Register of Debates*, 23rd Cong., 1st sess., (Dec. 30, 1833), 78, 81 (Senate).

sense, an executive department," but immediately added, "every provision was inserted which could tend to make it subservient to the legislature, and not the executive will." The head of the State, War, and Navy departments answered to the president and Congress received information on matters pertaining to those departments from the president, not the department heads themselves. These departments were clearly executive. But what of the Treasury? "Not so," the former Navy secretary observed:

> It takes care of the public money. But how? As the Legislature directs. It disburses the public money. But how? As the Legislature commands. It reports the state and condition of the treasury, and the situation of the finances. But to whom? Not to the Executive, but to Congress. Congress calls for information, plans, systems of finance. But on whom, and through whom? Not on or through the Executive, but immediately and directly upon the Secretary. He is required to look into the disbursement of the public money. But by whose orders? The President's? No, sir, no; by the command of law.[1]

Although Southard did admit it unavoidable that the Treasury maintain certain elements of an executive department, the effectiveness of his legalistic approach conveying the subordination of the department and its secretary to Congress and not the president surpassed even that of Clay. In fact, his whole speech should be regarded as equal to that of his more well-known peer. One friendly newspaper commented, "no speech in either house has been listened to with more attention, or more sincerely applauded for ability, manly spirit, and patriotic zeal," while another remarked that his "whole soul seemed to be engaged in the cause he was advocating."[2] Even the Richmond *Enquirer*, a news organ of the president, admitted that Southard "displayed some ability and spirit."[3] Indeed, the New Jersey senator proved just as able as any who took the floor to support or oppose Clay's resolutions.

William Rives offered an astute observation in refuting Clay and Southard's line of thinking. If reporting to Congress bestowed a legislative character to an office of government, what of the president? "[D]oes not the President himself," Rives questioned, "the chief Executive officer, report to Congress?...Do not the other heads of Departments, also, report, whenever required, to Congress?" The requirement to report to Congress was just one of several of the secretary's functions. The other functions the Treasury and he as department head were responsible for, such as preparing and reporting plans to improve the revenue, granting of warrants for the issuance of money, superintending the collection of the revenue, among others, were all execu-

---

[1] *Register of Debates*, 23rd Cong., 1st sess., (Jan. 8, 1834), 160 (Senate).
[2] *Alexandria Gazette* January 13, 1834; *Salem Gazette*, January 17, 1834.
[3] *Enquirer* (Richmond), Feb 3, 1834.

tive in character, and, the Virginian argued, "it certainly never could have been intended that Congress itself was to collect, to receive, to keep, to disburse, the public money." These duties were executive functions and ought to be performed by executive officers as provided by the law. Indeed, before the chartering of the current BUS, the Treasury department and specifically the secretary chose the place of deposit, as nothing regarding place was specified by law. The 1816 charter creating the BUS specified it as the new place of deposit, but the secretary retained power to move the deposits according to section sixteen of the charter. Congress' constitutional power over the purse, Rives held, was merely "the power of taxation and appropriation," but at the point its control ceased. Therefore, Rives determined that no usurpation of congressional power had occurred — Taney, whether operating under Jackson's direction or not, had merely exercised a power granted to him by law.[1]

Thomas Ewing fired back after Rives' keen display of constitutional reasoning. Speaking just after Rives, Ewing acknowledged the ambiguity of separation of power as laid out by the Constitution, especially between the legislative and executive branches. He held though, that when it came to power over the public treasury, the Constitution was quite clear. Ewing reminded his colleagues that Article Two, Section Two enumerated the president's general powers but absent from that enumeration was any "power over the treasury, or collection or disbursement of the revenue." Such power was vested to Congress in Article One, Section Eight. Further inspection of Article One, Ewing continued, revealed that Congress was granted power "whenever the fiscal concerns of the nation are subject to provision... in all things relating to the public treasure, its levy, collection, safe-keeping, and disbursement, Executive interference has been carefully excluded by the framers of the constitution." Divesting from the executive branch the safe-keeping and disbursement of the public treasure flew directly against the contention advanced by Rives a few days prior.

Continuing his attack on Rives' claims, Ewing maintained that the secretary's responsibility to Congress went beyond simply reporting directly to it; he "is made subservient to no commands except those of the House of Congress, and is charged with no duties except such as the constitution enjoins upon them." It was with Congress where the secretary's duties originated and this created a connection between the two far more complex than merely reporting, thus distinguishing the secretary's relationship with Congress from that of the president whose only responsibility to that body was to provide an annual report. Consequently, Ewing concluded, "[t]hat Secretary is not an executive officer, and the President has no more right to

---

[1] *Register of Debates*, 23rd Cong., 1st sess., (Jan. 17, 1834), 287, 275-276 (Senate).

order and direct how he shall perform any of his appropriate duties...than either House of Congress has to interfere with the discharge of the appropriate duties of the Secretary of War."[1]

Ewing also "differ[ed] from [Rives] wholly and absolutely" regarding the executive nature of the secretary's duties. Rives had cited the secretary's duty to draw up plans for improving the nation's finances as one of his executive functions. Such planning, Ewing adroitly remarked "is legislation in its incipient stage." It was a precursor to law, an initial step in the law-making process. Executive duty and action "follows legislation, and carries into effect the law." Ewing thus understood the secretary as "bear[ing] the burden of legislation" and his other duties were assigned to him with the same burden in mind.[2] Tyler took the point even further when he reminded the Senate that the secretary's duty called upon him "to prepare plans — not to adopt them himself." The Virginian observed, "[i]nstead of submitting his plans to Congress he has put them in force of his own mere will; and in the very face of the law, claims authority to have done so."[3] In Tyler's estimation, Taney had misconstrued his legally granted power and in doing so, usurped power not from the president, but from Congress to whom he is responsible.

The rhetorical battle waged by the two senators continued following Ewing's speech, with Jacksonians repeating and building on the arguments of their allies. Forsyth asserted that the members of the 1st Congress would view with surprise Ewing's notion that the duties of reporting to Congress and planning for the improvement of the public revenue subjugated the secretary to congressional oversight. Instead, the Georgian countered, those who opposed granting these duties to the secretary in 1789 argued "that it gave power to the Secretary over Congress; not power to Congress over the Secretary." These fears were calmed only by the assurance that such duties were simply procedural, for the sole purpose of disseminating information. In no way were these duties meant to shift the secretary's responsibility from the executive to Congress. Forsyth commented that doing so "destroys all responsibility for the wisdom of his acts," since the secretary's removal could only be initiated by the president, to whom, according to this misguided theory, he is not responsible. This would create an untenable situation in which the secretary was responsible to Congress, but Congress would be powerless to remove him if he proved ineffective or corrupt. The president would have to initiate the removal, in all likelihood at the behest of Congress.[4]

---

[1] *Register of Debates*, 23rd Cong., 1st sess., (Jan. 20, 1834), 306 (Senate).

[2] *Register of Debates*, 23rd Cong., 1st sess., (Jan. 20, 1834), 306 (Senate).

[3] *Register of Debates*, 23rd Cong., 1st sess., (Feb. 24, 1834), 667 (Senate).

[4] *Register of Debates*, 23rd Cong., 1st sess., (Jan. 27, 1834), 347-348 (Senate); History has proven this argument incorrect. Cabinet department heads are considered civil officers

Felix Grundy of Tennessee commented that with Congress rested the crucial job of "prescribing the rules which are to regulate the conduct of officers and citizens. When this is done by the enactment of laws, our duties, our powers are at an end...Congress has nothing to do with the execution of the laws."[1] Tallmadge sought to characterize the Treasury as executive by likening it to the other departments whose executive nature no one would argue. The Constitution stipulated that the president may require from the department heads a written opinion on subjects pertaining to their office. Tallmadge observed that "the records of [the Treasury] abound with instances of the exercise of this power, from the days of General Hamilton...The provision applies equally to the Treasury as to the other Departments...whatever difference there may be in their respective duties, they are all equally Executive."[2] The Jacksonians cited precedent, employed deductive reasoning, and linked the Treasury to other departments to argue for its unquestionable executive character.

Another senator whose contributions have yet to be addressed but are of utmost importance is Peleg Sprague of Maine. Throughout the debate, no senator, Clay included, exhibited same the level of contempt for Jackson than did Sprague. The descendent of one of the first groups of settlers to arrive in Massachusetts during the Great Migration in 1629, Sprague first locked horns with Jackson over his Native American policies. The Bank provided Sprague with another opportunity to attack the Old General.[3] An observer's description called "[his] manner...grave, solemn, and emphatic; his language appropriate, his enunciation clear and distinct, his voice harmonious, his person pleasing; he is about the middle height, dark hair and eyes, and fair complexion."[4] While his strongest language was reserved for other matters, Sprague neatly laid out before the Senate how different the Jacksonians and anti-Jacksonians viewed the nature of the Treasury secretary. Jackson's opponents, Sprague explained, viewed the secretary as an agent "created, guided, regulated, controlled, restrained, and governed by known and fixed laws; subject to visitation by committees of Congress; bound to make frequent reports which Congress could reach; and liable to have its

---

and therefore subject to impeachment. Consequently, removal could be initiated by either the president or Congress. Even accepting the Treasury secretary as a creature of the legislature does not change that. He is still a civil officer and liable to impeachment. The first and only Cabinet member to be impeached was Secretary of War William K. Bellknap in 1876. He was acquitted by the Senate.

[1] *Register of Debates*, 23rd Cong., 1st sess., (Jan. 30, 1834), 419-420 (Senate).
[2] *Register of Debates*, 23rd Cong., 1st sess., (Mar. 12, 1834), 894 (Senate).
[3] William Willis, *A History of the Law, the Courts, and the Lawyers of Maine, From its First Colonization to the Early Part of the Present Century* (Portland: Bailey & Noiles, 1863), 626.
[4] *Boston Post*, February 4, 1834.

existence terminated upon process to be ordered by Congress, if it should transcend the law of its being." The Jacksonians, on the other hand, perceived the secretary as "the mere creature of the Executive will: appointed by him to do what he commands, to abstain from what he forbids; removable by him, governed by no law but his pleasure; subject to no visitation by Congress; bound to no statute to make any returns or expositions of its doings." Upon laying out the two alternatives, Sprague asked his colleagues regarding the future of the country's public treasure, "[s]hall it be under the control of Congress; limited, restrained, and surrounded by fixed laws? or shall it be left to the sole, unguided, ungoverned, undefined, will of one man?"[1] Sprague joined many of his anti-Jacksonian colleagues in insisting that the secretary of the Treasury was answerable to Congress and therefore divorced from the executive branch of government. But the true horror, Sprague believed, lay in the alternative — an alternative opponents of Jackson expended considerable energy to demonstrate — that if not responsible to Congress, the secretary and the country's purse were under the complete control of one very dangerous man.

The wild card in this aspect of the debate was John C. Calhoun. The avid Southern states' rights man joined the anti-Jacksonians in their denunciation of Jackson's and Taney's actions but in doing so, broke from his colleagues by denying congressional authority over the deposits. Calhoun viewed the premise Taney advanced that Congress ceded its control over the deposits to the secretary of the Treasury in section sixteen of the charter as "utterly untrue," not because it was never their intention to relinquish such power, but because it was not a power Congress had to give up.[2] Calhoun explained, "[t]he constitution gives to Congress the power to lay duties with a view to revenue" but that power "was perverted to a use never intended." The acerbic senator continued, it was "Congress [who] first removed the deposites into the public treasury from the pockets of those who made them...The Executive, in his turn, following the example, has taken them from that depository, and distributed them among favorite partisan banks."[3] The perversion of power, of course, was a reference to the 1828 Tariff of Abominations that had a disproportionally negative impact on the South and the ensuing Nullification Crisis over which Calhoun was still bitter. While the anti-Jacksonians warned of executive encroachment on liberty, Calhoun could not help himself but to include the danger of congressional encroachment as well.

---

[1] *Register of Debates*, 23rd Cong., 1st sess., (Jan. 29, 1834), 380 (Senate).

[2] *Register of Debates*, 23rd Cong., 1st sess., (Jan. 13, 1834), 209 (Senate). Taney viewed section sixteen of the Bank's charter as Congress ceding control over the government deposits to the secretary of the Treasury. Section sixteen is covered in great depth in Chapter 6.

[3] *Register of Debates*, 23rd Cong., 1st sess., (Jan. 13, 1834), 220 (Senate).

This dig at Congress served as a reminder that although the current debate centered on the illegal seizing of power by the executive, Congress too, in Calhoun's estimation, had been guilty of the same. Additionally, it was a sobering message to the anti-Jacksonians, intentional or not, that as a long-term ally in their fight against Jackson, Calhoun would be a loose cannon. His colleagues on both sides, perhaps disinclined to divert the conversation to a matter many felt already put to bed, allowed Calhoun's remarks to stand largely unchallenged.[1] Regardless of his feelings on congressional encroachment, however, the South Carolinian made clear his disgust with the power grab orchestrated by Jackson and Taney.

Here, Calhoun revealed himself to be a staunch opponent of the president, but one with different motives than those who would make their way into the opposition Whig Party. The country Clay and most of the anti-Jacksonians envisioned was a far cry from the one Calhoun hoped to create. Clay wished to maintain the strength of the national government to implement his American System, but weaken that of the president in favor of Congress. Calhoun, formerly an advocate for a strong national government, had since became a staunch defender of states' rights and disapproved of much of Clay's platform. As described above, Calhoun blamed the whole Bank crisis on the tariff and took a veiled swipe at Clay for inviting Jackson's actions against the Bank by acceding to his passage of the Force Bill. Calhoun scoffed, "if those who led in the compromise [on the tariff] had joined the State rights party in their resistance to that unconstitutional measure [the Force Bill], and thrown responsibility on the real authors, the administration, their party would have been so prostrated throughout the entire South, and their power, in consequence so reduced, that they would not have dared to attempt the present measure; or if they had, they would have been broken and defeated." Calhoun also took the opportunity to preemptively heap praise on the nullifiers for making the takedown of Jackson possible, should it happen. "[I]f the present struggle against executive usurpation be successful," the South Carolinian gloated, "it will be owing to the success with which we, the nullifiers... maintained the rights of the States against the encroachment of the General

---

[1] An exception was William Rives. The Virginian reminded Calhoun of a speech he gave when the Bank bill was under consideration which seemed to contradict his point that Congress had no control over the deposits outside of their safekeeping. Calhoun had stated, "[l]et the United States retain the power over its deposits, and over the receipt of the bank notes in payment of duties and debts to the Government, and it would possess sufficient control over the bank." Calhoun countered that the comments Rives referenced were made in 1814, before the Bank's creation, and therefore could not apply to the current situation. With no national bank at the time, Calhoun argued, the government of course had to control the deposits. Rives replied that he felt the reference still applied. For the full exchange, see, *Register of Debates*, 23rd Cong., 1st sess., (Jan. 17, 1834, Jan. 20, 1834), 267, 297-301 (Senate).

Government at the last session."[1] Calhoun's choice of words could not be clearer; although the current situation was about *executive* encroachment, it was the power of the national government as a whole that was threatening to liberty. As an attack dog against the president, Calhoun proved himself to be indispensable to Clay and the anti-Jacksonians, but, since, as one observer noted, "his brains [contained] so much of the fruits of Nullification," the alliance between the old nullifier and the National Republicans who would coalesce into the Whig Party would be shaky at best.[2]

---

[1] *Register of Debates*, 23rd Cong., 1st sess., (Jan. 13, 1834), 221 (Senate).
[2] Henry Thomas Shanks, ed., *The Papers of Willie Person Mangum: Volume II* (Raleigh: NC State Department of Archives and History, 1952), 103.

CHAPTER 4: AND THIS IS REPUBLICANISM!!!

Being one most astute and able members ever to serve on the Senate, Henry Clay must have sensed the inadequacy of resting the whole defense of his first resolution on the questionable assertion that the Treasury department and its secretary were not under the umbrella of executive control. Therefore, operating under the concession that the Treasury was executive, Clay also endeavored to explain the various ways that Jackson's and Taney's actions still constituted a usurpation of congressional power. First, Clay had to establish that the removal of the deposits amounted to an illegal act. If the redirecting of the public funds from the BUS to the chosen state banks did not constitute an illegal act, the argument that a usurpation of power had occurred would be groundless. The most important step in determining that an illegal act had occurred was to establish that the funds had actually been removed from the Treasury.

Clay's resolution charged Jackson with usurping illegitimate power over the Treasury by removing the public deposits through his surrogate, Secretary of Treasury Roger Taney. To sustain his claim that the deposits were illegally removed from the Treasury, Clay had to explain what he believed the Treasury was, as its definition was quite ambiguous. If the money had not left the Treasury, then nothing illegal had taken place. Pinning down what the Treasury actually was proved a challenging task, since, as was often the case in matters concerning the early years of the Republic, the Constitution and the laws were not entirely clear. How the senators defined the Treasury in many cases informed their thinking on whether Jackson or Taney did anything wrong or if in fact a removal had actually occurred.

Establishing what the Treasury was first required an examination of the purpose of the Treasury department and its makeup. Clay pronounced that the power over the public treasure had always been in the hands of Congress and such authority had never been questioned. Congress created the Treasury department and in doing so, created both the offices of the Treasury secretary and the treasurer. To the treasurer, Congress assigned the duty "to receive and keep the monies of the United States, and to disburse the same upon warrants drawn by the Secretary of the Treasury, countersigned by the Comptroller, recorded by the Register, and not otherwise."[1] The treasurer also had to provide security for the deposits in the form of a bond of $150,000. It appeared obvious to Clay this meant that the once the money entered the Treasury, it could not be removed without the consent of the treasurer. Prior to the establishment of the Second Bank of the United States, Congress had passed no law designating where the public money should be deposited and therefore, such discretion was left up to the treasurer. However, the charter creating the Bank stipulated that all public funds be deposited in its vaults, and thus, Clay argued, "[w]hen the existing bank was established, it was provided that the public moneys should be deposited with it, and consequently that bank became the treasury of the United States."[2]

Other anti-Jacksonians, such as Southard agreed. He commented that "before the bank was formed there were more than ninety State banks in which the money was placed, and these were all one treasury; and withdrawing money from any of them was taking it out of the treasury...and so it is since the bank was created." Southard continued, "[the BUS] is the treasury now...and if the Secretary withdraws one dollar of it, with or without the executive sanction, it is a breach of the law."[3] Likewise, John C. Calhoun remarked, "[w]hen paid into the place designated by law as the depository of the public money, [it] then is in the treasury of the United States." At that point, Calhoun added, "it passes to the credit of the Treasurer."[4] The argument establishing the BUS as the Treasury followed that the funds deposited there became custody of the treasurer, not the Treasury secretary.

The Jacksonians, though, were not convinced that the BUS became the Treasury upon its chartering. Benton rebuked "the new fangled conception that the Bank of the United States was the treasury of the United States."[5] Virginia's William Rives attributed the anti-Jacksonians' misguided notions about what constituted the Treasury to an "error [of] annexing an idea of

[1] Stat. 65. 1st Congress, 1st Session, Ch. 12.
[2] *Register of Debates*, 23rd Cong., 1st sess., (Dec. 26, 1833) 61 (Senate).
[3] *Register of Debates*, 23rd Cong., 1st sess., (Jan. 8, 1834), 173 (Senate).
[4] *Register of Debates*, 23rd Cong., 1st sess., (Jan. 13, 1834), 214 (Senate).
[5] *Register of Debates*, 23rd Cong., 1st sess., (Jan. 2, 1834), 101 (Senate).

fixed locality to it; whereas, in the true constitutional and financial sense, it is not a place, but a state or condition." The condition to which Rives spoke that constituted the Treasury was that of money being to the credit of the treasurer as ascertained by law. The money was considered removed from the Treasury "only when it passes from [the treasurer] to some creditor of the Government, to whom it is paid under a warrant of disbursement." Taney's actions had not changed that the deposits were still to the credit of the treasurer. All he had done was to transfer the money from the BUS to various state banks which prompted Rives to question, "where is there any thing to give even a color of plausibility to the charge that the public moneys, in being removed from the Bank of the United States to other places of deposite, have been taken out of the public treasury?"[1] If such a flawed construction of the Treasury as conceived by the anti-Jacksonians be adopted, Shepley argued, "you could have no money but at the place where it was first paid in...Civil war, commotion, fire, and flood, may all come upon it, and you could not, according to this doctrine, remove it, without violating the constitution."[2] The Jacksonians clearly denied that the Treasury resided within the BUS, believing instead that it existed wherever the public funds were deposited. Taney decided that the public funds would no longer reside in the BUS and instead be spread amongst the chosen state banks. These state banks, Jacksonians reasoned, became the Treasury once the public money entered their vaults. Since the money had not left the Treasury, the Jacksonians contended, nothing illegal had taken place.

In espousing this view of the Treasury, the Jacksonians provided cover for Taney's actions by citing section fifteen of the Bank's charter. In one of the debate's early speeches, Benton quoted the aforesaid section that stated, "whenever required by the Secretary of the Treasury, the bank should give the necessary facilities for transferring the public funds from place to place." "This clause," Benton continued, "puts to flight all the nonsense about the United States Bank being the treasury, and the Treasurer being the keeper of the public moneys."[3] Calhoun fired back at the Missouri senator for attempting to construe section fifteen "as to confer on the Secretary the power to withdraw the money from the place of deposite, and loan it to favored State banks." For if the BUS is not the Treasury, Calhoun inquired, "[a]re we to understand that none of this money is, in truth, in the treasury? — that it is floating about at large subject to be disposed of — to be given

---

[1] *Register of Debates*, 23rd Cong., 1st sess., (Jan. 17, 1834), 276-277 (Senate).
[2] *Register of Debates*, 23rd Cong., 1st sess., (Jan. 14, 1834), 244 (Senate).
[3] *Register of Debates*, 23rd Cong., 1st sess., (Jan. 2, 1834), 101 (Senate).

away — at the will of the Executive, to favorites and partisans?"[1] The location of the Treasury, whether a physical place or abstraction, factored largely
into the senators' thoughts on if the deposits could legally be removed from
the BUS by the secretary of the Treasury. The anti-Jacksonians, arguing
that the BUS by the act of incorporation had become the Treasury, refuted
Taney's claims to authority to move the deposits to various state banks. The
Jacksonians, by contrast, viewed the Treasury simply as any place public
money was deposited at a given moment. These differences created another
debate over the authority Congress vested in the secretary versus that vested
in the treasurer vis-à-vis the removal of the deposits and the choice of their
new location.

When the 1st Congress created the Treasury department and with it,
the offices of the secretary of the Treasury and the treasurer, it vested in
the treasurer the duties outlined by Clay above. Anti-Jacksonians cited this
section of the law to argue that upon deposit in the Treasury, only the treasurer could remove the funds and choose a new place of deposit. Accepting
this explanation divested from the secretary any control over the money
once deposited in the Treasury. He may issue warrants for its disbursement
according to appropriations made by Congress that must be signed by the
treasurer before any money can be withdrawn, but nothing more.

Perhaps the most forceful declamation downplaying the role Congress
envisioned for the Treasury secretary over the removal of and location of
the deposits came from Samuel Southard. In his report submitted at the
start of the session, the senator argued that Taney had incorrectly conflated
his powers as secretary with the powers of the Treasury department as a
whole. "The Treasury Department," Southard corrected, "is a creature of the
law and the constitution, and consists of several officers, whose separate
and respective duties are prescribed; of whom the Secretary is but one, and
with no more undefined and unlimited powers than the others. Each has
his sphere of authority and service; and neither properly interfere with the
rest, except in the mode and to the extent which the law has established."
To demonstrate Taney's mingling of the two, Southard referenced the secretary's argument that since the Treasury department had been entrusted
with administering the finances of the country, it was therefore his duty as
secretary to oversee the safe-keeping of the public deposits. Southard called
this principle "unsound" and asked, if the Treasury department's duty is as
described, "does it follow that the Secretary alone is to perform the functions thus claimed?" Taney, it seemed, felt this a power deriving from the
nature of his position. Southard called such a perception of his responsibili-

---

[1] *Register of Debates*, 23rd Cong., 1st sess., (Jan. 13, 1834), 215 (Senate).

ties, "absurd, and an assumption of undelegated authority." The authority Southard accused Taney of usurping belonged to the treasurer, whose "very duty of safe-keeping is expressly assigned." As argued by Clay earlier, prior to the chartering of the Second Bank of the United States, the treasurer chose where the deposits would reside and was held responsible for their safety through his bond. Upon Congress establishing the BUS and designating it as the place of deposit, the treasurer was no longer responsible as long as the public money remained there. However, Southard explained, "if, from any cause, it be taken from thence, without the order of Congress where it shall be kept, the rights, and duties, and responsibilities of the Treasurer revive." Congress did not prescribe Taney's moving of the deposits from the BUS to the state banks nor was the action authorized by the treasurer. Therefore, Southard deduced, Taney's actions carried no legal authority but left the treasurer in a precarious legal situation as he, not the secretary, would be held financially responsible should the money be lost.[1]

Other arguments anti-Jacksonians brought up revolved around Taney having misconstrued his duties, believing that he had the power to take care of the public money once deposited. That duty, Clay stated, was "expressly, by the act organizing the department, assigned to the Treasurer of the United States."[2] Thomas Ewing of Ohio further clarified the point. The secretary's duties dealt with the collection of placing the revenue in the public treasury so "[w]hen placed there the collection of it has ceased, and the superintendence over that collection, given to the Secretary, ceases to confer on him any power over it."[3]

William Wilkins, John Forsyth, and Felix Grundy provided able counters to these points. The three blasted the argument brought up by Clay and his cohorts that the treasurer chose the place of deposit as directly contradicting how the deposits of the country had been handled since the creation of the Treasury department. Wilkins characterized this notion as "[a] strange and novel doctrine, subversive of every principle of the Treasury Department and of uniform practice of the Government!" Indeed, the continental ordinance of 1779 creating the Board of Treasury (which later morphed into the Treasury Department) conferred on the board of directors, whose duties were passed onto the Treasury secretary upon creation of the department, the authority of choosing the place of deposit while the treasurer was assigned the duty to receive and keep the money once deposited. Furthermore, during the major debates involving both national banks, "the control of the Secretary over the

---

[1] *Register of Debates*, 23rd Cong., 1st sess., (Jan. 8, 1834), 157-158 (Senate).
[2] *Register of Debates*, 23rd Cong., 1st sess., (Dec. 30, 1833), 78 (Senate).
[3] *Register of Debates*, 23rd Cong., 1st sess., (Jan. 20, 1834), 311 (Senate).

deposites was not only acknowledged, but his right to select the place of deposite was admitted with equal unanimity." This prompted Wilkins to question what secretary would ever bear the responsibility of removing the deposits if their ultimate landing spot was out of his hands.[1]

Forsyth quoted lengthy passages from reports and letters drafted by Hamilton in the early 1790's to prove that Taney's actions matched those of the first secretary of Treasury and aligned with the vision the creators of the department had for the office. Prior to the chartering of the First Bank of the United States, the public moneys were kept in several state banks. Upon its creation, Hamilton moved the funds to branches of the new bank. Forsyth observed, "Mr. Hamilton changed the place of deposite after the U. States Bank was chartered, as he had directed the deposites to be made in the State banks previously, without legislative direction, as none thought was necessary, for not one, even in the time of strong prejudice and party excitement against him, considered it as even an act of doubtful propriety." To answer the claim that Taney had seized power not granted to him over the deposits, Forsyth turned again to Hamilton who wrote, "[t]he Treasurer never has any public money in his possession or custody, which is not in fact deposited in bank, from the moment his possession or custody commences till it ceases by disbursement of it for public purposes...The Secretary of Treasury...never has the possession or custody of any part of the public moneys...And the possession or custody of the Treasurer is, as already stated, exercised through the banks."[2] Grundy also cited precedent to show that the treasurer was never meant to choose the place of deposit. In addition to Hamilton, the Tennessean referenced similar examples of transfers ordered by former Treasury Secretary Albert Gallatin, whose transfers from bank to bank were met without opposition. These transfers, Grundy argued, revealed that "[Congress] has obviously relied that the Secretary of the Treasury would find depositories sufficiently safe, as he found them for the last forty years...the Treasurer of the United States, acting under the orders of the head of his department, has incurred no responsibility [for the deposits' safety]."[3] Because the money had not been disbursed for public purposes and still resided in various state banks, the deposits had not left the custody of the treasurer and therefore, Taney had taken no illegal control over them. Once again, the perception of what constituted a removal from the Treasury informed the Senators' thoughts on whether or not Taney (and by extension Jackson) did anything wrong.

---

[1] *Register of Debates*, 23rd Cong., 1st sess., (Feb. 17, 1834), 579 (Senate).

[2] *Register of Debates*, 23rd Cong., 1st sess., (Jan. 27, 1834), 359-363 (Senate).

[3] *Register of Debates*, 23rd Cong., 1st sess., (Jan. 30, 1834), 423-424 (Senate).

***

Having laid out his claim that an illegal removal had occurred, Clay and the anti-Jacksonians next fixed upon the course of arguing how the removal was a usurpation of congressional authority. Who the senators chose to focus their ire upon, Jackson or Taney, unsurprisingly corresponded to who they believed prompted the removal. The case against Jackson revolved around two of the most ambiguous clauses found in the Constitution: "The executive Power shall be vested in a President of the United States of America," and "he shall take Care that the Laws be faithfully executed."

Clay, of course, was the first to attack the president's claim to power over the deposits. He posited that such power could derive from only two sources, the law and the Constitution. Clay quickly dismissed that Jackson was granted any power by the law that created the BUS. The president was only mentioned twice in the charter — as having the power to appoint the government directors to sit on the board and to order a *scire facias* to initiate proceedings to investigate the Bank for charter violations.[1] For Jackson to have any claim to authority over the public deposits, it must then be found in the Constitution, but Clay argued that no such claim existed there either. In regards to the department heads under him, the Constitution only bestowed on the president the power to call on them for their opinions on matters pertaining to their departments. Any other power the president may claim over the department heads came from the individual laws creating them and with the exception of the Treasury, these laws did place all the secretaries under control of the president. Since their creation, laws also conferred upon the department heads certain individual duties beyond the president's control (such as found in section sixteen of the Bank's charter). This principle, Clay contended, was upheld by the *Marbury v. Madison* decision. Chief Justice Marshall wrote that when acting as agents of the president, department heads must act in accordance to the president's will, but when performing duties ascribed to them by law, the officer must be free to act according to his own will.[2] By claiming total responsibility for removing the deposits, Jackson had violated the opinion of the court by seizing upon a duty granted to the Treasury secretary by section sixteen of the law creating the BUS.

Clay thus established that the president's control over the department heads was constrained by both the Constitution and laws Congress passed outlining specific duties to be independently carried out by the secretaries.

---

[1] A *scire facias*, as it relates to the BUS charter, means that the president could order an investigation into the Bank's affairs if wrongdoing was suspected. The Bank would have to prove it had not acted improperly or risk losing its charter.

[2] *Register of Debates*, 23rd Cong., 1st sess., (Dec. 26, 1833), 66-67 (Senate).

But what of the constitutional stipulation that the president take care that the laws be faithfully executed? Did that clause wrap the president in a blanket of power over the execution of all laws, extending to matters of the Treasury? The Jacksonians, Clay insisted, maintained a construction of this stipulation hazardous to the continuance of constitutional government. Clay's words are provided here in their entirety:

> It has been contended that under [the stipulation that the laws be faithfully executed], that the executive aid or co-operation ought not, in any case, to be given, but when the Chief Magistrate himself is persuaded that it is to be lent to the execution of the law of the United States; and that, in all instances where he believes that the law is otherwise than it has been settled or adjudicated, he may withhold the means of execution with which he is invested. In other words, this enormous pretension of the Executive claims that if a treaty or law exists, contrary to the constitution, in the President's opinion; or if a judicial opinion be pronounced, in his opinion repugnant to the constitution, to a treaty, or to a law, he is not bound to afford the executive aid in the execution of any such treaty, law, or decision.

> To assent to such a doctrine, Clay continued, would be to accept "that every thing revolves itself into the President's opinion." This would amount to "an end to all regulated government, to all civil liberty."[1]

To Clay's understanding, this doctrine was a gross overestimation of what was meant by, "to take care that the law be faithfully executed." In his view, the clause simply meant that the president could "employ the means intrusted to him to overcome resistance whenever it might be offered to the laws."[2] Those means, Clay clarified, were invested to him through the command of the armed forces and the militia and to this end and no further did the clause mean to extend. Over the executive departments, the president's eye was that of a parent, surveying their operation. He had no right to interfere directly with their functions prescribed to them by law. Clay magnanimously conceded Jackson's place as a "high and glorious station," but added, "it is one of observation and superintendence." To strengthen his claim, Clay reached back to the ratification process, researching *The Federalist Papers*, the Convention Debates, and other contemporary publications. He could find no mention by any of the nation's founders suggesting such wide expanse of executive power the president and his allies were now espousing.[3]

---

[1] *Register of* Debates, 23rd Cong., 1st sess., (Dec. 26, 1833), 67-68 (Senate).
[2] *Register of Debates*, 23rd Cong., 1st sess., (Dec. 26, 1833), 68 (Senate).
[3] *Register of Debates*, 23rd Cong., 1st sess., (Dec. 26, 1833), 69 (Senate).

Clay concluded his point on this particular matter by taking a jab at Jackson for seemingly violating his own constitutional rationale for his actions. The president and his friends had applied the aforementioned clause as cover for his actions regarding the deposits. But, those very actions impeded the proper enforcement of the law. The secretary of the Treasury was the one who the Bank's charter authorized to remove the deposits. Therefore, Clay declared, "if the President was bound to take care that that law should be faithfully executed, then his duty exacted of him to see that the Secretary of the Treasury was allowed the exercise of his free, unbiassed [sic], and uncontrolled judgement in removing or not removing the deposites. *That* was the faithful execution of the law." (Clay's emphasis) By consulting with his entire cabinet on the matter of removal and then replacing two secretaries who made it clear they would not remove the deposits, Jackson had overtly stood in the way of the faithful execution of the law.[1]

Jacksonians, predictably, attacked Clay's views on executive power from all angles. Shepley failed to understand how the president could perform his constitutionally mandated duties under Clay's narrow interpretation of the clause. "How can the Executive take care that the laws be faithfully executed, without an examination into, and a decision upon the manner of executing?" To Shepley, faithfully executing the laws required the president to closely monitor and examine the manner in which his subordinate officers performed their duties. Divesting this power from the chief executive would create a government in which "the President has no power to examine into their conduct and enforce obedience; the whole Government is divided in its responsibility; the officers are let loose, to follow their own judgement without either guide or control; the President cannot remove them, and there is no remedy." If Clay were correct that the president's role was that of an observant parent, Shepley argued, a faithful execution of the laws would be beyond his grasp. The senator imagined how such a narrow interpretation may look; "it might be the opinion of the collector of New York that the revenue laws were unconstitutional, and therefore, ought not to be executed. And what then...? Why a faithful execution of your laws becomes — what? Why a faithful execution becomes no execution at all, according to this interpretation." While admitting that each officer was charged with personal duties, Shepley held that this "does not take away the right of the President to examine into the manner in which that personal duty is performed, and decide upon it."[2] In regards to the Treasury secretary specifically, Forsyth echoed his colleague from Maine. To the secretary, "discre-

---

[1] *Register of Debates*, 23rd Cong., 1st sess., (Dec. 26, 1833), 70 (Senate).
[2] *Register of Debates*, 23rd Cong., 1st sess., (Jan. 14, 1834), 241 (Senate).

tion [over the deposits] was given with the well understood qualification, that it was to be exercised in subordination to the duty of the President, who is bound by the most solemn of all obligations to see the laws faithfully executed."[1] To Forsyth, this meant that the secretary's individual discretion over the deposits could be exercised only if it coincided with that of the president, who had ultimate control.

Clay too faced criticism for his contention that the president's duty to enforce the laws of the nation were confined to the use of force only when the laws were being forcibly resisted. Rives protested that this construction of the clause was far more dangerous than anything the president's detractors accused of him. It was Congress, Rives reminded, who was tasked with calling forth the militia. The president commanded once called upon, but his power to unilaterally call upon the armed forces of the country himself would be a violation of the Constitution. Therefore, the clause could not apply as Clay had described. Instead, Rives corrected, the execution of the laws occurred "by the intervention of officers appointed for the purpose, whose fidelity in the discharge of their duties may be secured by the superintendence of the chief Executive officer."[2] Later in the debate, William Wilkins also pounced on Clay's narrow interpretation of the president's power to take care the laws be faithfully executed. "Surely the power was not suspended until some open rebellion had broken out against the constitution," he wondered aloud. "Surely this power was never absent. Surely in all cases it was a part of his duty to attend to the revenue and to the finances."[3]

Rives next took aim at Clay's declaration that no such construction of the clause as Jackson had applied it existed in any writings of the founding era. The Virginian sarcastically jabbed that "[i]f [Clay] had taken the trouble to turn to the most obvious source of information on the subject — the proceedings and debates of the first Congress on the organization of the Executive Departments — he could not have failed to see that this clause appealed to in the sense, and for the purpose, which the President has done." James Madison wrote that the laws of the nation could be enforced only by "officers appointed for that purpose" and being the chief executive responsible for the enforcement of the law, the president naturally had the authority to control their actions. Jackson, Rives insisted, had merely exercised his power of superintendence over a subordinate officer, a power that founders such as Madison had envisioned for the office.[4]

---

[1] *Register of Debates*, 23rd Cong., 1st sess., (Jan. 27, 1834), 348 (Senate).
[2] *Register of Debates*, 23rd Cong., 1st sess., (Jan. 17, 1834), 282-283 (Senate).
[3] *Register of Debates*, 23rd Cong., 1st sess., (Feb. 6, 1834), 491 (Senate).
[4] *Register of Debates*, 23rd Cong., 1st sess., (Jan. 17, 1834), 283-284 (Senate).

Forsyth continued the assault on Clay's position throughout his address. The Kentuckian had argued that Jackson interfered with the faithful execution of the law by consulting with other members of his cabinet and making his feelings on the matter known to the Treasury secretary, thus impeding the unbiased performance of his duties over the public treasure. Forsyth reminded Clay that consultation of this sort was normal, quipping, "is it not in the experience of that Senator that Secretaries of the Treasury have been consulted about the plans of campaigns and the movements of the military and naval force of the United States? Is it not every day's practice to call upon him for opinions relating to the duties of all other Secretaries?"[1] If the founders meant to qualify the president's power to execute the laws, they certainly would have included language in that clause to do so. But no such language existed. For what other reason but to judge the performance of the secretaries would he be granted the power to seek out their opinions? And for what other reason would he form such a judgement if not for the express purpose of controlling their actions to ensure the laws be faithfully executed? Therefore, Forsyth concluded, "Congress cannot divest the Executive of control over those who are his eyes and hands to perform his appropriate functions."[2]

In refuting Clay's speech, Grundy spoke of the importance of unity for the government to function properly. Grundy argued that the only way to secure American liberty was for harmony to exist within each of the government's three branches, with each "having but one will, which must have effect whenever it is regularly expressed." The Supreme Court may hand down a judgement in conflict with that of an inferior court, but it would be expected that the inferior court would abide by the higher court's mandate. When the legislature passed a law, those who voted against it must still acknowledge and obey it and submit to the singular voice of legislative will. Similarly, the executive branch must operate through a singular voice. Because the department was tasked with carrying forth the nation's laws, Grundy believed unity of this branch was of greatest importance. For this reason, Grundy alleged, the founders decided upon a singular executive "to prevent discord and the confliction of a number of wills." He continued, "[i]f you permit any of his subordinate officers to counteract the wishes of the Chief Magistrate upon his important measures, you destroy his responsibility, which is the greatest security you have for a faithful discharge of his duties." Tallmadge too stressed the importance of executive unity to sound

---

[1] Forsyth is likely referring to Albert Gallatin, who during his time as secretary took an active role in many executive decisions outside financial matters including travelling with Clay to Ghent to negotiate the treaty that ended the War of 1812.

[2] *Register of Debates*, 23rd Cong., 1st sess., (Jan. 27, 1834), 342 (Senate).

government and invoked the failed Articles of Confederation to do so. One of the most obvious lessons drawn from the Confederation years was that sound government could not exist without a national executive. And after some debate among the convention goers who authored the Constitution, it was decided that a single executive was preferable to a plurality for "in every instance [in history], it was found that the division of executive power had led to the most disastrous results...Unity, therefore, in the Executive department of the Government, was deemed essential to secure energy and responsibility." This unity, Tallmadge continued, disintegrated "by conferring on any officer in either of the departments, a power, executive in nature, to be exercised independent of the Chief Executive himself. Such independence on the part of such officers, is destructive of the very principle on which the Executive department was founded."[1] In assigning the singular voice of the executive department to that of the chief executive, Grundy and Tallmadge made the most forceful case advocating for the unquestionable supremacy of presidential authority.

Jackson's final bastion of defense on this matter was Silas Wright, a man who before the deposits were removed expressed his desire that the decision be delayed.[2] Speaking just two days before the vote, the somber attorney took his time picking apart Clay's resolution piece by piece, repeating much of what had been argued previously. Wright did, however, add another layer of defense not argued by his fellow Jacksonians. The president was accused of assuming power over the Treasury not granted to him by the Constitution. Wright pointed out, however, that in order to take control of the Treasury, simply removing the secretary would not be enough. Beyond the secretary was also the treasurer "who keeps the keys of the public treasury." Controlling the public treasury required the removal of this officer as well, and as Jackson had not done this, it is not possible that he attempted to seize the power he was accused of.[3]

Some of Jackson's defenders did not merely stop at justifying his actions through constitutional means. A few took to hero worship. Wilkins argued that had the president wanted to take control of the public treasure like his opponents alleged, he easily could have. "Where would he have gone?" the Pennsylvanian asked his fellow senators. "To the Bank of the United States. Would he have gone to the local banks? Not at all. He would have gone to the bank which rules the nation — to the bank which was capable of producing all the sensation, all the influence which was now perceived in the

---

[1] *Register of Debates*, 23rd Cong., 1st sess., (Mar. 12, 1834), 893 (Senate).
[2] Schlesinger, *The Age of Jackson*, 100.
[3] *Register of Debates*, 23rd Cong., 1st sess., (Mar. 26, 1834), 1160 (Senate).

country." Instead, just as Jesus resisted Satan's temptation of all consuming power in the wilderness, Jackson cried, "[n]o...to the Bank of the United States, Begone from me. I know your power in the country, I know your influence, but, begone from me."[1] The biblical reference could not have been clearer; the Bank was a temptress, drowning weaker souls in its allure of all-encompassing power. But Jackson, the embodiment of good and of moral strength not only resisted the seductive pull of the Bank's power and riches, but sought to vanquish its evil from the face of the Earth. To be in the mind of Clay and the anti-Jacksonians when these words left Wilkins' mouth!

New Hampshire's Isaac Hill too chose to defend Jackson by reveling in the Old General's greatness. In 1829, the former newspaper editor was appointed second comptroller of the Treasury and covertly initiated an investigation into mismanagement at the Portsmouth branch of the BUS.[2] An avowed opponent of the BUS, Hill took his Senate seat in 1831 and served as one of Jackson's closest advisors in his Kitchen Cabinet.[3] Given his history with the Bank and his close relationship to Jackson, it is unsurprising that Hill would quickly dismiss the charges against the president and devote most of his attention instead to admonishing the Bank. The loyal Hill though did not conclude his speech without genuflecting before his beloved leader. Not merely content with comparing his contributions to the country with those of Washington and Jefferson, Hill insisted Jackson had "gone beyond both in securing for the nation the confidence and respect of all the principal kings, princes, and potentates of the world." Hill's final line captured the intense devotion Jackson's followers felt for him but also demonstrated a level of idolatry for one man dangerous to maintaining a republican form of government: "Hereafter shall his fame be transcended but by few men whose deeds have shed lustre upon their species."[4]

No one, however, took to hero worship more shamelessly then Thomas Benton. According to correspondents in the chamber, the broad-faced Missourian concluded his speech predicting that the Old General would be cast "hereafter in marble, brass, and bronze," "a peroration so ridiculous that even his own partisans laughed in his face." The exultation was so outrageous that either Benton's friends convinced him to leave it out of the final printed speech or the *Globe* chose not to include it.[5]

Anti-Jacksonians offered a starkly different vision of how Jackson's actions would impact the country. The same unity in the executive branch

[1] *Register of Debates*, 23rd Cong., 1st sess., (Feb. 6, 1834), 487 (Senate).
[2] See, Catterall, *Second Bank*, 171-175.
[3] Remini, *Jackson and the Bank War*, 52-53.
[4] *Register of Debates*, 23rd Cong., 1st sess., (Mar. 3, 1834), 801-802 (Senate).
[5] *Baltimore Patriot*, January 9, 1834; *Baltimore Patriot*, January 7, 1834.

that the Jacksonians regarded as essential to good government, their opponents viewed as destructive to that end. Southard called "the substitution
of a single will in place of the will of the whole...the essence of despotism...
and whenever it shall be approved by the American people, they will be
slaves, who may sing paeans to their despot over their chains, but they will
not thereby render them less strong, nor, in the end, less galling."[1] Southard
made clear his belief that the people were being bamboozled. They were so
blinded by their affection for Jackson that they could not see the chains he
had foisted upon them. The point of idolatry was taken up by Sprague as
well. The senator from Maine observed, "[the people] are not infallible...It is
of the nature of man to worship the work of their own hands, to bow down
to idols which they have set up. Feeble, fallible mortals like themselves are
canonized and deified." Sprague then shifted to the idol the American people
had created, his description of such being so impeccable that only his exact
words do the senator justice:

> And oftentimes a military chieftain, having wrought real or fancied
> deliverance by successful battles — fervent gratitude, unbounded
> admiration, the best feelings of our nature, rush towards him; the
> excited imagination invests him with a glorious halo, circling around
> him all the splendid perfections and dazzling attributes of heroes and
> patriots; — and then the strongest facts, the clearest evidence, and the
> most cogent reasoning, which expose his errors and ambition, excite
> only indignation and resentment towards their authors, as impious
> and sacrilegious revilers of the idol of their hearts. In the paroxysm
> of their devotion, they are ready at his shrine to sacrifice their rights,
> their liberties, their children, and themselves.

> Sprague did follow up this bleak outlook though with optimistic
> belief that the "delusion will vanish" and that the people will eventu-
> ally wake up from the nightmare they have created for themselves.[2]
> Until then, it would be up to Congress to save the people from their
> false idol.

While Clay certainly pilloried the president with great frequency, the
Kentuckian's fire was surpassed by Sprague, who pelted Jackson throughout
his speech with a furious attack unmatched by any senator who rose in
opposition to the chief magistrate. Usurpation of the public treasure was, in
Sprague's estimation, just the tip of a much larger iceberg. "The measure," he
remarked, "momentous as it in itself, is of still more portentous import when
viewed in its connexion as part of a system, as the last only of a series of acts
all running in the same direction, swelling the same current of patronage,

---

[1] *Register of Debates*, 23rd Cong., 1st sess., (Jan. 8, 1834), 150 (Senate).
[2] *Register of Debates*, 23rd Cong., 1st sess., (Jan. 29, 1834), 387 (Senate).

and accumulating power in one great and all-absorbing reservoir." Sprague lamented that the presidency had become "an all-pervading disease" and that while the power of the government was at an all-time high, the power of the legislature and judiciary had never been less; the power of the executive, meanwhile, had grown exponentially. "How is it at this moment?" the exasperated senator asked. "Is not the whole nation becoming agonized in every fibre, at the tones of his single voice?...His breath is spreading blasting and mildew over this fair and happy land, shrouding its bright and beaming surface in darkness, gloom, and dismay." Jackson had defied the Supreme Court's Cherokee decision; now he had proven he would defy all legislative action with the unbridled wielding of the veto.

After listing several of the more than forty vetoes Jackson handed down to that point, all issued for the simple purpose of gratifying his own will, Sprague exploded, "[a]nd this is republicanism!!!...The whole statute book is at his mercy." Not only was the president seeking to unify the executive departments under his singular will, he was now reaching to join the Senate to his will as well.

The Senate, though, stood firm against the General's assault. For defying Jackson's meddling, his supporters claimed the Senate was "committing suicide." That "[t]he storm of calumny and violence is raging upon [the Senate], because...we have dared to resist Executive encroachment. We may be prostrated; but if we are, the best hopes of the human race will be extinguished. Liberty herself will perish in the fall. Her last shriek will echo from the ruins of the Senate."

Sprague believed the Senate to be the last citadel of defense against an elected monarchy, at least until the people woke up to the danger their hero posed to their own freedoms. In closing, he warned, "[t]he progress of Executive power and prerogative must be arrested...And if it be not done now in this generation, by the peaceable means of constitutional resistance, it will hereafter by the convulsive throes of posterity — convulsions which will baptize our children in their own blood!"[1] The words of Peleg Sprague are generally lost among those of the men of greater consequence who comprised the Senate at this time. However, none among them approached the level of conviction in their words, urgency for the future of the country, and willingness to denounce the Old General for his assault upon liberties of the nation as did the ardent senator from Maine.[2]

---

[1] *Register of Debates*, 23rd Cong., 1st sess., (Jan. 29, 1834), 381-397, (Senate).

[2] Sprague's remarks certainly did not go unchallenged. Speaking next, Grundy took exception Sprague's implication of Jackson expanding the power of the government. It was Jackson who opposed the American System that would require a great expansion of federal power to implement. Grundy also voiced disgust that Sprague would have so low

Thomas Ewing took a more measured and lawyerly approach in rebuking Jackson's illegal claim to power. While the speech may have lacked the guttural fire of Sprague's, it was no less effective. Ewing sought to define what constituted executive power to expose Jackson for wantonly seizing power beyond its definitive bounds. Such a definition proved elusive. Ewing conceded that he "never saw a definition from which a distinct conception of its essence or qualities could be gathered." One who ventured to define executive power was the French statesman, Jacques Necker. Necker characterized executive power as uniting action to will, with the legislative power constituting the will. However, Ewing explained, unlike in France where government action and will resided in the same hands, the American system of government separated the legislative from the executive. For this definition to work in America, the executive would have to suppress his own will in carrying out that of Congress. "[I]n the case of our executive, Ewing continued, "[he] has a will of his own, [and] if it extend to and penetrate every portion of the body politic, that will, accompanied with efficient action, must, as a necessary consequence, overturn and absorb all powers of the legislative will, which is destitute of action." This was not the type of executive the framers had in mind when drafting the Constitution. The executive power of the president could not then be compared to that of kings in Europe who exercised both the will and the action of government, as some Jacksonians had sought to do in his defense.[1] Instead, a deep examination of the Constitution to ascertain what powers were meant for the president and what powers were not would be required to determine the rightness of his actions.

Ewing's examination took him several directions, some of which were discussed earlier. On this point, he compared the clauses granting powers to both Congress and the president to reveal a small, yet important difference. Article One stated "ALL legislative power herein granted shall be vested in a Congress of the United States," while Article Two indicated that "the executive power is vested in the President of the United States." The omission of the word, "all," from the president's grant of power was a crucial distinction. Although Congress was granted all legislative power, in practice, this power was limited — the president's veto power certainly encroached upon legislative authority. However, Ewing opined, by excluding the word

---

an opinion of the people that they would allow Jackson to usurp all power of the government and trample on their liberties. The people had greater sense than that, Grundy argued, and if Jackson were guilty of what he was accused of, the people would turn on him and cast him out of office. See, *Register of Debates*, 23rd Cong., 1st sess., (Jan. 30, 1834), 430 (Senate).

[1] *Register of Debates*, 23rd Cong., 1st sess., (Jan. 20, 1834), 303-304 (Senate).

"all" from the executive grant of power, it was clear that the founders did not intend the president's power to be more comprehensive than that of Congress, power that was in actuality limited despite the use of the word "all." The enumeration of power in the ensuing clauses of Article Two served as further evidence of the intention of the founders to limit the president's power. The Ohioan remarked, "[h]ad that grant been intended to carry with it all the powers now said to be in their nature executive, the subsequent clauses would have contained words of restriction instead of enumeration." Enumerating the president's powers implied that he was excluded from any powers not listed — such as that over the Treasury — whereas a restriction of certain powers would have implied universal authority outside of what was specifically restricted.[1] Ewing utilized his semantic understanding of the Constitution to deny the president any power over the public treasure.

Frelinghuysen went beyond the Constitution to the Bank charter itself to prove executive encroachment over the public treasure. Nowhere in the charter was any power over the deposits conferred to the president, instead, "it detaches the subject from the range of executive authority, and puts it under the immediate supervision of Congress." The president's authority over the Bank was confined to ordering a *scire facias* for charges of wrongdoing. The granting of power to the president in this regard was clear, and therefore, the silence as to any power over the deposits vested in the president was equally clear. This begged the question, why include such a specific delineation of power "if, as contended, [the President] has general control, by virtue of his office, over the money of the Government and every officer?" By assuming power beyond what was granted to him by the charter, Frelinghuysen explained, "[t]he rights of Congress and of the Secretary, and the chartered privileges of the stockholders of the bank, are all alike invaded."[2]

The final anti-Jacksonian to speak was future president, John Tyler. The Virginian called Jackson's claim to power, "alarming," and that sanctioning his removal of the deposits "is to arm him with all power — with the power over life and death — to punish all offenders whose offences he may consider dangerous to the community." By withholding the public deposits, Jackson had unilaterally killed the BUS and in its place, installed a deposit system of banking consisting of state banks reliant upon him for their existence. The money men of the country were forced to grovel at Jackson's feet for "a small pittance" and for an opportunity to be embraced by the safe arms of the president's patronage network. Patronage, Tyler defined as "the sword and the cannon by which war may be made on the liberty of the human race." By seizing

---

[1] *Register of Debates*, 23rd Cong., 1st sess., (Jan. 20, 1834), 303, 327 (Senate).
[2] *Register of Debates*, 23rd Cong., 1st sess., (Feb. 3, 1834), 453-454 (Senate).

control of the public purse, Jackson had made himself "every inch a king"[1] — a king, Tyler warned, with an army of 40,000 retainers "who live only by his smile, and perish by his frown" — more powerful than any found in Europe. Indeed, Jackson had styled himself a modern day Caesar and if allowed to continue, the American republic would meet with the same fate as did Rome.[2]

Tyler likening Jackson to Caesar was not unique among the senators who attacked the president. Clay first made the comparison in his opening speech and most of the anti-Jacksonians who followed made some allusion to Jackson's rule resembling that of the Roman dictator. The senator who orated the connection between the two most impressively was former Vice President John C. Calhoun, who was undoubtedly still stinging from the fallout over the Peggy Eaton affair and his run-in with Jackson over the Nullification Crisis. He remarked that "the analogy between the two...is complete, varied only by the character of the actors and the circumstance of the times." A marked difference though, Calhoun contended, distinguished the two cases. Caesar operated as "an intrepid and bold warrior, as an open plunderer, seizing forcibly the treasury of the country, which, in that republic, as well as ours, was confided to the custody of the legislative department of the Government." Jackson and his partisans, on the other hand operated differently — as "artful, cunning, and corrupt politicians, and not fearless warriors. They have entered the treasury, not swords in hand, as public plunderers, but, with false keys of sophistry, as pilferers under the cover of midnight." Caesar sought money to get men which he used to successfully strike down the Republic; Jackson sought money to attract partisans and votes which he would use "to choke and stifle the voice of American liberty" through corrupting the press, suppressing the other branches of government, and creating a corrupt party of loyal partisans to continue the line of Jacksonian succession for years to come. "[W]hen the deed be done," Calhoun fumed, "the revolution be completed, and all the powers of our republic, in like manner, be consolidated in the President, and perpetuated by his dictation."[3]

***

Of the topics covered in this debate, the discussion of Jackson's illegal seizure of power was the most varied, both in style and substance, especially amongst the anti-Jacksonians. This was likely because some, such as Clay, Sprague, Tyler, and Calhoun, attacked the president not just on his specific actions regarding the Treasury, but for the pattern of executive encroachment

---

[1] Tyler here is quoting from Shakespeare's *King Lear*.
[2] *Register of Debates*, 23rd Cong., 1st sess., (Feb. 24, 1834), 664, 672-675 (Senate).
[3] *Register of Debates*, 23rd Cong., 1st sess., (Jan. 13, 1834), 220 (Senate).

they perceived as pervading Jackson's entire presidency. They used their speeches as an opportunity to condemn Jackson on matters such as overuse of the veto, defying the Supreme Court, and the corrupt spoils system. Their speeches were fiery and combative, if not always accurate in their constitutional argument, but impactful nonetheless. Others, such as Ewing and Frelinghuysen, took a more scholarly, analytical approach to impugn Jackson's behavior by playing with semantics and digging into the nitty-gritty of the Constitution. Their words may have lacked the sheer firepower of those previously mentioned, but their detailed dissection of the issue did not lack in effectiveness. The key thread though tying the anti-Jacksonians together was their universal agreement that a supreme danger to American liberties lay in the president gathering too much power. They all felt that the clause, "to take care that the laws be faithfully executed," was not a blanket grant of power giving the president free reign to do as he pleased. Jackson was constrained by both the laws and the Constitution and actions he had taken throughout his whole presidency, were a blasphemy to the office the framers of the Constitution sought to create.

Jackson's defenders too took different courses in the defense of their embattled president. Some, such as Benton and Hill, chose to ignore the charges against the president, assert that the Senate had no right to investigate the matter, and instead attacked the BUS. Those who addressed Clay's charges, chief among them, the often overlooked William Rives, blasted Jackson's opponents for effectively neutralizing the presidency with their restrictive view of the office. The Jacksonians took to the Constitution and precedent to argue for executive unity to secure good government, unity achieved only through adherence to presidential will. Without the singular voice of the president to guide the branch, they argued, the executive departments would be responsible to no one with the president reduced to nothing more than a hopeless parent vainly trying to corral a litter of wild children. Another effective method of defense employed by the president's men was hero worship. Jackson was the most popular man outside of Washington to have served the office and his partisans, Wilkins, Hill, and Benton most conspicuously, reminded the chamber of his triumphs and the glory he had and would continue to bestow upon their great nation. Given this view of the man, how could he be guilty of the gross charges his enemies had spewed at him?

Chapter 5: A New and Detestable Feature

There were very few points regarding Clay's first resolution on which the opposing sides of the Senate agreed. Did Jackson order the removal of the deposits or did Taney? Was the Treasury department responsible to the legislature or the executive? How much control did the president have over the actions of the department heads? What was the Treasury? These questions polarized the Senate into camps that feverishly defended what each believed to be irrefutably correct. One thing though requiring no debate was the mechanism by which the deposits were removed. Even Jackson, who steadfastly believed his mandate of power was without limit, knew he could not directly implement his will over the deposits. The president needed an agreeable Treasury secretary and when it became clear that William Duane would not accede to Jackson's wishes, the president removed his obstinate subordinate and replaced him with one he knew would comply.

Clay's first resolution charged that Jackson abused his power of removal in the manner described above to impose his will over the public treasury. The Constitution is silent on the removal of officers — only the power to appoint officers with the consent of the Senate is explicitly listed — thus opening the door for the Senate to debate from where was the president granted the power to remove officers, whether this power was constrained in any way, whether Jackson's use of it in this case was an abuse of such power, and if this use be accepted, how it could impact the country going forward.

Clay focused on that final question in his speech. To invade the public treasury, Jackson removed a secretary who was simply exercising his legally granted discretion over the public deposits but whose views clashed with those of the president. In his place, Jackson installed a new secretary willing to move forward with the president's reprehensible scheme. Acceptance of these actions would lead to the creation of a president whose powers knew no limit. Clay warned, "[i]f the President may, in a case in which the law has assigned a specific duty exclusively to a designated officer, command it to be executed, contrary to his own judgement, under the penalty of an expulsion from office, and, upon his refusal, may appoint some obsequious tool to perform the required act, where is the limit to his authority?" Specific to the Treasury, according to the practice of the current administration, all officers of that department must acquiesce to the will of the president under the threat of removal. "What is to prevent whenever he desires to draw money from the public treasury," Clay asked, "his applying the same penalty of expulsion...to every link down the chain, from the Secretary of the Treasury down, and thus obtain whatever he demands?"[1] The president's ability to interfere in all executive matters would be unstoppable. He could patrol the departments, armed with the sword of removal and unsheathe his weapon of obedience at the first sign of defiance. If the sight of its shimmering blade failed to bring the insolent officer in line, he would strike the subordinate down and replace him with one who knew and respected the sword's power.

One aspect of the discussion centered on whether the power to remove officers was granted to the president by the Constitution or the law. The distinction was important for two reasons. First, a constitutional grant of power denoted a level of sacredness and authority to it, such that anyone who dare question it would subject themselves to severe ridicule. Secondly, a legal grant of power could be rescinded by statute, a more conceivable prospect compared to the implausibility of getting passed the constitutional amendment required to revoke a constitutional grant of power.

This debate first transpired in 1789 during the 1st Congress and both Jacksonians and anti-Jacksonians called on the wisdom of their esteemed political ancestors more than forty years later in the advancement of their own views. The Jacksonian who offered the firmest argument that the power of removal was constitutionally granted was William Rives. Rives, perhaps the most meticulous defender of Jackson, laid before his colleagues a detailed review of those early debates to prove that the framers intended for the president to have unquestioned authority to remove officers as one of his vested executive powers granted by the Constitution. The Virginian first argued that entrusting all executive power with the president gave him the authority to control officers to ensure the proper exercise of that power. Rives bolstered

---

[1] *Register of Debates*, 23rd Cong., 1st sess., (Dec. 26, 1834), 73 (Senate).

his claim by citing the highest of constitutional authorities, fellow Virginian, James Madison. "It is evidently the intention of the constitution that the First Magistrate should be responsible for the Executive Department," Madison remarked, and "[t]he principle of unity and responsibility in the Executive Department, is intended for the security of liberty and the public good." Additionally, Rives quoted another member of Congress who stated, "[i]n the constitution, the heads of Departments are considered as mere assistants of the President in the performance of his executive duties," and yet another who said, "[t]he executive powers are delegated to the President, with a view to have a responsible officer to superintend, control, inspect, and check, the officers necessarily employed in administering the law." Undoubtedly, Rives contended, the power to control officers was granted to the president by the Constitution and the authority to remove officers, being the ultimate tool to control executive officers, was a natural consequence of that grant of executive power. Therefore, logic dictated that removal was also granted to the president by the Constitution. Because the framers made no mention of removal when establishing the executive branch, Rives observed, the 1st Congress took steps to make clear this power too flowed from the Constitution and not the law. When creating the departments in 1789, it was originally written that "Secretaries should be appointed, 'to be removable by the President.'" This wording though implied that the power to remove was granted by the law only. To guard against this, the clause was stricken from the final law and instead, an incidental reference to removal was included — "whenever the principal officer shall be removed from office by the President..." — to establish the power as a pre-existing one granted by the Constitution.[1] The slight, but crucial adjustment from "to be removable" to "whenever...shall be removed" detached the grant of power from the law, instead suggesting the power originated from another source, that being the Constitution.

Thomas Ewing, who locked horns with Rives repeatedly throughout his speech, opposed him on this point as well. While the president undeniably retained the power of removal, Ewing contended, it did not originate with the Constitution as Rives had argued. Ewing pointed out that the power to appoint and remove officers was not common for executives in 18th century Europe. In England, where the power to appoint was granted, the Ohioan cited the writings of a mid-18th century commentator to show that appointment power was added following the general grant of executive power to the King. The addition of the power to appoint suggested that it was not considered one of the executive powers normally granted. The framers,

---

[1] *Register of Debates*, 23rd Cong., 1st sess., (Jan. 17, 1834), 289-290 (Senate).

who borrowed extensively from Europe in structuring the federal government, therefore, had very little precedent directing them to vest appointment and removal powers in the chief executive. The structure of the state governments, Ewing remarked, colored much of the framers' thinking for the national government as well. To his knowledge, few states conferred on their governors the power of appointment and even fewer the power to remove. This mentality of reluctance to give such power to the president revealed itself when opposition arose against Madison's suggestion that the chief executive was vested with the power to appoint and remove during the debate forming the State Department. After Madison spoke of the executive powers he envisioned for the president (some of this Rives quoted above), William Loughton Smith responded that he could find no state in which the powers suggested by Madison were granted to a governor. Elbridge Gerry agreed, wondering from what precedent Madison was drawing upon to confer such power on the president and in fact, all precedent on the matter pointed to the contrary. Madison ventured no response to either man's concerns.[1]

The power to appoint, of course, found its way into the Constitution, but it was not granted solely to the president. Nomination was the sole responsibility of the president but appointment was shared with the Senate. Ewing pointed out that the precise wording of this clause in the Constitution was analogous to the British statute that shared appointment power between the king and Parliament. If removal power was a natural consequence to appointment, as Rives had contended, "that power vests in the President, by and with the advice and consent of the Senate, and not the President alone." To show that removal was never intended to rest solely in the president's hands, Ewing quoted *Federalist 77*, in which Alexander Hamilton said, "[i]t has been mentioned as one of the advantages to be expected from the co-operation of the Senate in the business of appointments, that it would contribute to the stability of the administration. The consent of that body would be necessary to displace as well as appoint; a change of the Chief Magistrate, therefore, would not occasion so violent, or so general a revolution in the officers of the Government as might be expected if he were the sole disposer of office." This paper, among others sharing a similar sentiment, were circulated throughout the country for the purpose of explaining to all who wanted to learn how the newly formed government would function.[2] It was apparent to Ewing that although removal was a presidential power, it was not one granted to him by

---

[1] *Register of Debates*, 23rd Cong., 1st sess., (Jan. 20, 1834), 327 (Senate). The exchange between Madison, Smith, and Gerry can be found in *Annals of Congress*, 1st Cong., 1st sess., (June 16, 1789), 479-492 (House).

[2] *Register of Debates*, 23rd Cong., 1st sess., (Jan. 20, 1834), 328 (Senate).

the Constitution. Peleg Sprague took Ewing's point further and suggested that the American people had been duped by the 1789 enactment. Sprague claimed that above quoted passage in *Federalist 77* was meant to inform the people that removal "would not be possessed by the President alone; that as appointments could be made only with the approbation of the Senate, the same concurrence would be necessary to effect a removal." The Constitution was then adopted, along with that understanding of removal. The 1789 decision to grant the President sole removal power was accomplished by the tie-breaking vote of John Adams in direct defiance to the manner presented by Hamilton to the American people.[1]

Grundy undertook to refute the anti-Jacksonian contention that like appointment, removal was a power meant to be shared with the Senate and, like Rives before him, he referenced Madison from the famous 1789 debate to do so. After acknowledging the exception to the president's appointment power spelled out explicitly in the Constitution, Madison asked, "[h]ave we a right to extend this exception? I believe not...If the constitution had not qualified the power of the President in appointing to office, by associating the Senate with him in the business, would it not be clear that he would have the right, by virtue of Executive power, to make such appointment? Should we be authorized, in defiance of that clause in the constitution — the Executive power shall be vested in a President — to unite the Senate with the President in the appointment to office? I conceive not. If it is admitted we should not be authorized to do this, I think it may be disputed whether we ought to associate them in removing persons from office, the one power being as much of an Executive nature as the other."[2] A clearer expression of the president's duty to control his subordinate officers Grundy could not find. The Constitution qualified the president's appointment power, but it was beyond the duty of the legislature to assign the same exception to another executive power, as similar to appointment as it may be.

When Nathaniel Tallmadge broached the matter, he recognized "there was a difference of opinion on the subject in the first Congress, when this important question was agitated" and conceded that Hamilton's stature added weight to the side of sharing the power of removal between the president and the Senate. However, the debate concluded with the decision to vest sole power of removal in the president, "was deemed conclusive...and the matter has been considered at rest." Tallmadge referenced others who agreed the issue resolved, such as Immanuel Kant, who stated that the wording, "'whenever the Secretary shall be removed from office by the Presi-

---

[1] *Register of Debates*, 23rd Cong., 1st sess., (Jan. 29, 1834), 389. (Senate).
[2] *Register of Debates*, 23rd Cong., 1st sess., (Jan. 30, 1834), 417-418 (Senate).

dent'...amounted to a legislative construction of the constitution, and it has ever since been acquiesced in and acted upon, as of decisive authority in the case." Likewise, a 1797 Congressional resolution regarding the deliverance of laws stated that those bound for the various secretaries were to go to their successor in the event of their "death, resignation, or dismission from office."[1] That no opposition arose to the inclusion of the words, "dismission from office" made clear to Tallmadge that removal had become accepted and only now has its validity been questioned.

Theodore Frelinghuysen, despite the outcome of the 1789 proceedings and the precedent established by the ensuing forty years remained unconvinced. The New Jerseyan pointed to another clause of the Constitution to cast doubt on the generally accepted notion that removal was among one of the president's exclusive executive powers. Article Two, Section Two, Clause Three allows for the president to make recess appointments. The inclusion of this clause, according to the theory of power advanced by the Jacksonians, perplexed Frelinghuysen. He mused, "if [the president] may, by his general executive powers, create a vacancy, and then fill it, without the Senate, why was the above clause inserted into the constitution of the United States?" Any construction of the Constitution granting removal power was implied. Therefore, Frelinghuysen surmised, "[t]he question was not then, nor has it since been, directly decided and settled; so that it remains, at the most, a doubtful matter."[2]

The ideas advocated by Ewing, Frelinghuysen, and Sprague were certainly tenuous; even many anti-Jacksonians conceded that Jackson had the constitutional right to remove Secretary Duane, instead focusing their contempt on his reasons for doing so. But future events would prove Frelinghuysen at least somewhat correct; the question was not as settled as the majority believed. In 1867, Congress passed the Tenure of Office Act which prohibited the president from removing certain federal officers without Senate approval. Andrew Johnson promptly violated the act by removing Secretary of War, Edwin Stanton without consent of the Senate and was impeached. The law was repealed in 1887. Two prominent 20th century Supreme Court cases tackled the thorny removal issue as well. The 1926 decision in *Myers v. The United States* upheld the Jacksonians' argument that the president had sole authority in removing appointed officers and did not require Senate approval, but the 6-3 outcome indicated that some were still unconvinced. Nine years later, in *Humphrey's Executor v. United States*, the court ruled unanimously that the president must have cause to remove any officer who is not

---

[1] *Register of Debates*, 23rd Cong., 1st sess., (Mar. 12, 1834), 899-900 (Senate).

[2] *Register of Debates*, 23rd Cong., 1st sess., (Feb. 3, 1834), 453 (Senate).

purely executive in their function.[1] A century separated the debates over Duane's removal and these court cases. That the matter of removal required Supreme Court intervention so many years after the Jacksonians declared it a settled issue serves as vindication for Frelinghuysen, Ewing, and Sprague who views were considered unsound by even some of their own allies.

***

Some of the anti-Jacksonians accepted the president's right to remove officers without Senate approval. Instead, they charged that the president's removal of Duane was unwarranted, against the spirit of what the founders intended removal to be used for, and if allowed, dangerous to the existence of a free government regulated by a clear separation of power.

Samuel Southard summarized the fear of most anti-Jacksonians when he asked, "the President has the power of dismissing...and, therefore, has power to discharge the Secretary, unless he thinks as the President thinks, and acts as the President directs; and that, by this means, he has control over all the actions of all the officers under the Government. Is this...true? Is this power of dismission supreme and irresistible? If it be...no time should be lost in erasing it." To Southard, it was not the existence of such power that bothered him, but the use of it as employed by Jackson. He continued, "[t]here was not then a man in the Congress of the United States [in 1789] who believed that this power could or would be used for mere personal or party purposes, for personal or party revenge; much less to obtain control of the treasury of the country." During his own speech, Sprague added that "predictions that this prerogative would be exerted" in the manner Southard described "were treated as chimeras of a gloomy imagination...if the President remove a valuable officer, it would be an act of tyranny."[2] Tyler summed up the feeling concisely; "if properly exerted to get rid of incompetent or unfaithful agents, [removal] is beneficent in its results. But if used merely to bestow rewards on favorites and to punish opponents...the consequences are most fatal."[3]

All previous presidents had indeed exercised the power of removal but in the estimation of the anti-Jacksonians, none to extent and for the purely partisan purposes that Jackson had.[4] By Sprague's count, the six presidents preceding Jackson had removed seventy-three officers. Within one year of

---

[1] *Humphrey's Executor v. United States*, 295 U.S. 602 (1935).

[2] *Register of Debates*, 23rd Cong., 1st sess., (Jan. 29, 1834), 390 (Senate).

[3] *Register of Debates*, 23rd Cong., 1st sess., (Feb. 24, 1834), 673 (Senate).

[4] Arthur Schlesinger has argued that the scale and the partisan designs behind Jackson's removal of officers were overblown and that this was merely a tool used by the anti-Jacksonians to paint him as a loyalty-seeking authoritarian. Regardless of accuracy, during Jackson's time and since, this charge has been an effective weapon for his opponents to use against him. See, Schlesinger, *The Age of Jackson*, 47.

Jackson taking office, he had removed no fewer than one hundred ninety-six, nearly three times the total of the previous forty years combined.[1] Jackson had perverted the use removal was meant to serve and brought into reality the dangers its opponents forewarned that its supporters never dared to envision. The proper use of removal, Southard declared, "must exist in the law," or "to relieve from the fraud and mental incapacity to discharge the duties arising under circumstances which could not otherwise be controlled." If Congress has vested in an officer a specific duty, such as was vested in the secretary of the Treasury over the deposits in section sixteen of the BUS charter, removal cannot be used "to take away from [Congress's] agent and trustee the right to judge their wishes and intentions. The Executive can never say how the officers of the law shall discharge their duties." Extend the current administration's construction over the power to remove out to other officers and see what shred of free government would remain, Southard cautioned. By this construction, "he may direct a marshal how he shall execute his writs, and whom he shall summon on juries...Where, then is our security? where our protection? where our legal liberties? where the trial by jury — the last and most efficient guardian of the citizen in his dearest interests?...There is no right or privilege which this construction of the power of dismission will not reach...You may boast of your liberties, but they are in the hands of an individual."[2]

Calhoun too acknowledged that the president had the constitutional right to remove officers and actually joined Jacksonians in the opinion that his removal power should be used for the general supervision of the executive officers and could be "exercised in relation to the deposites." However, in this case, Calhoun believed "that the President's conduct is wholly indefensible; and, among other objections, I fear he had in view, in the removal, an object eminently dangerous and unconstitutional." That "eminently dangerous" object was to snuff out the BUS before Congress could act to save it and "give an advantage to his veto."[3] The veto of the Bank recharter bill merely ensured the current bank would no longer exist. Along with removal, however, came the creation of a new banking system, one where the public funds would now reside in chosen state banks. These state banks, in Calhoun's estimation, were subservient to Jackson and therefore, the president had taken an unconstitutional hold over the public purse. Ewing concurred, remarking, "[t]he President has no right to touch or control a single dollar of the public funds, unless it be in pursuance of an appropriation made by law; but he

---

[1] *Register of Debates*, 23rd Cong., 1st sess., (Jan. 29, 1834), 391 (Senate).
[2] *Register of Debates*, 23rd Cong., 1st sess., (Jan. 8, 1834), 161-162 (Senate).
[3] *Register of Debates*, 23rd Cong., 1st sess., (Jan. 13, 1834), 216 (Senate).

has now, by means of another power, with which the law has invested him for other purposes, (the power of appointment and removal,) obtained the potential control over the collection of the revenues, and their custody when collected."[1] Although the two men differed on the source of the president's removal power, both agreed that its use in this case was to secure an unconstitutional object — the seizing of the public purse.

The clearest summary of how Jackson abused of his removal power to take control of the Treasury came from Senator Frelinghuysen. He stated, "[i]n a case where the Secretary of the Treasury reported that the deposites were safe, and that he found no cause to disturb them, the President, in his power, threatens him with expulsion unless he find reason to remove them. The President forces himself between Congress and its officer, and actually drives him from office because he had the manly firmness to follow dictates of his own judgement and conscience...Not only this, but the Executive persists in his interference until he is provided with a Secretary who will put his name to the rescript, and violently abstract eight or nine millions of dollars from the accredited depository of our moneys...[t]here is no parallel for such arbitrary encroachment."[2] Frelinghuysen's concise summary hinted at another area where anti-Jacksonians felt the president could be charged with abuse. The removal of Duane was only side of the equation; the appointment of Taney while the Senate was out of session was the other side. Recess appointments were explicitly granted to the president by the Constitution, but the manner in which Jackson employed it raised eyebrows among his opponents. Because recess appointments could serve until the end of the following congressional session without confirmation, they could hold their position for over a year without Senate approval. Senator Sprague argued that Jackson was taking advantage of this constitutional loophole to bypass the Senate in the appointing of officers. By utilizing his power of removal, Sprague maintained, the president "may cause a vacancy to happen in the recess, which he may fill until the end of the next session of the Senate, and then the vacancy, which commences with the recess, is construed to be one happening in it, to be again filled by the President until the end of another session, when the same process may be repeated." Sprague alluded to the case of Samuel Gwinn to demonstrate Jackson's abuse of the recess appointment. Gwinn had been appointed during a recess to a land office in Mississippi. When the Senate reconvened, his nomination was rejected. Gwinn was then renominated, but the Senate, having already made their feelings on Gwinn clear, tabled the nomination. When the session ended, Gwinn was

---

[1] *Register of Debates*, 23rd Cong., 1st sess., (Jan. 20, 1834), 307 (Senate).
[2] *Register of Debates*, 23rd Cong., 1st sess., (Feb. 3, 1834), 454 (Senate).

appointed during recess again to the same position. Should this manipu-
lation of the recess appointment become standard, Sprague warned, "the
power of the Senate over appointments is annihilated."[1] The senator from
Maine feared that Jackson would use the same tactic to keep Taney in office
should his nomination be rejected by the Senate.[2]

Similar to their defense of the president on other matters, the Jacksonians'
methods to vindicate the exercise of his removal power varied considerably
but they all agreed that exerting that power was critical for the president to
accomplish his duty to see that the laws be faithfully executed. Benton, in
alignment with his general handling of any direct charges against Jackson,
was characteristically dismissive. "From the foundation of the Government," he curtly explained, "it had been settled that the President's right
to dismiss his Secretaries resulted from his constitutional obligation to see
that the laws were faithfully executed." Every prior president had exercised
their removal power but it was only now that a charge of abuse stemming
from the use of such power had occurred. Benton argued that an abuse could
not have occurred since the "Senate cannot assume to know for what cause
the Secretary in question was dismissed," and even if such reasons could
be ascertained, "the President may dismiss his Secretaries without cause."[3]
With that, his discussion of the matter ceased. Benton's terse treatment of
the serious charges against Jackson perhaps spoke louder than the more long
winded, detailed defenses offered by his other allies. The Missourian felt the
charges against Jackson and the Senate's claim to authority to discuss them
so flimsy that he would barely condescend to address them. A similar course
was pursued by Senator Hill of New Hampshire who had little desire to offer
a complex, detailed exoneration of the president. Speaking towards the end
of the three month debate, Hill stated simply on the question of the president's removal power, "[i]f there was any uncertainty, at the commencement
of the discussion of the resolutions offered by the Senator from Kentucky, as
to the constitutional power of the Chief Magistrate to remove a Secretary of
the Treasury, or any other head of a Department, that uncertainty no longer
exists."[4] While the two Jackson stalwarts avoided an intricate exposition on

---

[1] *Register of Debates*, 23rd Cong., 1st sess., (Jan. 29, 1834), 386 (Senate).
[2] Sprague's fears did not come to fruition. Jackson held Taney's official nomination until
the very end of the session in hopes of giving his staunch ally a chance to be confirmed,
but the Senate, without debate, rejected the nomination on June 24, 1834, by a 28–18 vote
along partisan lines. Taney was the first cabinet nomination to be rejected. Days later,
Jackson nominated Levi Woodbury as Secretary of Treasury; he was confirmed by the
Senate on June 27. See, James F. Simon, *Lincoln and Chief Justice Taney: Slavery, Secession, and
the President's War Powers* (New York: Simon & Schuster, 2006), 24.
[3] *Register of Debates*, 23rd Cong., 1st sess., (Jan. 2, 1834), 99, 100 (Senate).
[4] *Register of Debates*, 23rd Cong., 1st sess., (Mar. 3, 1834), 756 (Senate).

presidential power, the rest of those who spoke in his defense took the time to attack the incongruity of vesting executive power in the president but while limiting the power to remove.

To the question of whether the president can direct how an officer performs his duty, Shepley answered in the affirmative. "If he cannot say this," he observed, "then is the officer at liberty to act according to his own opinion; and, however unlawful, however unconstitutional that action may be, the President cannot say he does wrong." Limiting the president's removal power would make it impossible for him to perform his own duty to see that the laws be faithfully executed. Southard had previously imagined a scenario in which the president could direct a marshal which jurors to appoint to affect the outcome of a case under the threat of removal. But consider the opposite, Shepley cautioned. Suppose a marshal appointed a jury of those friendly to the accused — would the president be able to properly execute the laws if he could not step in and direct the marshal otherwise? Shepley reasoned, "[i]f he cannot do this, then indeed is the law and justice prostrated, and all offenders are released from the restraints of law; for the officers may not execute the laws, and the President may not examine how they shall do it, and, of course can have no cause to remove them."[1] Directly related to the situation at hand, Rives proposed an imagined scenario in which the secretary of the Treasury wanted to remove the deposits from the BUS to several questionable banks for no apparent reason and against the wishes of the president. What would have been said had the president not acted in that situation? "We should have heard...denunciations not less loud and vehement than those which have been uttered on the present occasion, thundering against him, but upon a different principle," Rives predicted. He continued, "[w]e should have then been told, sir, that the President had been recreant to his high trust; that he had been armed with the power of removal expressly to protect the public interests from the faithlessness or incapacity of public officers, and, that in failing to exercise it, he had weakly and wickedly betrayed his duty to the constitution and to the country."[2]

It is impossible to know how the counterfactual scenario imagined by Rives would have played out had it occurred but it certainly would have put Clay and his allies in a tricky position between defending the Bank for which they felt genuine affinity and sanctioning an exercise of presidential power that they felt he did not have. It is possible that the constitutional arguments over the president's removal power would have fallen silent and instead, Clay allies would have remarked that while the power to remove is

---

[1] *Register of Debates*, 23rd Cong., 1st sess., (Jan. 14, 1834), 242-243 (Senate).
[2] *Register of Debates*, 23rd Cong., 1st sess., (Jan. 17, 1834), 288-289 (Senate).

not absolute, in this case, Jackson used removal the way the members of the first Congress envisioned it. This, of course, is pure speculation.

Another method of defense for removal employed by the Jacksonians was to attack William Duane. Ether Shepley first introduced this curious defense, but merely hinted at it. The senator remarked that although the president had final say over how executive officers performed their duties, this did not absolve the officers of their own responsibility. However, Shepley added, "[i]f the subordinate officer were to form a judgement of what constituted his duty different from the opinion of the President...it was the duty of the subordinate officer to yield to the opinion of the President, or to retire from office."[1] Without speaking specifically to Duane, Shepley implied that it was the secretary's responsibility to resign his position if his views did not line up with those of the president. Other Jacksonians were more overt in their condemnation of Duane. Forsyth reminded the Senate that the secretary had initially agreed to resign if Jackson decided to move forward with his plan to remove the deposits. When the president made clear he intended to move forward, Duane reneged on his pledge to resign, claiming Jackson's insulting of his professional independence as his reason to stay. Forsyth rebuked Duane for staying on, asserting that had he truly felt mistreated, "he should have thrown back upon the President his commission from respect to himself."[2] How impudent for Forsyth to suggest how Duane best defend his own honor!

The harshest reprimand of Duane, though, came from William Wilkins. The Pennsylvanian all but accused the former secretary of trying to sabotage Jackson's presidency. "The Secretary came into office," Wilkins explained, "holding towards the President unjust and unjustifiable sentiments: that General Jackson was the most unfit man in the country for our Chief Magistrate; that he was the victim of passion and arbitrary feeling; that he was guided, not by his own judgement, but by a secret cabal; that he never carried out, and never intended to carry out, any political opinion which he had professed."[3] The basis for Wilkins' accusations towards Duane stemmed from attacks the latter sustained at the hands of the Jacksonian press machine following his removal. One Philadelphia paper claimed that Duane referred to Jackson as "a RUTHLESS DESPOT," along with the warning, "Jackson is King over all; all must succumb to his mandate, or beware of the consequences!" Another publication accused Duane of intrigue, alleging "that he accepted the office, not to serve the President and the people, but

---

[1] *Register of Debates*, 23rd Cong., 1st sess., (Jan 14, 1834), 242 (Senate).
[2] *Register of Debates*, 23rd Cong., 1st sess., (Jan. 27, 1834), 349-350 (Senate).
[3] *Register of Debates*, 23rd Cong., 1st sess., (Feb. 6, 1834), 490 (Senate).

to serve Nicholas Biddle and the foreign gentry, who own so much of the bank."[1] Duane's surviving letters would suggest these charges were blatantly false and the scorned secretary took measures to defend his reputation.[2] But, as was often the case when it came to Jacksonian politics, the truth lagged secondary to the message his partisans desired for public consumption and Wilkins' message was clear; what other choice did Jackson have but to remove a man so clearly hostile to the president's designs?

***

So important was the matter of removal to the anti-Jacksonians that on March 7, 1834, more than two months into the debate, Henry Clay presented four resolutions aimed at weakening the president's power to dismiss federal officers while strengthening the role of the Senate. The first resolution denied that the Constitution conferred on the president the power to remove offi-cers at his pleasure. The second gave Congress the power to prescribe tenure to any positions whose tenure is not prescribed by the Constitution. The third asked the Judiciary Committee to look into a law that would require Senate approval for all removals and that while the Senate is out of session, the president could only suspend an officer until the Senate reconvened. At that point, the Senate could order the officer removed should they agree with the president or reinstate him if they do not. Lastly, the Committee on the Post Office would look into a provision requiring Senate approval in the appointment of deputy postmasters. The key concerns that his allies had been harping on for the last two months all made their way into Clay's resolutions. The Kentuckian conceded that the 1st Congress had granted the president the power to remove, but that the propriety of that decision had not been examined since. He attributed the concession of removal to the president to the reverence held by the 1st Congress to George Washington; a man so esteemed as to render null, even among his opponents, the concern that the power may be abused. The current chief magistrate, Clay argued, had no such integrity. The unlimited removal power that the Jacksonians maintained would give their standard bearer an army of forty thousand government officials, all reliant on him for their existence. This boundless danger compelled Clay to propose these resolutions to "invite a deliberate review of the constitutional powers of the President and of Congress; and to ascertain if the wisdom of our fathers had really rendered subservient to the will of one man, a vast power, capable of totally changing the character

---

[1] *Philadelphia Gazette*, October 9, 1833; *New Hampshire Patriot and State Gazette*, October 14, 1833.

[2] For Duane's answer to the Jacksonians' charges, see, Duane, *Correspondence*, 113-126.

of the Government, and rendering it, although in form a republic, in fact a despotism."[1]

It is unclear exactly why Clay chose to propose these resolutions when he did, especially when considering his initial resolutions had yet to be voted on. Some clues can be found in his correspondence with Littleton Tazewell, the former senator from Virginia and the state's soon-to-be governor. Clay wrote on February 1, 1834, that he had read the communication between Tazewell and former Secretary Duane that the former had sent him and that it "expose[d] a new and detestable feature in the affair of the deposites."[2] What the "new and detestable feature" Clay was referring to is not revealed. The letter which Clay appears to have referenced was written by Duane to Tazewell on January 15. Duane wrote, "[t]he true nature of the service required, consisted, not in the mere removing of the deposites, but in removing them, from an unwillingness to await the action of congress, or to resort to the appropriate agency of the judiciary, upon questions connected with the bank of U.S. — not in the mere substitution of one fiscal agent for another, but in exercising, for penal ends, a power given solely for conserva-tive purposes."[3] It is likely the decision to remove Duane for refusing to enact a measure for the purposes he described was the "detestable" feature Clay alluded to and compelled him to propose the above resolutions. Clay then asked his former Senate colleague his thoughts on whether the Constitu-tion, decision of the 1st Congress notwithstanding, gave the president the power to remove officers and if Jackson therefore had the power to remove Duane for refusing to remove the deposites. Tazewell responded a few weeks later that he believed removal to be one of the president's constitutionally granted powers since, in his view, it was an executive power and all such power resided with the president. He continued that he felt it "manifestly absurd" for the president to be responsible for the acts of the officers under his watch but be unable to control and remove them if need be. He added that a president who abused such power would have to answer to Congress, the people, and the states, implying that the limit to the president's removal power would emanate from those sources.[4] Clay did not appear deterred by Tazewell's upholding of the president's removal power and went along with his resolutions anyway.

The resolutions reveal Clay's intense desire to kneecap the president, more accurately, *this* president, and make him subservient to the Senate

---

[1] *Register of Debates*, 23rd Cong., 1st sess., (Mar. 7, 1834), 834-835 (Senate).
[2] Clay to Littleton Tazewell, February 1, 1834, in *Papers of Henry Clay*, 693.
[3] William Duane to Littleton Tazewell, January 15, 1834, in Duane, *Correspondence*, 137.
[4] Tazewell to Clay, February 19, 1834, in *Papers of Henry Clay*, 699-700.

which at that time was comprised of a majority of anti-Jacksonians. Removal, however, was not a winning issue for the forlorn Kentuckian. While his colleagues, notably Ewing, Frelinghuysen, and Sprague, put forth a gallant effort in their attempt to divest constitutional authority from the president's removal power, the more effective arguments attacked Jackson's abuse of power, not whether he actually possessed it. Arguing against the wisdom of the 1st Congress, and specifically James Madison, was an Augean task. Accordingly, Clay's resolutions met with a quiet death. After presenting them on March 7, Clay moved that they be considered on April 7 and then he delayed further until April 21. By that point, the Senate was deep into its discussion of Jackson's protest message following the adoption of Clay's December 26 resolutions and the matter seems to have been ignored. On May 8, the resolutions were again considered, but on the motion of John Forsyth, were laid on the table. There is no record that the March 7 resolutions were considered again.[1]

Clay was presented with one more opportunity to limit to president's removal power during the next session. John Calhoun had proposed that a committee look into the extent of executive patronage in the government, as in his view it had been growing over the recent years. The bipartisan committee emerged with three resolutions, one being a bill to repeal two sections of an 1820 act that limited the terms of certain officers. Clay delivered a speech on February 18, 1835, which he began by expressing his gratitude that the issue of patronage had come up. At the previous session, Clay complained, the Bank issue was used "to deceive and blind the people as to the enormity of executive pretensions." Without the Bank issue, the Senate could now take up the matter of the expansion of executive power free from distraction. Clay took the opportunity during his speech to introduce an amendment to the repeal bill under consideration. After reading it, Clay commented that the proposed amendment was "substantially the same proposition as one which I submitted to the consideration of the Senate at its last session." However, astute enough to recognize that its inclusion could sink the bill he himself supported, Clay added that he would not force the amendment to appear in the final version of the bill against the wishes of those who crafted it.[2] The bill eventually passed by a 31–16 vote without Clay's amendment.[3] Thus ended the Kentuckian's valiant quest to erode the president's removal power by chaining it to the Senate.

***

---

[1] *Senate Journal*, 23rd Cong., 1st sess., Mar. 7, 1834, 175-176; Apr. 7 1834, 213; May 8, 1834, 253.

[2] *Register of Debates*, 23rd Cong., 2nd sess., (Feb. 18, 1835), 513, 523 (Senate).

[3] *Senate Journal*, 23rd Cong., 2nd sess., Feb. 21, 1835, 178.

It was very easy in 1835 for Clay to blame the Bank for distracting from the real issue of curbing executive power after the final nail had been driven into its coffin. However, his 1835 statements regarding the Bank were indicative of the Kentuckian's true purpose when he rose to present his resolutions on December 26, 1833. Clay understood by that point that the BUS could not be saved, at least not while Jackson was still in power. But he also believed that Jackson's maneuverings to kill the Bank would have a profound negative impact on the nation's finances. If Clay could draw a direct line from Jackson's usurpation and abuse of power to the distress the people were currently suffering, perhaps he could tear down the man he had failed to supplant by electoral means. Indeed, much of the language employed during the debate over the first resolution so resembled that of the previous presidential election that the session could be viewed as a continuation of that contest. Furthermore, Clay recognized the importance of unity among anti-Jacksonians in the Senate. He hoped this unity would coalesce into a permanent political party with national appeal to oppose Jackson, a party he hoped and expected to lead. Among the president's opposition existed those with varying affinities for the BUS so making it the prominent issue threatened to fracture the fragile anti-Jackson coalition that would become the Whig party. An aggressive defense of the BUS could also have had the additional effect of stigmatizing the new party as just a reincarnated version of the elitist National Republicans, a label long spoiled by defeat.[1] Clay and Biddle discussed as much as the former headed to Washington ahead of the opening of the session. The two men agreed usurpation and abuse of executive authority should take the lead to unite the opposition against the president.[2] Indeed, when halfway through the debate after it became clear that the discussion was drifting at times to the question of rechartering the Bank, Jackson defector, Willie P. Mangum, attempted to redirect the discussion back to the true question before the Senate. Speaking just above a whisper, the North Carolinian asserted that recharter "was not the question before the Senate, nor should it be made the question with his consent...The Senate ought now to look to the subject before them; to perform their duty at all hazards; the duty they owed to the constitution and the country, and to repair the violated majesty of our constitution and our broken faith."[3] This well-known remark encapsulated the anti-Jacksonian strategy ironed out between Clay and Biddle before the session began. But for Clay, there some-

---

[1] Frank Towers, "The Rise of the Whig Party," in *A Companion to the Era of Andrew Jackson*, ed. Sean Patrick Adams (Somerset: John Wiley & Sons, Inc., 2013), 342.
[2] Merrill D. Peterson, *The Great Triumvirate: Webster, Clay, and Calhoun* (New York: Oxford University Press, 1988), 239.
[3] *Register of Debates*, 23rd Cong., 1st sess., (Feb. 11, 1834), 536 (Senate).

thing more than just fear for the country's future and party unity that drove his first resolution; it was fueled by something that burned deeper in his soul. It was a fire that had been stoked twenty years earlier and had only intensified with time — his hatred of Andrew Jackson.

This hatred of Jackson culminating with the proposal of his first resolution forced an examination of executive power to a level unseen since the Republic's earliest days. The examination was warranted; Jackson had taken the presidency to a place the founders never envisioned it going. Modern observers would not recognize the presidency that Clay and his allies hoped to restore. To be sure, all the men who had assumed the office of the presidency prior to Jackson had enlarged its power in some way, but none so much as approached the height of expansion reached by Old Hickory.

Clay set the tone for the line of attack against the president, but in doing so, he put his allies in an extremely untenable position. Many of Clay's grievances against Jackson rested on shaky foundation and appear driven more by anger than by constitutional soundness. This made it difficult for his colleagues to sustain the attack at the risk of appearing to lack a basic understanding of how the government functioned. The anti-Jacksonian vision for the presidency was also at odds with the new flavor of egalitarian democracy that was evolving at the time (for white males, at least). The anti-Jacksonians, though, must be given credit for the creativity they employed in support of their leader and his resolution, and although their attempt to corral executive power ultimately failed, their willingness to stand in opposition to a man whose popularity was only matched by his vindictiveness to advance what they perceived to be in the best interest of the country, is commendable.

The outcome of the vote notwithstanding, the Jacksonians won the debate over Clay's first resolution on the back of forty years of precedent that the anti-Jacksonians, despite their best efforts, could not hope to erase. Clay's second resolution, a refutation of Taney's reasons for removing the deposits, would prove an easier case to argue, but as Clay feared, the Bank issue would reveal cracks in the anti-Jacksonian alliance.

CHAPTER 6: AT ANY TIME OTHERWISE ORDER AND DIRECT

Henry Clay's first resolution was an abstraction. He used Jackson's conduct towards the Second Bank of the United States as a vehicle to denounce his entire presidency. His second resolution, however, was far more concrete. Roger Taney had presented his reasons for removing the deposits from the BUS; Clay rejected those reasons as being insufficient to warrant such action. The debate over the first resolution at times wandered into theoretical discussions of constitutional principles — discussions in which some senators were reluctant participants. The debate over the second resolution was far simpler in its substance, however no less intense. Whereas some Jacksonians, such as Thomas Benton and Isaac Hill chose to let the absurdity of some of Clay's grievances against Jackson go unaddressed, their defense of Taney and corresponding attacks on the BUS were abundant and delivered with force. For anti-Jacksonians, upholding the resolution was their last ditch effort to secure a stay of execution for the BUS lingering helplessly on death row; for Jacksonians, denouncing the resolution was a rejection of that effort.

Before examining Taney's report and the debate that followed, it is important to note the developments that led to the submission of a report by the Committee of Finance on the expediency of the removal, as it weighed in heavily on many of the topics the secretary brought up. Daniel Webster chaired the committee of five; of the other members, three — Thomas Ewing, John Tyler, and North Carolina's Willie Mangum — were anti-Jacksonians. The lone Jacksonian of the bunch was William Wilkins. It was discussed earlier that just after Taney submitted his reasons for removal, some members of the Senate, led by Thomas Benton, wanted the issue immediately to be taken up by the Committee of Finance. To this end, Benton was voted down and Clay's resolutions, including debate over Taney's report, became the special order of the day moving forward.

The removal of the deposits prompted Biddle to shift BUS lending policies that created an economic panic lasting throughout the session.[1] Prices fell, wages decreased, defaults on loans edged upwards, businesses failed, unemployment rose, and although the panic hit some areas much harder than others, and in some places not at all, people were on edge.[2] Consequently, throughout the debate, the Senate was flooded daily with petitions, memorials, and testimonials from various parts of the country, expressing either support or opposition to the measures taken by the administration. The vast majority opposed the administration and requested the deposits be restored. Between December 30, 1833 and March 28, 1834 — the date Clay's resolutions came to a vote — no fewer than one hundred twenty-one petitions, memorials, and testimonials were presented expressing pro-Bank sentiments compared to just twenty-five in support of the removal. Once read to the Senate, the memorials were referred to the Committee of Finance for further examination. The outpouring from the public led to a parallel Senate debate on the level of financial distress burdening the country and what caused it.

This parallel debate on the distress of the country elicited some heated discussion matching the intensity of that over Clay's resolutions. One discussion in particular brought the Committee of Finance off the sidelines. After presenting resolutions passed by the New York legislature in support of the administration on January 30, Silas Wright, employing an earlier tactic used by Webster in which he spoke extemporaneously after submitting a memorial from his state, took the opportunity to offer his own feelings on the public distress. Wright placed the Bank at the center of the current distress, attacked its constitutionality, and made clear his desire to see no changes to the current state of things vis-à-vis the Bank and public deposits.[3]

Webster, who Wright referenced throughout his speech, took a moment to respond in defense of the Bank and its necessity to sustaining a stable economy. He charged that Wright's words were those "not of cheering or consolation, but of ill-boding signification," since Webster believed Wright, as one of the most authoritative Democrats in the Senate, had spoken to "the settled purpose of the administration on the great question which so much

---

[1] The specifics of the Bank's behavior and the two sides' commentary on it are covered in this and ensuing chapters.

[2] Campbell, *The Bank War and the Partisan Press*, 104.

[3] *Register of Debates*, 23rd Cong., 1st sess., (Jan. 30, 1834), 397-405 (Senate).

agitates the country." Wright immediately interjected that his words were his alone and "he had no authority to speak for the administration."[1] This was a blatant lie. The day before taking the floor, Wright met with Vice President Van Buren at the behest of Jackson. The Little Magician had been instructed to push his New York ally to make a statement on the Bank in line with that of the administration. The purpose was two-fold; the president felt his views on the Bank had not been fully articulated and Wright could rectify that. Of greater importance, Jackson needed a New Yorker to openly repudiate centralized banking to shake rumors that the administration's opposition to the BUS was part of a conspiracy led by Van Buren and the powerful Albany Regency to transport the nation's financial center to New York. Wright understood his task and as the loyal Jacksonian that he was, acquiesced and even asked Van Buren to jot down some specifics he wanted included in the speech. The speech served the desired purpose and helped coalesce Democratic support around the administration's policies towards the BUS among those who to that point had remained on the fence.[2]

The day after the two enemies clashed — Wright and Webster shared a mutual dislike for one another — George Poindexter of Mississippi rose and expressed dismay over the current state of the Senate. Like Webster, Poindexter correctly believed Wright's words to be those of the administration and it was clear that no matter what the Senate ruled in regards to the deposits, it would be vetoed if Jackson did not approve. The Mississippian lamented that "Congress was reduced to a mere legislative machine, for the preparation of business, to be consummated or not, by the power that assumes the right to rule the destinies of the country." Poindexter felt the only remedy was to refer the matter to the Committee of Finance, as they would have the ability to investigate fully and present to the people all the facts on the subject. He trusted the investigation would vindicate all that Clay and his colleagues had been arguing and reveal the removal of the deposits perpetrated by the administration as the source of the pecuniary distress that had befallen the nation. Poindexter therefore submitted five resolutions to the Senate to provide a framework for the investigation. The third resolution called for the Committee to investigate the appropriateness of both Taney's reasons for removal and of the power exercised by Jackson to facilitate it — the very essence of Clay's resolutions.[3]

On February 3, the Senate considered Poindexter's resolutions. Their author voiced concern that because the Committee would need Taney's orig-

---

[1] *Register of Debates*, 23rd Cong., 1st sess., (Jan. 30, 1834), 405 (Senate).
[2] Remini, *Jackson and the Bank War* 149, 161-164.
[3] *Register of Debates*, 23rd Cong., 1st sess., (Jan. 30, 1834), 434-435 (Senate).

inal report to complete its investigation, it might delay the Senate's debate on Clay's resolutions, a delay he did not want to provoke. Van Buren, as the presiding officer, ruled that as long as the secretary's original report was in the possession of the Finance Committee, the Senate debate on Clay's resolutions would be suspended. Clay and Poindexter both made suggestions that would allow the debate to continue while the Committee of Finance looked into the Mississippian's resolutions and Webster, as chair of the Committee, pledged to compile a report by the following evening so the order of the day could resume with minimal interruption. The Jacksonians, of course, were not silent on the matter. William Rufus King of Alabama questioned the purpose of Poindexter's resolutions and Forsyth insisted that the debate must halt for an extended period while the Committee examined all that the resolutions instructed. This was a tacit swipe at Webster for suggesting that the Committee report could be completed in a single day.[1]

Webster doubled down on the promise the next day. He moved that the Committee of Finance take up not Poindexter's resolutions, but Taney's report and Clay's second resolution and that their findings would be presented the following day. This amounted to an adoption of Poindexter's third resolution that he presented a day earlier, excluding the piece instructing the Committee to investigate Jackson's abuse of power (Poindexter would later modify his resolution to omit that piece). Webster's motion passed; the Committee of Finance would evaluate Taney's reasons for removal. Although the Mississippian's resolutions were ultimately left to die on the table, in introducing them, he was instrumental in procuring the authoritative report of the Committee, presented by its chair, the powerful Daniel Webster.[2]

***

Taney listed the reasons for his actions in the report he submitted to Congress at the beginning of the session. Taney first established his authority to remove the deposits from the BUS by quoting section sixteen of the Bank's charter. The section read, "[a]nd be it further enacted, that the deposites of the money of the United States, in places which said bank and branches thereof may be established, shall be made in said bank or branches thereof, unless the Secretary of the Treasury shall at any time otherwise order and direct; in which case, the Secretary of the Treasury shall immediately lay before Congress, if in session, and if not, immediately after the commencement of the next session, the reasons for such order and direction."[3] He went

---

[1] *Register of Debates*, 23rd Cong., 1st sess., (Feb. 3, 1834), 445-447 (Senate).
[2] *Register of Debates*, 23rd Cong., 1st sess., (Feb. 5, 1834), 466-467 (Senate).
[3] *Register of Debates*, 23rd Cong., 1st sess., Appendix 59.

on to comment that this power of removal "be absolute and unconditional" and, perhaps anticipating his detractors' arguments, that his requirement to report his reasons to Congress "cannot be considered as a restriction of the power" and, "as the Secretary of the Treasury presides over one of the Executive Departments of the Government, and his power over this subject forms a part of the executive duties of his office, the manner in which it is exercised must be subject to the supervision of the officer to whom the constitution has confided the whole executive power."[1] Simply stated, Taney claimed unlimited power over the country's public deposits and that while he must report his reasons for removing the deposits, it was merely for information-giving purposes and Congress had no right to judge upon the expediency of those reasons. Furthermore, being an executive officer, Taney must defer to the supervision of the president, to whom the Constitution conferred all executive power.

Taney contended that by adding section sixteen to the Bank's charter, Congress effectively waived its power over the place of the deposits and ceded such power to the secretary of the Treasury, a move he viewed with surprise. Under this reading of the charter, if Congress, for whatever reason, deemed the public deposits unsafe in the BUS, section sixteen would impede their authority to remove them. Therefore, in order for the deposits to be removed, the secretary would have to share Congress's view as to the safety and remove them himself. If the secretary disagreed with Congress's desire to remove the deposits, it would have no recourse. Nevertheless, Taney understood the contract, and specifically section sixteen, as Congress ceding its power and granting him unlimited control over the deposits. He had merely acted according to that understanding.[2]

Taney construed this power over the deposits to mean removal could come at any time he felt it would serve the public interest, even if the safety of the deposits was not in question. Specifically, Taney asserted, "[i]t is not necessary that the deposits be unsafe, in order to justify the removal. The authority to remove is not limited to such a contingency. The bank may be perfectly solvent, and prepared to meet promptly all demands upon it; it may have been faithful in the performance of its duties, and yet the public interest may require the deposites to be withdrawn."[3] This construction of the charter further exemplified Taney's belief that his power over the deposits was limitless; perfect behavior by the Bank could not ensure the deposits remain in its

---

[1] *Register of Debates*, 23rd Cong., 1st sess., Appendix, 60.
[2] *Register of Debates*, 23rd Cong., 1st sess., Appendix 60.
[3] *Register of Debates*, 23rd Cong., 1st sess., Appendix 60.

vaults if the secretary decided, under the broad umbrella of public interest, that they should be deposited elsewhere.

To support such an interpretation of the charter's meaning, Taney employed precedent, citing a postscript from an 1817 letter written by former Secretary of Treasury, William Crawford, to the President of the Mechanics' Bank of New York. Crawford wrote, "[t]he Secretary of the Treasury will always be disposed to support the credit of the State banks, and will invariably direct transfers from the deposits of the public money in aid of their exertions to maintain their credit."[1] Although Crawford later stated that the current situation warranted no such transfers, his willingness to transfer public moneys to maintain the credit of the state banks would seem to support Taney's claim that solvency and safety of the deposits were not the sole factors necessitating their removal.

The construction of section sixteen as understood by Taney, effectively granting him sole jurisdiction over the deposits and the authority to remove them for reasons beyond their safety, drew heavy criticism from the anti-Jacksonians. Clay recognized the general nature of the clause Taney referred to but cautioned that it must be considered within the context of the whole contract. The charter stipulated that the secretary of the Treasury act as an agent or representative of Congress. How could Taney, being the agent, possess more authority over the deposits than Congress, the principal, who in the previous session recommended against the removal of the deposits? Instead, Clay reasoned, Taney's role was to uphold the government's end of the contract — to deposit its revenue in the BUS. Contract law forbids one party from breaking a contract if the other is fulfilling the terms agreed upon. The Bank was bound by the charter to serve as a safe depository for the public funds and facilitate payment of government expenditures in a timely manner. Both of these functions, even Taney admitted, the Bank had performed adequately. Yet Taney still removed the deposits. Clay asked his colleagues, "[s]uppose, when the citizens of the United States were invited by the Government to subscribe to the stock of this bank, that they had been told that, although the bank performs all its covenants with perfect fidelity, the Secretary of the Treasury may, arbitrarily or capriciously, upon his speculative notions of any degree of public interest or convenience to be advanced, withdraw the public deposites; would they have ever subscribed?" Clay believed removing the public deposits for any reason besides danger to their safety was a breach of the contract between the government and the Bank.

---

[1] *American State Papers: Correspondence Related to Public Deposits* 18: 501.

One of the purposes of this study is to highlight the contributions to this crucial debate of lesser known senators, but on this point, the marquee names spearheaded the opposition. Perhaps none joined Clay in opposition with more force or candor than John C. Calhoun. The South Carolinian condensed the whole argument down to just three words found in section sixteen: unless otherwise ordered. He referred to the clause in question as a trust power conferred upon the secretary as opposed to a chartered right or personal liberty. Trust powers, Calhoun continued, are limited in nature so the argument boiled down to the scope of power Congress intended to give to the secretary through the inclusion of section sixteen and the three words in question. "The whole section relates to...the safe and faithful keeping of the public funds," Calhoun explained. The Bank was determined as a safe depository for the revenue and the secretary was granted power to withhold the deposits as an added measure of security. The common thread between the Bank's responsibility and the secretary's power was the security of the deposits. Therefore, Calhoun reasoned, Taney clearly exceeded the trust power confided in him since "[i]t is not even pretended that the public deposites were in danger, or that the bank had not faithfully performed all the duties imposed on it in relation to them; nor that the Secretary placed the money in more faithful hands." Calhoun recognized that his opponents would argue that the charter did not confide a trust power to the secretary, but that the letter of law instead granted him a "chartered right, to be used according to his discretion and pleasure." Although he personally rejected this notion, Calhoun entertained it to prove that even accepting this, Taney exceeded the letter of the law. The charter granted the secretary the power to withhold the deposits but nowhere did it confer on him the power to choose an alternate place of deposit. Choosing the place of the deposits would then require Taney to resort to what he felt was the intention of the law. Simply stated, Taney and his supporters wanted it both ways — the letter of the law gave Taney the power to withhold the deposits and the supposed intention of the law allowed him to choose a new place of deposits. Such power as Taney claimed, in Calhoun's mind, was beyond that of even Congress to wield. Accepting this would confer on the secretary "extraordinary power...over the deposites, to dispose of them in such manner as he may think the public interest or the convenience of the people may require." The secretary's role instead, Calhoun concluded, matched that as described by Clay; "to withhold the deposites in the case that the bank should violate its stipulations in relation to them on one side, and, on the other, to prevent the

Government from withholding the deposites, so long as the bank faithfully performed its part of the contract[.]"[1]

The South Carolinian's narrowing of the charter dispute down to three words and his effortless dismantling of the opposing view showcased the greatness of Calhoun's legalistic mind. An observer commented that he spoke "with his usual fluency and fire...threw out many new and strong points, and was listened to with the most profound attention by all the Senate, every member being in his seat; and with anxious solicitude by the auditors, who crowded every accessible part of the chamber." Calhoun's entire speech lasted just ninety minutes and was delivered without the aid of notes, a "rare merit" when compared to most of his Senate colleagues who consumed multiple days to complete their speeches.[2] Despite its relative brevity, the South Carolinian delivered his message with aplomb, with one friendly newspaper commenting, "he had condense[d] more thought in a speech of one hour and a half, than others had in four days."[3]

The assault on the Jacksonian position by the Great Triumvirate concluded three weeks after Calhoun spoke, when Daniel Webster, in delivering the report from the committee he chaired, zeroed in on Taney's wild claims. Calhoun chose to focus his opposition on three words in section sixteen; Webster chose a wider examination of the charter in his refutation. The two Senate titans had chosen different tactics, but they were equally effective in dismantling the secretary's argument.

Webster reiterated his colleagues in charging that public interest could not serve as the impetus under section sixteen for the secretary to remove the deposits. "The keeping of the public money is not a matter which is left, or was intended to be left, at the will of the Secretary, or any other officer of the government," the Committee chair lectured. "This public money has a place fixed by law, and settled by contract; and this place is the Bank of the United States...To remove it, therefore from this place, without the occurrence of just cause, is to thwart the end and design of the law, defeat the will of Congress, and violate the contract into which the Government has solemnly entered." Instead, Webster observed, no proof existed in the charter — in section sixteen or beyond — or throughout the debates over the formation of the Bank to suggest Congress had any intention to grant the secretary the authority to judge what would serve the best interests of the public. Webster explained that "[s]uch a power, should he possess it, would necessarily make him the general superintendent of all the proceedings of

---

[1] *Register of Debates*, 23rd Cong., 1st sess., (Jan. 13, 1834), 208-209.
[2] *The United States Gazette*, Philadelphia, January 18, 1834.
[3] *Baltimore Patriot*, January 16, 1834.

the bank; because it would enable him to compel the bank to conform all its operations to is pleasure, under penalty of suffering a removal of the public moneys. This would be little less than placing all the substantial power of managing the bank in his hands." The charter conferred to the secretary no power over the management of the Bank and in fact, it stated quite the opposite. All power over the management of the Bank resided with the twenty-five annually chosen directors. Webster categorically stated, "[t]here is nothing in the charter giving the slightest authority to the Secretary to decide, as between the bank on the one hand, and the government or the people on the other, whether the general management of the directors is wise or unwise; or whether, in regard to matters not connected with the deposites, it has or has not violated the conditions of the charter." Had Congress intended to bestow on the secretary a general guardianship over the public interest in relation to the Bank and a right to judge its operations, it would have granted him far more extensive power than just over the deposits. The secretary's power was confined to judging the safety and solvency of the deposits and he was armed with the remedy of removal if he deemed their safety precarious. There, however, his power over the operations of the Bank ceased. The secretary had no authority to sell the stock of the Bank nor could he refuse to receive BUS notes as payment to the government, regardless of any depreciation the notes may have suffered. The power to remedy issues arising from those matters rested with Congress or the president, thus illustrating the limited scope of the secretary's authority over the Bank's operations outside of anything beyond the safety of the deposits.[1]

The vigor with which Clay, Calhoun, and Webster delivered their remarks and the talent they displayed in elucidating their positions showcased the great potential they had to lead a united front to stand up to Jackson. This alliance, however, was hamstrung by their own political ambitions and sectional ties. Webster had flirted with the Jacksonians since the Nullification Crisis in hopes of ascending to the presidency through an alliance with Unionist Jacksonians and was therefore reluctant at the start of the session to involve himself in the debate over Clay's first resolution. Only when it became clear by the end of January 1834 that his attempts to conciliate with the Jacksonians had failed, as one prominent historian described it, "Webster fell into line, kicking and screaming behind Clay's leadership."[2] As explained earlier, Calhoun was no stronger an ally for Clay. Although readily willing to join the Kentuckian in attacking Jackson and Taney for abusing their power, Calhoun broke with Clay and Webster on the future of

---

[1] *Register of Debates*, 23rd Cong., 1st sess., Appendix, 148-149.
[2] Peterson, *The Great Triumvirate*, 240.

the nation's currency and instead shared the vision desired by hard money Democrats. Had Congress worked with Jackson to develop a new system of banking and currency that was to his liking, the South Carolinian would have likely abandoned his soft money allies and fallen in line with the president despite his personal animus towards Old Hickory.

Despite its frail strands, the fabric of alliance between the three great senators held strong on this particular point. The clarity, force, and political clout behind it though did not shield it from rebuke from the Jacksonians. Shepley wondered why section sixteen would not indicate such, if the criteria for removal were based solely on their safety. The construction of the section advanced by Calhoun, Shepley argued, would "change the rights of the parties; giving the bank the right to say to the Government, You cannot remove the deposites unless they are unsafe." Both the Bank and government agreed to the general language of section sixteen as written and attempting to spin it otherwise now only suggests gross ineptitude on the part of the Congress when drawing up the charter.[1] Forsyth added that Calhoun's construction of section sixteen "is founded upon an assumption that the discretion of the [Treasury] department is necessarily limited by the nature of its duties, these being fiscal, his reasons for exercising the discretion must be fiscal reasons. Hence, it is concluded that the deposites must be in danger before he [the Secretary] can properly act." However, Forsyth contended, even if it was true that the secretary was limited in his authority to purely fiscal matters, "there might exist many and various fiscal reasons for changing the place of deposite, perfectly consistent with their safety in the bank."[2] To these Jacksonians, section sixteen could not be clearer; the secretary's power over the deposits was unqualified and without limit.

Other Jacksonians joined the chorus of attacks against triumvirate's construction of section sixteen by adding different subtleties to what had already been argued. Grundy found it ironic that Calhoun cited the shortness of the passage outlining the secretary's power over the deposits as the basis for his objections considering "the maxim on which he so successfully practises...is, that in expressions of thought, brevity gives strength. It is singular that he should make that objection which his friends declare to be one of the distinguished excellencies of his own style, which compresses *multum in parvo*." The Tennessean added that even the Bank accepted the power exercised by Taney as illustrated by its willingness to surrender the funds when ordered. If the Bank felt the secretary had exercised power beyond the limits of the charter, why then did it cooperate with Taney's order? The Bank had

---

[1] *Register of Debates*, 23rd Cong., 1st sess., (Jan. 14, 1834), 246 (Senate).
[2] *Register of Debates*, 23rd Cong., 1st sess., (Jan. 27, 1834), 351 (Senate).

demonstrated it would refuse to release public money if it thought improper when it declined to disburse funds to the War Department for pension payments in 1832.[1] The surrendering of the money in this case, Grundy reasoned, amounted to an acknowledgement of Taney's right to remove it.[2] Wilkins drew the Senate's attention to another section of the charter — section fourteen — to prove the secretary was granted full authority over the deposits. Section fourteen stipulated "that the bills or notes shall be 'receivable in all payments to the United States, unless otherwise directed by act of Congress.'" The charter clearly distinguished between areas left to the discretion of Congress — bills and notes — versus those to the discretion of the secretary — the deposits. "If the intention of Congress was otherwise," Wilkins questioned, "why were not the deposites and the bills and notes placed on the same footing?...why was it not also enacted, that the deposites should remain with the bank, 'unless otherwise ordered and directed by act of Congress!'"[3] Building on Wilkins' point, Tallmadge added that viewed as a contract, section sixteen was the sole clause granting the government authority to remove the deposits should the need arise and this power was given to the secretary. The New Yorker continued, "[i]f Congress had been inserted instead of the Secretary, Congress would have had the power, without limitation or restriction. The Secretary being inserted in the place of Congress, it follows, as a necessary consequence, that he must have the same power the Congress would have had."[4] Tallmadge also took issue with Webster's point that the grant of power, as Taney construed it, would give the secretary the authority over the total management of the Bank. He countered that while he agreed the secretary's power could not outstrip that of the board of directors, "it is his right, no less than his duty, to judge of that management, as regards the great and paramount interests of the country, and to correct it, if in his judgement, it be wrong, so far as his power over the public deposites may enable him to do it."[5]

In the same way they relied on interpretation and intent of the Constitution to charge Jackson with usurpation and abuse of power, anti-Jacksonians relied on interpretation and intent of the Bank's charter to assail Taney. Considering the challenge posed by trying to prove someone's intentions, the anti-Jacksonians deserve credit for their bold and often convincing attempts to do so. The Jacksonians, predictably, countered by reading no more into the charter than what was written. The dispute therefore mirrored

---

[1] More on this is found in Chapter 12.
[2] *Register of Debates*, 23rd Cong., 1st sess., (Jan. 30, 1834), 420-421 (Senate).
[3] *Register of Debates*, 23rd Cong., 1st sess., (Feb. 17, 1834), 578 (Senate).
[4] *Register of Debates*, 23rd Cong., 1st sess., (Mar. 12, 1834), 915 (Senate).
[5] *Register of Debates*, 23rd Cong., 1st sess., (Mar. 12, 1834), 912 (Senate).

the constitutional debates of the 1790's with the anti-Jacksonians playing the role of the loose constructionist Federalists and the Jacksonians cast as the strict constructionist Democratic-Republicans. To bolster their argument that the charter should be read strictly, the Jacksonians called upon the precedents established by prior secretaries. The anti-Jacksonians, however, were prepared for this tactic, deployed effective counters, and essentially nullified the Jacksonians allusions to precedent.

Taney mentioned specifically a post script from a letter written by former Treasury Secretary, William Crawford in 1817 to establish precedent for his own actions. The letter itself deserves some context to fully understand its implications for the debate. One of the first tasks before the Second Bank of the United States upon its chartering was the resumption of specie payments from state banks in accordance with a joint resolution requiring that all payments to the government be in specie starting February 20, 1817. When it became clear that the state banks would not cooperate in a timely manner, the BUS invited representatives from the bigger state banks to meet on February 1 to discuss the situation. They emerged with an agreement that although not being overly advantageous to the BUS, achieved its goal of resuming specie payments.[1] The Mechanics' Bank of New York, however, resisted an aspect of the agreement and appeared unwilling to cooperate. This prompted Crawford to send the letter to the bank's president that Taney cited in his report.

Clay hammered Taney on the use of Crawford's letter as a model for his own actions and claimed the secretary had not told the whole story. The government was fearful that the Bank alone would not be able to force the state banks to resume specie payments. Believing the state banks would require a stronger push than the BUS could provide, Congress passed a resolution on April 30, 1816 giving the secretary of the Treasury the authority to take whatever steps necessary to collect from the state banks all payments to the United States in the acceptable forms of currency prescribed by the law. The state banks that resisted the February 1 agreement described above seemed to require the push the resolution meant to provide. The authority Crawford exercised over the deposits described in the letter Taney cited, Clay reasoned, derived from the resolution of 1816, not from the Bank's charter. With the resumption of specie payments long since established, Taney's use of the Crawford letter as precedent for his own actions no longer applied.[2] Southard added more details to bolster Clay's position. The New Jerseyan brought to the Senate's attention a circular letter written by Craw-

---

[1] Catterall, *Second Bank*, 24-26.
[2] *Register of Debates*, 23rd Cong., 1st sess., (Dec. 19, 1833), 52 (Senate).

ford and distributed amongst state banks that had demonstrated opposition to the resumption of specie payments by the February 20 deadline. The letter warned the banks that should they not adhere to the date prescribed by Congress to resume specie payments, Crawford would have no choice but to remove any government funds on deposit in *their* vaults. Clearly, Southard reasoned, the power Crawford claimed in these letters Taney now used as cover for his own actions were in compliance with a very specific resolution no longer in effect. Furthermore, Crawford spoke of removing government deposits in the *state* banks. "[The letters] had no relation to the deposites made in the Bank of the United States," Southard continued, "nor do they furnish any assertion of authority by Mr. Crawford to touch deposites accruing after the charter went into operation." To conclude his point, Southard directed the Senate to refer to letters and reports written by Crawford outlining all transfers made during the early years of the Bank's existence. All transfers ordered by Crawford were either from one state bank to another or of funds on deposit before the Second Bank of the United States was created, "and above all...he did not claim the unlimited power which has recently been exercised."[1] Clay revisited the subject again during his final speech the day prior to the vote on his resolutions. He summed up succinctly that Crawford's actions meant to "break all [government] connexion with the local banks, and to form a connexion with the Bank of the United States exclusively" whereas Taney was driven by the opposite — "to cut loose from the Bank of the United States, and attach himself to the local banks."[2] To equate the two men's actions and thus sanction Taney's removal by the precedent set by Crawford was simply wrong.

Ewing took the subject down a slightly different path, refusing to speculate whether Crawford's actions were informed by the resolution (as Clay and Southard had) or by a general grant of power now claimed by Taney. If inspired by a general grant of power, Ewing blamed the trap many who reach positions of power fall into — overestimating one's authority. Regardless of motive, Ewing called Crawford's conduct "a most unfortunate step; one that stands as an example to be shunned, not as a precedent to be followed," as much of the money transferred was ultimately lost.[3]

Several Jacksonians offered perfunctory support of Taney's use of the Crawford letter to establish precedent for his actions, but the detailed analysis of the anti-Jacksonians shook much of the foundation upon which the argument was built. Instead, they conjured up other instances of past secre-

---

[1] *Register of Debates*, 23rd Cong., 1st sess., (Jan. 8. 1834), 169-170 (Senate).
[2] *Register of Debates*, 23rd Cong., 1st sess., (Mar. 27, 1834), 1175 (Senate).
[3] *Register of Debates*, 23rd Cong., 1st sess., (Jan. 20, 1834), 318.

taries wielding the power of removal in the same way Taney had to justify his behavior. Tallmadge, speaking towards the end of the debate, referenced a new authority to bolster Taney's claim to past precedence, that of former Secretary, Samuel Ingham.[1] In an 1829 letter to Biddle, Ingham expressed the same willingness to threaten removal to keep the Bank in line as did Taney. Ingham wrote, "'if it should ever appear to the satisfaction of the Secretary of Treasury that the bank used its pecuniary power for purposes of injustice and oppression, he would be faithless to his trust if he hesitated to lessen the capacity for such injury, by withdrawing from its vaults the public deposites.'" The secretary later voiced his pleasure with the "flourishing condition" of the institution he helped create but cautioned that if the Bank began using its power and resources adverse to liberties of the people, "'no consideration of a personal nature will curb me in exercising the legal power with which I may be invested, to check its tendencies, and reform its abuses...'"[2] To Tallmadge, Ingham's letter served as irrefutable proof that precedent had been established to validate Taney's course of action.

Forsyth introduced several examples of precedent, unsurprising given he was one of the few Jacksonians who served in Congress when the charter was created. The charter required that a large percentage of stockholder deposits to the BUS be paid in specie. This stipulation proved difficult for many stockholders, so the board of directors skirted the measure by passing a resolution allowing stockholders to pay their second installment to the Bank in notes rather than specie. Congress empowered the House Committee on the Currency to investigate the matter and when that investigation fell short of remedying the situation to his liking, Forsyth, then a member of the House, introduced two resolutions effectively authorizing the secretary of the Treasury to remove the deposits if the charter was not adhered to. The resolutions were rejected and when another committee was appointed to look into the matter, they recommended no congressional action was needed "because, by the provisions of the charter, the Secretary of Treasury has full power to apply a prompt and adequate remedy whenever the situation of the bank shall require it." In essence, the Committee deemed Forsyth's resolutions superfluous since the secretary already possessed the remedy to remove the deposits whenever he felt it necessary.[3] To Forsyth, this proved conclusively that the charter did not mean for the safety of the deposits to be the sole factor guiding the secretary's authority to remove them. The senator also referred to the well-known 1830 pro-Bank report written by BUS supporter,

---

[1] Ingham served under Jackson from March 6, 1829 until June 20, 1831, when he was ousted for his involvement in the Peggy Eaton Affair.

[2] *Register of Debates*, 23rd Cong., 1st sess., (Mar. 12, 1834), 921-922 (Senate).

[3] *Register of Debates*, 23rd Cong., 1st sess., (Jan. 27, 1834), 351-353 (Senate).

George McDuffie. The Major General wrote, "[i]t is true that the Secretary of the Treasury, with the sanction of Congress, would have the power to prevent the bank from using its power unjustly and oppressively, and to punish any attempt on the part of the directors to bring pecuniary influence of the institution to bear upon the politics of the country, by withdrawing the deposites from the offending branches." The significance of these words was strengthened, Forsyth believed, by McDuffie's friendliness to the Bank and the "golden influence" attributed to the report.[1] The acknowledgement of a general grant of power over the deposits existing within the pages of a report celebrating the BUS, to Forsyth, amounted to the strongest evidence yet that Taney's actions were rightful.

Peleg Sprague spoke the day after the conclusion of Forsyth's speech and the Mainer was quick to confront Forsyth directly on the examples of precedent he employed to defend Taney. He first commented on the rejected resolution that Forsyth himself introduced in 1817, and, in a clear swipe at the Georgian, described it as "carrying with it no other authority than the unsupported opinion of the mover." The resolution gave the secretary the power to remove the deposits, as per the directions of Congress. "How this tends to show unlimited power in the Secretary, to the exclusion of Congress," Sprague wondered, "is not easily perceived." Sensing the senator had misunderstood his aim for citing the resolution, Forsyth interjected, explaining that had not meant to deny Congress the power to remove the deposits; he meant to show that the secretary, in addition to Congress, could remove the deposits. Sprague shrugged off the clarification and continued to the McDuffie report, which the Georgian had cited with "peculiar emphasis." The report stated that the secretary could remove the deposits for various reasons with the sanction of Congress. Lost on Sprague was how this could be argued as a precedent upon which Taney could base his own actions. He cried out, "[w]ith the sanction of Congress! And yet it is now contended that no such sanction is necessary; the Secretary's power is sole and exclusive — absolute and uncontrollable."[2] Both instances of precedent cited by Forsyth indicated that the secretary could not move on the deposits without congressional approval. Neither example, in Sprague's opinion, established precedent under which Taney could justify his actions.

While several anti-Jacksonians attacked specific examples of precedent, Calhoun and Tyler condemned Taney's and the Jacksonians' general use of prior conduct to justify the removal. Calhoun allowed for instances where an officer could cite precedent to defend their own actions but only "[i]f

---

[1] *Register of Debates*, 23rd Cong., 1st sess., (Jan. 27, 1834), 353-354 (Senate).
[2] *Register of Debates*, 23rd Cong., 1st sess., (Jan. 29, 1834), 394-395 (Senate).

the infraction be a trivial one, in a case not calculated to excite attention." But in cases "of the utmost magnitude, involving the highest interests and most important principles," as was the case before Senate, an officer could not "avail himself of the plea of precedent to excuse his conduct." Calhoun argued that to rely on precedent in this case was shameful, for "[i]f the Secretary's right to withdraw public money from the treasury be clear, he has no need of precedent to vindicate him." Although he chose not to analyze Crawford's letter or even mention it by name, it seems possible that Calhoun accepted the letter as proof that the former secretary believed his power over the deposits to be absolute. At one point, the South Carolinian commented, "[this] is a case where false precedents are to be corrected, not followed," the inference being that Crawford *had* established a precedent validating absolute control over the deposits but it was one to be shunned, not embraced.[1]

The fiercest attacks on the use of precedent came from John Tyler. In fact, his denunciation of its use was perhaps the strongest aspect of his speech. Despite battling the lingering impact of a disease that affected "his frame and countenance," the future president delivered his diatribe with the eloquence and verve generally attributed to Clay or Webster.[2] Tyler derided the Jacksonians for parading out every expression uttered by a former secretary that could provide cover for the removal. Tyler called precedent the worst way to argue the rightness of present actions. "[Precedent] may be found to justify every act, however bad, in private or public life — and yet," the Virginian inquired, "what would be thought of a private citizen, who, upon being arraigned in a court of justice for an offence against the law, should rest his defence upon the fact that this or that man had done the same thing before him?"[3]

Tyler also made sure to clarify a misrepresentation of the Committee report he helped compile in 1819 that Forsyth cited. The Georgian had quoted from the report to prove that Taney had acted in accordance with the Committee's judgment — that the secretary could remove the deposits for any reason. Tyler blasted his fellow senator for attempting "to convert a single sentence of it into the declaration, that the Secretary possessed unlimited power over the deposites." Bank mismanagement had put the deposits in a precarious spot, Tyler explained. The Committee called for a change of directors responsible for putting the deposits in danger; if the Bank did not comply, the secretary would be asked to exercise his power to remove. This was the context of the sentence Forsyth quoted and nothing more. Indeed,

---

[1] *Register of Debates*, 23rd Cong., 1st sess., (Jan. 13, 1834), 215 (Senate).

[2] *The Charleston Mercury*, March 3, 1834.

[3] *Register of Debates*, 23rd Cong., 1st sess., (Feb 24, 1834), 665 (Senate).

the Bank had committed other flagrant violations of the charter but it was Congress, not the secretary, where the Committee looked for the remedy. "[N]ever for a moment," Tyler concluded on this point, "[did he believe] that the Secretary of the Treasury could do more than watch the condition of the bank, with a view to decide on its safety as a place of deposite."[1]

Tyler though saved his strongest attacks on precedent for Jackson and his partisans in general. If his vote against the Force Bill was his official break with the party, the sarcastic tirade that cut to the very core of Jacksonism, served as his audition to join the opposition. "[Jackson] came into office on the principle of reform," Tyler began. "He was to be a very Theseus, destined not only to pierce the labyrinth of error, but to destroy the monster — to draw vigor from the stream of change — to collect from the past the scattered fragments of defeated innovation, and lead them against the future. And yet," Tyler persisted with biting sarcasm, "how ludicrous the figure he is made to cut; drums and trumpets announce the coming of the great reformer. His banner waves above his head with Reform inserted in large characters upon it, and yet, when he opens his lips, the only cry which issues from them is Precedent, precedent, good or bad, sound or unsound — still Precedent, precedent."[2] Tyler's words were not just a repudiation of one particular action taken by the administration and their attempt to justify it; it was a repudiation of Jackson, his supporters, and the foundation upon which his appeal was supposedly built. Tyler, only a reluctant soldier for Jackson, had seen past the façade. His denunciation of Jacksonism as a front to expand its standard bearer's power beyond all limits carried more weight than that of others who always opposed the Old General. And although he would eventually betray them when he, by chance, ascended to the presidency, Clay and the soon-to-be Whigs were happy to welcome Tyler into their fold with open arms.

The clash over whether or not Taney had the authority to unilaterally remove the deposits inspired passionate argument from both sides. Taney's reasons for exercising his perceived authority to actually remove the deposits produced debate of equal, if not greater, fervor within the Senate which found itself locked in a bitter struggle for the country's economic future.

---

[1] *Register of Debates*, 23rd Cong., 1st sess., (Feb. 24, 1834), 666 (Senate).
[2] *Register of Debates*, 23rd Cong., 1st sess., (Feb. 24, 1834), 665-666 (Senate).

CHAPTER 7: THE BANK HAS FALLEN

Taney cited section sixteen of the Bank's charter and the precedent set by former secretaries of the Treasury to explain why he believed he possessed sole legal authority over removing the deposits. The secretary had also argued that other factors beyond the deposits' safety, such as public interest, could induce him to remove the funds. It was therefore crucial for Taney to explain why removal of the deposits at that time was in the best interest of the public. The first of these reasons involved the nearing termination of the Bank's charter. Set to expire on March 3, 1836, the Bank would have less than three years to wrap up its affairs. Taney acknowledged that the law allowed the Bank to settle its accounts and liquidate its assets for two years from the final day of the charter, but, for all other purposes, the Bank's existence ceased with the expiration of the charter. Therefore, to prevent sudden financial shock and distress upon the people, Taney determined that removing the deposits early to allow the Bank to slowly settle its affairs over time would best serve the public interest.

Renewal of the charter would negate the Bank's need to wrap up its affairs and due to this possibility, Taney was compelled to further explain the approaching termination of the charter as a reason for his decision to remove the deposits. "It is the duty of the Executive Departments of the Government," Taney explained, "to exercise the powers conferred on them, and to regulate the discretion confided to them, according to the existing laws; and they cannot be allowed to speculate on the chances of future changes, by the legislative authority."[1] Taney removed the deposits based on the current laws which set when the BUS would cease operations, and it would be irresponsible of him to factor the possibility of Congress renewing the Bank's charter into that decision.

The secretary did concede that certain situations could allow an executive officer to act in the anticipation of future legislation but only in "cases in which the principles of justice, or public interests, manifestly call for an alteration of the law; or where some expression of the public opinion has strongly indicated that a change will probably be made."[2] Taney saw no principles of justice, public interest, or expression of public opinion to convince him the Bank would be unquestionably rechartered. In fact, he saw quite the opposite; all the evidence present convinced Taney that the bank would not be rechartered. According to the secretary, the reelection of Andrew Jackson served as a mandate from the people that the Bank ought not to be renewed, as its "voluntary application to Congress for the renewal of its charter four years before it expired, and upon the eve of the election of the President, was understood on all sides as bringing forward that question for incidental decision at the then approaching election."[3] Since Jackson had vetoed the recharter bill passed by Congress just months prior to the election, he firmly established himself as being the candidate in opposition to the Bank's renewal. That Jackson won by sweeping margins confirmed in Taney the people's overwhelming sentiment against the BUS.

Acting under the assumption that the BUS would not be renewed, Taney next explained why leaving the deposits in the Bank until the expiration of the charter would create economic chaos for the country. The sudden redemption of several millions of dollars coupled with the removal of funds by private investors to be placed in other institutions would severely hinder the Bank's ability to make its payments to the government. In addition, as the most common circulating medium used by the people, the abrupt withdrawal and deprecation of BUS notes in the absence of a viable substitute "would certainly produce extensive evils, and be sensibly felt among all classes of society."[4] According to Taney, the credit and confidence attached to the notes of the BUS was not based upon the management of the Bank itself; it resulted from the acceptance of the people to make receivable BUS notes in all payments to the United States. Therefore, Taney believed, a circulating medium receivable for all payments to the United States furnished by

---

[1] *Register of Debates*, 23rd Cong., 1st sess., Appendix 60.
[2] *Register of Debates*, 23rd Cong., 1st sess., Appendix, 61.
[3] *Register of Debates*, 23rd Cong., 1st sess., Appendix, 61.
[4] *Register of Debates*, 23rd Cong., 1st sess., Appendix, 61.

state banks would instill the same confidence among the people. But this could not occur suddenly; gradual shifting from BUS notes to this new form of currency would provide the best chance to avoid widespread distress caused by the closure of the Bank of the United States. Thus formed part of Taney's reasoning for removing the deposits when he did. Even friends of the Bank expressed the urgency of taking up charter renewal early during the December 1831 congressional session as time would be needed for the Bank to close up should the charter be allowed to expire. Nearly two years had passed since those concerns were raised and a new charter for the BUS had been vetoed with no chance for an override. Taney had simply acted upon the concerns set forth regarding the Bank's impending dissolution.[1]

Taney hinted that perhaps he would not have needed to take the action he did had the Bank taken steps on its own to wind up its business when it became clear that its charter would not be renewed. Instead, the Bank enlarged its business between December 1, 1832 — just after Jackson's reelection — and August 2, 1833. On the former date, the Bank's discounts amounted to $61,571,625.66. Just eight months later, they had ballooned to $64,160,349.14, an increase of roughly two and a half million dollars. The only explanation Taney could muster for such an expansion of business in the face of certain termination was a desperate attempt by the Bank to create an economic atmosphere necessitating its renewal as the only means to avert financial ruin.[2]

At the same time that the Bank was expanding its business, the former Treasury Secretary, William Duane, had appointed Amos Kendall to investigate whether the state banks would be willing and able to take on the duties of the BUS once it ceased operations as well as assess the ability of four major commercial cities, Baltimore, New York, Philadelphia, and Boston to serve as adequate depositories for the public funds. The Bank may have viewed this action as a precursor to total withdrawal of the public deposits, thus prompting the expansion of credit that the secretary had railed against. Taney, in a litigious manner befitting a future Supreme Court Chief Justice, sought to downplay the veracity of the Bank's fears. First, it would be natural for the government to begin preparing for life without the BUS, given that Jackson's veto of the recharter bill and his lopsided reelection victory indicated the extreme unlikelihood that the Bank would continue after the expiration of its charter. Such important financial changes required time to implement so the government making the necessary preparations should not have come as a shock to the Bank and certainly should not have compelled a

---

[1] *Register of Debates*, 23rd Cong., 1st sess.,, Appendix, 61-62.
[2] *Register of Debates*, 23rd Cong., 1st sess., Appendix, 62.

drastic change in lending policies. Secondly, the inquiry into the state banks came at a time when the BUS was flush with cash due to higher than expected customs duties (specifically on woolens), and therefore, Taney stated, "[t]he capacity of the bank...at this time, to afford facilities to commerce, was not only equal, but greatly superior to what it had been for some time before; and the nature of inquiry made of the State banks, confined as it was to four principal commercial cities, showed that the immediate withdrawal of the entire deposites from the bank, so as to distress it, was not contemplated."[1] Based on these two facts, it appeared to Taney that the Bank's fear stemming from the inquiry of the government agent into the condition of some state banks as a sign of removal of the deposits was altogether unfounded. The Bank's behavior in response to these unfounded fears forced Taney to remove the deposits earlier than he originally planned.

The behavior Taney alluded to consisted of the Bank's actions between August 2, 1833, the end of an eight-month period of bank's expansion of loans, and October 2, the day after the order to remove the deposits came down. As previously stated, on August 2, 1833, the extension of the bank's loans stood at $64,160,349.14. By October, that number had shrunk to $60,094,202.93, a reduction of $4,066,146.21. Over the same period, the Bank collected $2,268,504.11 in public debt, thus increasing its public deposits by that amount. Therefore, Taney concluded that between the curtailment of loans and the collection of public debt, over the two month period under scrutiny, the Bank took $6,334,650.32 out of circulation.[2] This action alone would produce considerable distress but in addition, the BUS called on loans due from state banks in specie (mostly from the financial centers of New York, Philadelphia, and Boston), forcing those banks to call in their own debts to protect themselves, thus adding to the distress. These developments convinced Taney "that if the public moneys received for revenue had continued to be deposited in the Bank of the United States for two months longer, and it had adhered to the oppressive system of policy which it pursued during the two preceding months, a widespread scene of bankruptcy and ruin must have followed."[3] Taney would have preferred to wait to act until Congress reconvened in December but because of the Bank's oppressive measures, he had no choice but to move swiftly and remove the deposits from BUS immediately to rescue the country from pecuniary embarrassment.

Timing undoubtedly played an important role in Taney's decision to remove the deposits when he did. The rapid approach of the expiration of

---

[1] *Register of Debates*, 23rd Cong., 1st sess., Appendix, 62.
[2] *Register of Debates*, 23rd Cong., 1st sess., Appendix, 63.
[3] *Register of Debates*, 23rd Cong., 1st sess., Appendix, 63.

the Bank's charter with no evidence to support the eventuality of its renewal coupled with the desire to avoid sudden shock to the country's finances upon closure of the Bank compelled Taney, in the best interest of the public, to begin forcing the gradual closure of the Bank by ordering the removal of its public deposits. The expansion of the Bank's loans around the time of the previous presidential election and its ensuing curtailment of business which produced undue financial distress on the country required Taney to remove the deposits immediately rather than wait for Congress to reconvene or else watch the nation succumb to economic ruin.

***

The timing of the removal incited heated debate within the Senate. Taney's explanation opened the door to two disputes, one over the decision to remove the deposits just sixty days before Congress was to meet, the other over removal as being necessary for the Bank to quietly wrap up its affairs. Clay questioned the secretary's judgement to remove the deposits when he did. "Was the urgency for the removal of the deposites so great that he could not wait sixty days, until the assembling of Congress?" Clay reminded the Senate that by Taney's own admission, the deposits were perfectly safe. Clay also referenced the previous session, when the House "had declared its full confidence in the safety of the deposites," leading him to wonder, "[w]hy not wait until it could review the subject, with all the new light which the Secretary could throw upon it, and again proclaim its opinion?[1]

The indignant Samuel Southard provided answers to Clay's questions. The New Jerseyan called the timing of the removal, "[a] trick, a cunning device...to cheat the legislative power of the country of its rights." If Southard's explanation for why the removal happened when it did was correct, his characterization of the timing was indeed accurate. Southard blasted Taney for cowardly removing the deposits while Congress was out of session because he knew full well that Congress would not approve. "The deposites could not be removed by the joint action of the Executive and Legislature, without a majority of the latter in favor of removal," Southard explained. "But if [removal] was made by the authority of the President or Secretary alone, [the deposits] could not be restored; as a single word, veto, would prevent that majority from accomplishing their wishes. Two-thirds would then be required; and this, the [veto], the wishes of the President, and the force of party, would prevent. The act was done therefore...for the sole purpose of preventing Congress...from exercising their judgement and powers in relation to this question, and the management and control of the

---

[1] *Register of Debates*, 23rd Cong., 1st sess., (Dec. 30, 1833), 81 (Senate).

public treasure." He then challenged the Senate to find in history an "act of lower cunning, or haughtier scorn...towards the legislative body."[1]

Tallmadge took umbrage with the senators' insistence that the timing of the removal was to purposely circumvent Congress. "If [Taney] deemed there was good ground for removing them," Tallmadge argued, "it was his duty to act without regard to the time when Congress was to assemble." The New Yorker blamed the anti-Jacksonians' flawed case on a misguided interpretation of the sixteenth section of the Bank's charter. The section, "instead of confining the Secretary's power to a time when Congress is not in session, it expressly recognises his right to remove them when Congress is in session." Regardless of whether Congress was in session or not, the power to remove the deposits belonged to the secretary. Therefore, Tallmadge reasoned, "[h]ad the deposites remained till now in the Bank of the United States, and it should be generally conceded that they ought to be removed, still Congress, though in session, could not interfere; the Secretary alone could perform that duty."[2] Waiting for Congress to convene would not have stopped the deposits from being removed if Taney felt it necessary.

One Jacksonian, John Forsyth, did admit that had he been an advisor to the administration, he would have recommended waiting to take action until Congress reconvened. Despite winning reelection impressively, Forsyth said he would have advised that Jackson (and by extension, Taney) "not to take it for granted that you understand the opinions of the House of Representatives" because "[i]t is possible that the people may have continued you in place, and yet desire the continuance of the [the BUS]." Forsyth continued, "wait until a vote of the House of Representatives renders their opinion not a matter of argument, but of undisputed and indisputable fact."[3] The Georgian advised in this manner because of his confidence that the House ushered in by the voters of 1832 would uphold the administration's opposition to the Bank. Having their opinion on record as being in support of removal would have created an airtight case and would have removed the impetus for Clay's resolutions and the subsequent debate. Of course, Forsyth had the cover of the results of the congressional elections to shield his controversial stance from backfiring. Benton communicated previously that of the two hundred and forty victorious congressional candidates, roughly one hundred and sixty had publically opposed recharter.[4] Armed with this knowledge, Forsyth could make his statement without concern that the Bank would

---

[1] *Register of Debates*, 23rd Cong., 1st sess., (Jan. 8, 1834), 154 (Senate).
[2] *Register of Debates*, 23rd Cong., 1st sess., (Mar. 12, 1834), 921 (Senate).
[3] *Register of Debates*, 23rd Cong., 1st sess., (Jan. 27, 1834), 345 (Senate).
[4] *Register of Debates*, 23rd Cong., 1st sess., Jan. 2, 1834), 137 (Senate).

bring the issue of recharter before the newly elected Congress, as the new makeup of the House would surely doom the measure to failure. Regardless of the cover the election of an anti-Bank majority provided for his statement, Forsyth's break with the Jacksonians over the choice to remove the deposits ahead of the congressional session created an opening for BUS supporters to pounce. One pro-Bank publication called the Georgian's address, a "half-sided speech, which gives no satisfaction to his party, and no dissatisfaction to us."[1] Another claimed that some "expressed astonishment at the moderate tone which he used" and others "who were wondered that he should have risen at all."[2]

***

Taney had hinted, disingenuously, that he would have waited for Congress to reconvene before acting had the Bank's behavior not created a danger to the public interest if the deposits were allowed to remain there. To this charge, Thomas Ewing responded with disdain. Ewing rationalized the Bank's behavior that amid "rumors...of the impending blow, accompanied with predictions that when the blow should come it would crush its victim," the Bank had no alternative but to "adopt the strongest possible defensive and protective measures." At any time, the Bank could be called upon for between seven and ten million dollars in the form of transfer drafts and threats of runs on its branches only added to the danger.[3] Taney had issued these drafts to some of the chosen state banks, some for as high as $500,000, to be used as protection, if need be, against aggressive tactics by the BUS. Had the BUS acted in ways detrimental to their safety, the state banks could present these drafts to BUS branches to stay afloat. However, Taney did not inform the BUS of these drafts and when some of the draft recipients cashed them in against the secretary's wishes, the BUS had to react. When confronted on the issuance of these drafts, Taney did not reveal their true purpose, effectively keeping the BUS in the dark and forcing it to "measures otherwise unnecessary and contrary to the public interest."[4] In addition, the Bank had no way of knowing when these drafts would be cashed or from where. Therefore, Ewing added, had the Bank waited until Congress convened before deploying its defensive measures, as suggestion offered by William Wilkins, "the bank would have been crushed at once."[5]

Frelinghuysen expounded on the thoughts of his Ohio colleague and turned the secretary's own words against him. Taney warned of widespread

---

[1] *Baltimore Patriot*, February 1, 1834.

[2] *The United States Gazette*, Philadelphia, February 1, 1834.

[3] *Register of Debates*, 23rd Cong., 1st sess., (Jan. 20, 1834), 315 (Senate).

[4] Hammond, *Banks and Politics*, 422-423.

[5] *Register of Debates*, 23rd Cong., 1st sess., (Jan. 20, 1834), 315 (Senate).

bankruptcy and ruin had the Bank been allowed to continue its curtailment policies. However, at the time Taney removed the deposits, Frelinghuysen remarked, "there was not the slightest indication of [ruin]...and [Taney], by this rash act, produce[d] the wide-spread ruin and bankruptcy that he so much feared." It was Taney's actions, not the Bank's curtailment, that produced the distress felt around the nation. But what of this curtailment? The Bank, Frelinghuysen argued, only curtailed the amount under threat prior to removal, and after Taney's act, by the amount actually reduced.[1]

Perhaps no Jacksonian senator despised the BUS more than New Hampshire's Isaac Hill. Unsurprisingly, he vehemently defended his fellow Kitchen Cabinet ally's choice to act prior to the beginning of the session. Curtailment began on August 13, over a month before the removal occurred, Hill reminded his colleagues. Even though the anti-Jacksonians argued that the Bank's measures were a preemptive defense against what was to come, Hill insisted curtailment meant to serve a more nefarious purpose than simple self-defense. Had Taney not intervened, the distress heaped upon the country would have been felt "with tenfold vengeance [and] the cry at this session of Congress for relief would have been directed to the single point of a renewal of the charter." Hill believed the Bank's true goal was to circumvent the president's veto and the will of the people by creating such pressure on the community that their only option for relief was recharter. It then followed that the secretary had done the people a great service by limiting the distress the Bank could produce by restricting its means. To Hill, curtailment was not about defense, it was about recharter. "The bank had taken measures to bring about pressure and embarrassment," Hill lectured, and added sarcastically, "I am not now to believe that her disposition to do justice would have been greater with increased than with diminished means."[2]

What was the true motive behind the Bank's curtailment, self-defense or to force recharter? Nicholas Biddle's words seem to indicate both. In late January, the embattled bank president wrote, "[t]he ties of party allegiance can only be broken by the actual conviction, of existing distress in the community...Our only safety is in pursuing a steady course of firm restriction — and I have no doubt that such a course will ultimately lead to a restora-

---

[1] *Register of Debates*, 23rd Cong., 1st sess., (Feb. 3, 1834), 457 (Senate). Frelinghuysen began his remarks on February 3. By that point the BUS had curtailed its operations by roughly $9,500,000 since it began in August while its deposits had been reduced over that same period by about $8,000,000, so his statement here was somewhat accurate. However, over the next several months, the deposits remained steady while curtailment increased by nearly $10,000,000. See, Catterall, *Second Bank*, 323.

[2] *Register of Debates*, 23rd Cong., 1st sess., (Mar. 3, 1834), 776-777 (Senate).

tion of the currency and the recharter of the Bank."[1] Referring to curtailment as a means to ensure safety implies that the measures taken were defensive in nature. However, while Biddle only hinted at self-defense, he minced no words in espousing what he believed would result from the Bank's actions — recharter.

It is plausible that Biddle may have acted initially in self-defense but it is certain that as winter gave way to spring as 1834 wore on, recharter had become his true goal. One prominent historian of the Bank War wrote, "[t] he enormous reductions made by the bank were certainly in excess of any possible danger, and were continued after any such danger threatened...The president and company of the Bank of the United States were, in fact...vindictive with calculation. They hoped to force a re-charter, or at least a restoration of the deposits."[2] Another commented, "Mr. Biddle was concerned not merely to defend the Bank but to pursue its course in the hope of reversing the advantage gained by the President from vetoing new charter and removing the deposits," while a third said bluntly, "Biddle meant to squeeze until the suffering was unbearable, and in so doing...to win recharter."[3]

**

While the decision to remove the deposits just two months before Congress reconvened produced spirited discussions from both sides, those discussions paled in comparison to those over the explanation for why Taney felt it necessary to remove them due to the approaching termination of the Bank's charter. Taney cited the president's veto of the Bank bill coupled with his decisive reelection as a mandate from the people that the BUS would not be rechartered. Anti-Jacksonians refused to make this connection. The Webster-chaired Committee of Finance called Taney's claim to be guided by electoral mandate "unusual...for public and official acts."[4] There was no way to discern what influenced individuals to vote as they did. "One man may think that a candidate has been elected on account of his opposition to the bank; another may see only that he has been chosen, notwithstanding such opposition." Webster continued, "[o]ne may regard the opposition, or the support, of any measure, by a particular candidate, as having been, itself, a promoting cause of the success of his election; another may esteem it as a formidable objection, overcome, however, by more powerful reasons; and others, again, may be of the opinion that it produced little or no effect on

---

[1] Nicholas Biddle to Wm. Appleton, of Boston, Jan 27, 1834, quoted in, Catterall, *Second Bank*, 330.

[2] Catterall, *Second Bank*, 329.

[3] Hammond, *Banks and Politics*, 433; Remini, *Jackson and the Bank War*, 127.

[4] As Webster was the chair of the Finance Committee and he presented the report to the Senate, references to the report will be conveyed as Webster's words.

the one side or the other." An electoral mandate, regardless how clear it may appear, was not a proper basis for the presumption of what laws may or may not be passed by the Legislature. Webster felt that assuming so much demeaned the "constitutional independence and dignity" of Congress.[1]

Other anti-Jacksonians made similar statements disparaging the election results as a cover for Taney's actions. Southard lamented that the secretary thought so little of the American people to think, "in the performance of their highest and most sacred function, that of election, descended to the degra-dation of trying an issue between the bank and a candidate for the presi-dency[.]" Assuming as much rendered the American voters as caring only about the single issue of the Bank, unconcerned with any other matter before them. This assumption, Southard was unwilling to make. Furthermore, in reducing the election to a mandate against the Bank, Taney had actually diminished the role of Jackson's wider appeal in bringing about his reelec-tion. "Had he no other merits?" the senator asked. "Had he no constitutional principles to secure regard? no acts of reform to win favor?...Does any man believe he would not have received a single vote on this ground, which he would not have received had there been no quarrel with the bank? No...The President was chosen for other and stronger reasons, however unfounded and misguided I may regard them."[2] Southard displayed his political chops by spinning Taney's mandate argument as degrading to the president. The effectiveness of this tactic was less impressive than the political brilliance the New Jerseyan exhibited in employing it.

Clay and Calhoun both argued that treating the election as a mandate to kill the Bank had wider implications beyond just the future of the BUS. The South Carolinian wondered under what authority Taney believed he could act as the voice of the people. Calhoun sarcastically remarked that being the astute lawyer he was, the secretary surely knew that the voice of the people could be claimed by the government's three branches only "within the respective limits assigned by the constitution." He warned, "[a] claim on the part of the Executive to interpret, as the Secretary has done, the voice of the people, through any other channel, is to shake the foundation of our system."[3] Clay too viewed Taney's reasoning with unease. "I am surprised and alarmed at the new source of executive power which is found in the result of a presidential election," Clay commented. He was under the impression that an election merely put the president in office and granted him "neither more nor less power, in consequence of that election, than the constitution

---

[1] *Register of Debates*, 23rd Cong., 1st sess., Appendix, 151.
[2] *Register of Debates*, 23rd Cong., 1st sess., (Jan. 8, 1834), 175-176, 179 (Senate).
[3] *Register of Debates*, 23rd Cong., 1st sess., (Jan. 13, 1834), 211 (Senate).

defines and delegates." Were the people to believe that any opinion put forth by a candidate prior to an election, would, upon their victory, "incorporate themselves with the constitution," regardless of the nature of the opinion?[1] Forsyth and Wilkins provided able, albeit historically inaccurate ripostes to this point. The Georgian called Clay's complaint that the election conferred upon the president new power "a most wonderful misconception of a very simple and unpretended truth, that the result of the election proved that the principles which had governed the administration were approved by the people."[2] Similarly, but more specific to the Bank, Wilkins added, [i]t is not pretended that the re-election of the President gave him any new power. It only told to the world that the people did not expect a renewal, during his term, of the charter of the bank."[3] To Forsyth and Wilkins, the election merely signaled approval from the people for Jackson to continue on in the manner he had for the previous four years. The near universal acceptance by historians that the expansion of presidential power became one of Jackson's most enduring marks on the office would suggest that Clay may have been on to something.

As the candidate Jackson defeated in 1832, Clay argued against the election as a mandate from an incredibly awkward position. Indeed, before attempting to prove that the election was not a mandate at all, Clay made a discomfiting statement — coming from a candidate so roundly defeated — about elections in general. "The winners ought to forbear making any complaints, and be satisfied, whatever the losers may be," he began. Then, riding atop the hindsight of his own defeat like Attila across the plains of Mongolia, he added, "[a]fter an election is fairly terminated, I have always thought the best way was to forget all the incidents of the preceding canvass, and especially in the manner in which the votes had been cast."[4] Three more failed attempts at the presidency certainly put this sunny outlook to the test.[5]

Following his disclaimer, Clay dove into the more pressing issue at hand. Unlike some of his allies who spoke after him to argue that Jackson's stance on the Bank was just one of many issues before the people and assigning his victory solely to that one was foolish, Clay sought to prove that Jackson never made his stance on the Bank clear. Therefore, he said, the issue was not clearly put before the people so his victory could not serve as a mandate to dissolve it early. Clay meticulously detailed Jackson's public messages to

---

[1] *Register of Debates*, 23rd Cong., 1st sess., (Dec. 30, 1833), 84-85 (Senate).

[2] *Register of Debates*, 23rd Cong., 1st sess., (Jan 27, 1834), 356 (Senate).

[3] *Register of Debates*, 23rd Cong., 1st sess., (Feb. 17, 1834), 585 (Senate).

[4] *Register of Debates*, 23rd Cong., 1st sess., (Dec. 30, 1833), 82 (Senate).

[5] Clay lost the presidential election in 1844. In 1840 and 1848 he sought the presidency but failed to win his party's nomination.

prove his point. In his 1829 address, Jackson claimed that a large segment of the population questioned the Bank's usefulness and constitutionality. Jackson himself, though, did not share his own opinion. Later in the address, the president admitted his openness to *a* national bank if it be determined one was needed for the stability of the nation's finances. The following year, Jackson again spoke of the qualms that many people had with the Bank, omitting any mention of his own feelings on the subject and although he did voice displeasure regarding the advantages of the present bank, he objected only to the Bank as currently constructed, not the idea of a national bank. His 1831 message was equally non-committal. Then came the famous recharter veto message of 1832. Here, Clay sardonically assured the chamber, the president would certainly reveal his true hostility to the Bank and make clear to the people that a vote for him would be a vote against the BUS. But it was not to be. Clay quoted several pieces, paraphrased here: that a national bank is convenient to the government and the people, that only some of the powers and privileges it possesses are unconstitutional, that the president felt duty-bound to ask Congress to organize a national bank to fix the problems with the current one, that he regrets this charter does not accomplish that end, that a national bank that fits his vision can, without a doubt be furnished, and that had he been called on to help create this new national bank, he would have gladly obliged. Clay then wryly observed, "[t]he message is principally employed in discussing the objections which the President entertained to the particular provisions of the charter, and not to the bank itself...Does the President, even in this message, array himself in opposition to any Bank of the United States? Does he even oppose himself to the existing bank?...On the contrary, does he not declare that he does not entertain *a doubt* that the bank may be constitutionally organized?" (Clay's emphasis.) How could the people have an accurate view of Jackson's personal feelings on the Bank based on these statements? Instead, Clay insisted, "the various messages of the President conclusively evinces that they were far from expressing frankly and decisively any opinions of the Chief Magistrate, except that he was opposed to the amendments of the charter contained in the bill submitted to him for its renewal." Even in his second inaugural, Jackson made no mention of any mandate from his constituents to destroy the Bank. On this point, Clay concluded, "[t]he President, then, and the Secretary of the Treasury, are without all color of justification for their assertions that the question of the bank or no bank was fully and fairly submitted to the people, and a decision pronounced against it by them."[1]

---

[1] *Register of Debates*, 23rd Cong., 1st sess., (Dec. 30, 1834), 83-84 (Senate).

The Jacksonians found Clay's assessment laughable. Benton reminded the proud Kentuckian that when addressing the Senate in the last session he himself claimed the Bank veto forged "the issue of life and death joined between President Jackson and the bank." Following the veto, the friends of the Bank pushed the issue to the public "and fought [Jackson] a pitched battle throughout the Union for victory or death. This was known to every body; and broad denials or special pleading evasions were equally unavailable to obscure the fact, or obliterate its recollection."[1] During the same Clay speech, Tallmadge recounted, the Kentuckian spoke of being asked to make public statements on the Bank two years prior to the veto. Even then, it appeared, the Bank question was squarely before the people. To Clay, "'[i]t seemed as if a sort of general order had gone out from head-quarters, to the partisans of the administration every where, to agitate and make the most of the question.'"[2] Jacksonians called upon the words of other Bank partisans besides Clay in demonstrating the clearness of the issue before the people. Forsyth referenced Daniel Webster, who in response to Jackson's veto message pronounced, "'[t]here is no longer doubt of the President's opinions — the bank has fallen, or it is to fall.'" All that could save the Bank would be "'a change in the councils of the nation.'"[3] Isaac Hill added, alluding to the same Webster quote, "[t]here has been no 'change in the public councils' since the veto of the President. The bank, on [Webster's] own showing, has become defunct. The state of things precisely has occurred which the gentleman had represented as putting an end to the bank, and all other banks entitled to the name."[4] Tallmadge quoted Delaware's John Clayton, who speaking after Webster during the veto message debate declared, "'[i]t was not merely the question whether the present Bank of the United States should be re-chartered, but whether any bank whatever should be established by the Government after the expiration of the act of Congress incorporating that institution...I repeat then...that from the opinions of the President, as fully developed in this paper, it is not to be expected that, during his administration, and while these sentiments remain unchanged, any bank whatever can be established by this government.'"[5] If Clay could not claim to know Jackson's explicit views on the Bank prior to the election, despite evidence suggesting otherwise, it seemed his political allies did. Forsyth did admit that although Clay had been correct in his judgment that Jackson did

---

[1] *Register of Debates*, 23rd Cong., 1st sess., (Jan., 1834), 136-137 (Senate).
[2] *Register of Debates*, 23rd Cong., 1st sess., (Mar. 12, 1834), 927 (Senate).
[3] *Register of Debates*, 23rd Cong., 1st sess., (Jan. 27, 1834), 344 (Senate).
[4] *Register of Debates*, 23rd Cong., 1st sess., (Mar. 3, 1834), 774 (Senate).
[5] *Register of Debates*, 23rd Cong., 1st sess., (Mar. 12, 1834), 926 (Senate).

not take the issue of the Bank directly to the people, Clay's party did, and did so "distinctly and intelligibly."[1]

Despite his best efforts, Clay's attempt to divorce the Bank from the ballot fell on deaf ears.[2] It was true that Jackson preferred the Bank remain out of the election as he knew it would cut into his electoral margin regardless of his stance on its future. But if his statements were, as Clay characterized them, "non-committal," it was only by design to offend as few voters as possible. Any objective analysis of the election reveals conclusively the Bank's presence on the ballot, and although its impact on voting behavior and the outcome of the election is hard to determine, both sides tried to paint their candidate as being the defender against or hero for the BUS. It was possible, but challenging, to argue that Jackson's victory did not signal a mandate from the people to crush the Bank. Arguing that the people did not know what their vote meant for the future of the Bank was an exercise in futility.

***

Even accepting the inevitably of the charter's expiration coupled with public endorsement of the Bank's demise as demonstrated through the vote, anti-Jacksonians argued fiercely that this did not warrant removing the deposits two and a half years early. Clay remarked that Congress certainly had been aware that the charter would expire when it was created but armed with that knowledge, chose not to provide for an early withdrawal of the deposits to prepare for the Bank's closure. "Whence does the Secretary derive an authority to do what Congress has never done?" Clay questioned. "Whence his power to abridge in effect the period of the charter, and to limit it to seventeen and a half years instead of twenty?"[3]

Of greater significance, anti-Jacksonians were puzzled as to why Taney believed it would be dangerous to allow the Bank's charter to expire naturally, and they assailed his position from all angles. Ewing drew on precedent to discredit Taney, which is ironic given the latter's reliance on precedent in his own defense. The Ohioan reached back to 1811 and then Treasury Secretary, Albert Gallatin, who "exercised what must be admitted a sound discretion as to the time, previous to the termination of the charter, at which it should cease to be a place of deposite. And how long," Ewing asked mockingly, "do you suppose he thought sufficient? Just seven days, neither more nor less." Ewing concluded his point with a not so subtle swipe at Taney, remarking that he would not venture to compare the financial acumen of

---

[1] *Register of Debates*, 23rd Cong., 1st sess., (Jan. 27, 1834), 344 (Senate).
[2] See Chapter 1.
[3] *Register of Debates*, 23rd Cong., 1st sess., (Dec. 30, 1833), 81 (Senate).

the two secretaries but recounted that "Mr. Gallatin had watched over and governed its affairs with distinguished ability, for more than nine years. Mr. Taney had been Secretary just three days."[1]

Anti-Jacksonians also assaulted Taney's contention that early removal was necessary to prevent shock to the community upon the Bank's sudden termination. Webster maintained that the deposits would be "as safe the last day of the existence of the bank...as any previous period." The Bank would expect that its deposits would be withdrawn as its termination drew nearer and ready itself accordingly. Webster resumed, "[t]he operation, if made gradually, produces, when thus conducted, the least possible disturbance to the business community."[2] Frelinghuysen agreed. "[I]t is discount and circulation that endanger deposites," he argued. "It is when these are expanded that concern should be felt, and not when they are constantly and gradually contracted." As the Bank slowly wound up its affairs, more money would be safely within its vaults rather than lent out to return only on the promise of repayment.[3] To Taney's concern that the BUS notes would depreciate in the months and weeks leading up to the charter's expiration, the Finance Committee was dumbfounded and "utterly at a loss to see the slightest foundation for such an opinion." Webster explained, "[t]here is nothing to render it in any degree doubtful that the bills of the bank will be in as good credit the last day of its charter, and even after that time, if any shall be outstanding, as they are now; and there is as little to render it doubtful that then, as now, the bank would be competent to answer all demands upon it."[4]

Sprague assailed Taney from a different perspective. The senator observed that the purpose of the BUS since its creation was to serve a fiscal agent for the government. By separating the Bank from its role as depository for the public revenue it no longer would function as a fiscal agent for the government. In essence, without government deposits, the BUS would become nothing more than a commercial bank. Suppose Congress had acted as Taney had. Would anyone dare argue that Congress had the authority to create a commercial bank? Sprague asserted, "[t]he boldest advocates of latitudinarian constructions never advanced such an extravagant claim to power." Yet, Taney did just that. He "divorc[ed] the bank from the Government — to dismiss it from its agency, and yet continue its being for all other purposes — to establish a mere commercial bank."[5]

[1] *Register of Debates*, 23rd Cong., 1st sess., (Jan. 20, 1834), 318 (Senate).

[2] *Register of Debates*, 23rd Cong., 1st sess., Appendix, 151.

[3] *Register of Debates*, 23rd Cong., 1st sess., (Feb. 3, 1834), 456 (Senate).

[4] *Register of Debates*, 23rd Cong., 1st sess., Appendix, 151-152.

[5] *Register of Debates*, 23rd Cong., 1st sess., (Jan. 29, 1834), 395 (Senate).

Sprague also found ways to contradict the secretary. Taney had argued that two and half years was not enough time for the Bank to wind up its affairs without shock to the community; that a sudden removal of public money as would occur when the charter expired would produce consider-able distress. Sprague could barely contain his amusement with this position. To prevent public distress, "[t]he Secretary instantly intercepts all future deposites, threatens the immediate withdrawal of the whole, and actually takes from the vaults, all, excepting a small fraction, within a short period of four months; and yet tells us that two years, six times as long, would be too short, and assigns that as a reason for his speedy action!" The secretary also warned that since the Bank would be curtailing its business at the approach of the charter's end, the additional blow of removing the deposits would create distress. Calling in the deposits early, Taney argued, would mitigate the distress. "[Y]et," Sprague continued, "during the months of August, September, and October, the bank was rapidly curtailing its loans, and this was known to the Secretary at the moment he gave his sudden order. He tells us so himself, and that it stimulated him to instant action; that he could not even wait till the meeting of Congress!"[1] The often overlooked senator from Maine shined here once again. At least one publication recognized his abilities, calling his speech "a brilliant and powerful effort, and commanded all eyes and ears. Argument, declamation, retort, and sarcasm have all been displayed with great force and in beautiful words and illustrations."[2] His sharp wit and bulldog tactics were of immense value to the anti-Jacksonian cause.

Both sides made great efforts to both discredit and defend Taney over the timing of the removal, but in some respects, the debate was unnecessary and argued in circles. Much of the case the anti-Jacksonians built revolved around the safety of the deposits increasing as the expiration of the charter neared. While the financial logic behind their case was sound, the deposits' safety factored very little into Taney's decision to remove them when he did. Taney's decision to remove the deposits arose from his desire to shift the nation's currency from a national banking system to that of the states to prepare for the demise of the BUS and radically alter the relationship between the government and banking as well as move the country down a path to hard currency that many Jacksonians promoted. But perhaps the greater motivation for his decision stemmed from his desire to cripple a moneyed power eminently dangerous to the well-being of the common farmer, mechanic, and laborer — the very backbone of Jackson's support.

---

[1] *Register of Debates*, 23rd Cong., 1st sess., (Jan. 29, 1834), 395 (Senate).
[2] *The National Gazette*, Philadelphia, February 1, 1834.

Chapter 8: Sentinels in this Institution

Had the Bank exhibited perfect conduct, the nearing expiration of its charter alone would have been reason enough for Taney to remove the deposits. That the Bank exhibited troublesome conduct in recent years only made it easier to move forward with the removal. According to Taney, the Bank was established to serve the public and any benefits bestowed on private investors were nothing more than rewards for the public services rendered and "it was never supposed that its own separate interests would be voluntarily brought into collision with the public," nor "that it would seek, by its money, to obtain political power, and control the action of the Government."[1] Furthermore, if the Bank were at any time guilty of violating its duties as a public agent, it was the responsibility of the secretary of the Treasury to rescue the public moneys from the offending institution. Having presented the supposed purpose for the BUS and its duties, Taney next outlined how the offending institution violated its supposed purpose, failed in its duties as a public agent, and had consequently forfeited its right to serve as the depository for the public funds.

According to the charter, the United States government had the right to appoint five of the Bank's twenty-five directors. This provision was meant to provide oversight to ensure the Bank was serving the best interests of the public and if it did not, establish a mechanism to alert the proper government authorities of any transgressions. The fourth section of the charter required that a minimum of seven directors was needed to constitute a board

---

[1] *Register of Debates*, 23rd Cong., 1st sess., Appendix, 64.

to transact the business of the Bank (such as the discounting of bills) — a board the government-appointed directors had every right to serve upon, thus guaranteeing public representation for all Bank business.[1] Transparency being necessary to the trustworthiness of any moneyed institution, Taney asserted that no individual would trust their money in an institution that concealed its actions. Taney added that the public should require no less transparency for the safe-keeping of the country's deposits.

Taney argued that the Bank had failed to meet the transparency requirements needed to maintain the public's trust in its safeguarding of the nation's deposits. First, it violated the fourth section of the charter by conducting the majority of its business through a committee of exchange instead of a board of at least seven directors as stipulated by law. The violations of the charter by this committee were numerous and Taney took care to make them known. Of this committee, Taney complained:

> ...no one of the public directors has been allowed to be a member since the commencement of the present year. This committee is not even elected by the board, and the public directors have no voice in their appointment. They are chosen by the president of the bank, and the business of the institution, which ought to be decided by the board of directors, is, in many instances, transacted by this committee; and no one has a right to be present at their proceedings but the president, and whom he shall please to name as members of this committee...And this fact alone furnishes evidence too strong to be resisted, that the concealment of certain important operations of the corporation from the officers of the Government is one of the objects which is intended to be accomplished by means of this committee.

To this, Taney asked rhetorically what individual would trust their money in an institution that took measures to conceal its operations, such as the one just described. How could he, in executing his duties as the safe-keeper of the Treasury, allow the public's money to remain in the BUS?[2]

The Bank's actions regarding the payment of bonds bearing three percent interest (or 3 percents) was a specific example Taney used to expose its secretive conduct. In his message, Taney only mentioned the matter but went no further, citing the extensive attention it received in Congress previously. It is important though to take a moment to discuss the situation, as it became a topic in the subsequent Senate debate. Jackson had made exceedingly clear his desire to see the national debt retired during his term in office. In March 1832, the government informed the Bank of its intention to pay off half of the 3 percents, amounting to $6,500,000 of the government's

---

[1] *Register of Debates*, 23rd Cong., 1st sess., Appendix, 64.
[2] *Register of Debates*, 23rd Cong., 1st sess., Appendix, 65.

outstanding debt in July.[1] Due to over-lending throughout the previous year, Biddle was unexpectedly short on cash and was forced to appeal to the government for an extension on the payment; the government acquiesced and Biddle was granted an additional three months. The good news was short-lived, however, as Biddle learned later that the government planned to pay off the remaining 3 percents by January 1, doubling the amount owed by the bank to $13,000,000. Recognizing the clear danger of withdrawing such an enormous sum from the public coffers during an election year so critical to the Bank's future, the crafty Biddle concocted a shrewd way out of his jam. Biddle proposed negotiating with the foreign stockholders to surrender their 3 percent bonds to the Bank, which the Bank would then pass on to the government as evidence demonstrating the debt had been paid. The government's portion of the foreign debt thus retired, the BUS would be responsible for repaying the original bond holders with interest over the next year. This new loan, which amounted to $5,000,000, was entirely legal since the government was absolved of all responsibility. Indeed, the board of directors had already given Biddle and the exchange committee the green light to defer some of what it owed.[2] In essence, the foreign holders would receive an additional year on their bonds to collect interest except the debt holder changed from the United States government to the BUS.

Biddle's plan began to crumble, though, when negotiations to implement it commenced. When initial discussions with New York's T.W. Ludlow went nowhere, Biddle sent Thomas Cadwalader overseas to London to begin talks with Baring Brothers. Cadwalader and Baring Brothers struck a deal, but it was not the deal that Biddle conceived or authorized. Unable to convince enough bond holders to surrender their securities to the BUS, Cadwalader alternatively allowed Baring to buy up the 3 percents for no more than ninety-one cents on the dollar. Instead of transferring the bonds to the BUS to then pass on to the government as originally planned, Baring took possession of the bonds or they remained in the hands of the original holders. This new deal was an express violation of the Bank's charter which prohibited it from purchasing public debt. In addition, because the Bank would no longer be delivering the 3 percents, the government's goal of retiring its debt as soon as possible would have to wait. (Jackson announced the country was debt-free

---

[1] 3 percents refers to a type of Treasury bond sold by the government. The percent indicates the amount of interest the bond bears, so in this case, the government planned to redeem the bonds bearing 3 percent interest (the government also sold 6 percents and 4 ½ percents). Stephen W. Campbell, Twitter direct message, February 19, 2020.

[2] Remini, *Jackson and the Bank War*, 120.; Ralph C. Catterall, "The Charges Against the Bank," in *Jackson Versus Biddle: The Struggle Over the Second Bank of the United States*, ed. by George Rogers Taylor (Boston: DC Heath and Company, 1949), 47.

on January 8, 1835.) Public pressure forced Biddle to condemn Cadawalder for the illegal deal, but privately he wondered why there was such an outcry — considering the money had not left the Treasury and the government no longer had to pay the interest on the loan. Unsurprisingly, Jackson leapt at the chance to disavow the Bank for its actions and accused it of once again usurping control from the government over policy measures.[1]

Such is the story of the 3 percents that Taney referenced in his message to Congress. Aside from violating the Bank's charter and preventing the government from paying off its debt in a timely fashion, the whole scheme was concocted by Biddle and the exchange committee in secret. The situation exemplified the power over the Bank's affairs exerted by the exchange committee in defiance of the charter requiring business operations to be conducted by a board of no fewer than seven. Taney also submitted to Congress a report composed by three of the government-appointed directors detailing how "the power conferred by law on the board has been surrendered to the exchange committee."[2] If this blatant violation of the charter be allowed, Taney claimed the appointment of government directors to oversee the Bank's operations for the public interest was pointless.

To expand upon the case of the Bank's troublesome conduct, Taney also brought up the issues surrounding the French spoliation bill. The issue stemmed from a treaty signed by the French government promising to pay the United States indemnification for property destroyed during the Napoleonic Wars. The total amount to be paid to the United States was twenty-five million francs over six installments. When the first payment came due in February, 1833, rather than ask the BUS to take up the bill on its account, the government felt the best way to collect would be to sell the bill of the exchange to the BUS for the amount of $903,565.89.[3] When presented with the bill, the French government refused to pay and so it went into protest. The Bank sent the protested bill to the secretary of the Treasury (as the representative of the United States government, the drawer of the bill) along with a claim for restitution drawn up according to a Maryland law which applied to Washington D.C. as well. The claim was "for the principal, interest, cost of protest, re-exchange, and damages at 15 percent."[4] Then Secretary of the Treasury, Louis McLane paid the principal, but nothing else and upon assuming his duties as secretary, Taney — who had voiced considerable displeasure with the Bank over the matter as attorney general

---

[1] Remini, *Jackson and the Bank War*, 121.
[2] *Register of Debates*, 23rd Cong., 1st sess., Appendix 65.
[3] Remini, *Jackson and the Bank War*, 119.
[4] Catterall, *Second Bank*, 300.

— ignored the claim. Now, though, Taney revived the issue to demonstrate that "[The Bank's] own interests will be found to be its ruling principle, and the just claims of the public to be treated with but little regard, when they have come into collision with the interests of the corporation."[1] Indeed, the Bank was attempting to extract $158,842.77 in damages from the government, a sum Taney said far exceeded any losses incurred by the BUS. Instead of acting in the best interest of the public, the Bank's callously tried to profit from the situation, serving as additional confirmation of its inexcusable and dangerous conduct.

***

The debate over the Bank's alleged misconduct, more than any other debate during the session, pushed the warring factions firmly into their respective corners. Whereas the dispute over abuse and usurpation of power, subtleties of the Constitution, and interpretations of the Bank's charter allowed for some nuanced approaches that resulted in Jacksonians and anti-Jacksonians breaking with their colleagues on occasion, the dispute over the Bank's misconduct provided little room for nuance. This created perhaps the most polarized subject of the debate, with Jacksonians, to a man, lining up to assail the bank for its misconduct and the anti-Jacksonians likewise coming to its defense.

The Jacksonians followed Taney's lead in excoriating the secretive business conducted by the Bank's exchange committee and leading the charge was Thomas Benton. Benton, in contrast to the more passive role he assumed on the questions of power and the Constitution thus far discussed, on the question of sins committed by the Bank, took on the role of lead prosecutor. Speaking first after Clay allowed the Missourian to set the tone that his cohorts could follow in assailing the BUS. Benton felt the forcing of Taney's hand due in part to the secret maneuverings of the exchange committee the easiest plank to defend, as the task was "reduced to the mere occupation of reading the evidence which bore upon the case." The evidence the senator referred to was from two reports written by the government directors of the Bank, appointed in January 1833, to show that they had been intentionally cut off from the business of the BUS and thus divested of any authority legally granted by the charter. Benton read from one of the reports: "'It is the case of a subordinate corporation, spurning at, and virtually discarding, the agents of those by whom it was created; paying no sort of respect to the exalted public sources whence their appointment immediately emanates; denying the true nature of their trusts; and nullifying, by preconcert and pretence,

---

[1] *Register of Debates*, 23rd Cong., 1st sess., Appendix 66.

the law of the land and its ministerial officers."'[1] This passage suggests that the scheming on the part of the Bank to cut from the loop the government directors was intentional for the purpose of depriving the people of representation over the Bank's business. Instead, the exchange committee and other committees firmly in Biddle's grasp held the Bank's real power. The purposeful exclusion of the government directors from these committees, Benton reasoned, "was a dissolution of the connexion between the Government and the bank; it was the extinction of the only national feature of the institution; it was sufficient cause in itself for a removal of the deposites."[2]

The exclusion of these directors, according to their reports, started almost immediately. At the first meeting of the year, the newly appointed government directors were left off of every standing committee, a move they viewed as calculated by Biddle and the board of directors "'to deprive us of the best means of information in regard to the nature of its proceedings.'" The shunned officers quickly learned the exclusion they experienced at that first meeting was but a portent for a pattern that would ensue aimed at funneling power over all important Bank business into the hands of a few. The reports exposed several examples illustrating how this plot operated in practice, but to spare the Senate from the tediousness of hearing a recollection of them all, Benton communicated the details of just one. Near the end their one-year term of service to the Bank, the government directors offered a resolution for the creation of a committee to investigate printing expenses incurred for the time between July 1, 1829 and July 1, 1833 in an attempt determine if the BUS engaged in electioneering ahead of the 1832 presidential election. The resolution was tossed aside without consideration.[3] To Benton, no example better encapsulated the systematic exclusion of the government directors from participating in the business of the Bank while simultaneously hiding from them the particulars of its conduct.

Just days earlier, Clay had attempted to explain away the charges of misconduct by the exchange committee and the tactics used to allegedly exclude the government directors from exercising any authority over the Bank's dealings. Clay observed that the board of directors met on an intermittent basis and therefore, could not be expected to handle the day to day affairs of the Bank. Those responsibilities must necessarily devolve upon "some authority at the bank daily, to pass daily upon bills, either in the sale or purchase, as the wants of the community require." The committee of exchange was created for that very purpose and to Clay's knowledge, all

---

[1] *Register of Debates*, 23rd Cong., 1st sess., (Jan. 2, 1834), 125-126 (Senate).
[2] *Register of Debates*, 23rd Cong., 1st sess., (Jan. 2, 1834), 128 (Senate).
[3] *Register of Debates*, 23rd Cong., 1st sess., (Jan. 2, 1834), 126-127 (Senate).

banks had committees of the same nature and to serve the same purpose. Clay next rationalized the mode of appointment to these committees as being the same as the mode of appointment to committees in the national and state legislatures. Just as Biddle appointed members to the Bank's committees, the House speaker and chairs of public meetings generally appointed members to legislative committees. Clay reasoned that the omission of the government directors from these committees was due to their lack of "skill and experience, and standing in society to be put there." If Jackson had nominated men with great business acumen and experience, perhaps their presence on important committees would be more conspicuous. After all, the Kentuckian concluded, "[a] piece of coin, having even the stamp of the Government, will not pass unless the metal is pure."[1]

Benton did not allow Clay's explanation to go unchallenged, calling the differences between the operations of the BUS committees and of legislative committees "too obvious to escape the attention of any hearer." Legislative committees, Benton explained, functioned only to *prepare* business to be acted on by the full legislative body. The BUS committee of exchange, on the other hand, "had final and conclusive authority over the subjects on which they acted...In fact, the committee on exchange was the board of directors, or what the charter intended the board to be."[2] In Benton's eyes, the strands of correlation between the Bank's committee of exchange and legislative committees were frayed at best, and more accurately, non-existent. To Clay's contention that the government directors had been left off important committees due to their lack of qualifications, the Missourian reacted with sarcastic contempt. Benton mockingly described the scenario as painted by Clay: "The bank sets itself up above the constituted authorities, judges the appointments which it makes, and sets them aside when not agreeable to itself. Henceforth the bank must be consulted in the choice of Government directors, in the choice of those who are to represent the interests of the United States; and if the President and the Senate presume to make appointments contrary to her will, they will be set aside and nullified."[3] It is curious that Benton chose this phrasing considering he and his allies would argue that Jackson *had* the authority to set aside and nullify Duane since he acted contrary to his will, but so goes the hypocritical world of American politics.

Both sides continued sparring over this subject commenced by their de-facto leaders. Anti-Jacksonians generally avoided a direct defense of the committee of exchange and instead attacked the government direc-

---

[1] *Register of Debates*, 23rd Cong., 1st sess., (Dec. 30, 1833), 81 (Senate).
[2] *Register of Debates*, 23rd Cong., 1st sess., (Jan. 2, 1834), 128 (Senate).
[3] *Register of Debates*, 23rd Cong., 1st sess., (Jan. 2, 1834), 129 (Senate).

tors, suggesting that it was not the committee that was guilty of secretive dealings, but the government directors themselves. They argued that the directors' reports Benton had so heavily leaned on to spin his story of their systematic exclusion were ordered and compiled in secret, saddling themselves with the label of spies among some of the anti-Jacksonians. When the Bank was created by Congress, Southard asked, "[d]id it occur to them that [the government directors] were to act as informers under executive appointment and order? secret spies, who were to give information to the President, without the rest of the directors being aware of it?"[1] South Carolina's William Preston added bluntly that once the government directors' plot was discovered along with their ultimate goal to supply the president information with which to destroy the Bank, "[the Bank directors] would have been worse than idiots to have given their confidence to them."[2] Ewing carried the argument further, stating that if the government directors truly felt they had been conspired against, they had only themselves to blame. The charter specifically outlawed any director, government or otherwise, from disclosing information regarding the accounts of private individuals. Yet, the Ohioan noted, the government directors "made frequent and free communications to the Executive of those private affairs which the charter did not permit to be disclosed." Why then would Biddle appoint them to committees where they would be privy to additional information they could illegally share with the administration?[3] Calhoun, putting his oratorical gifts fully on display, purposely referred to the five government appointed men as directors so he could dramatically correct himself. "Directors!...did I say?" he exclaimed. "No! *spies* is their proper designation!"[4]

Despite the blatant violation of their authority, it appeared to Ewing that the government directors had access to the same information as any other director and that the nature of their complaint of being denied information stemmed from their mistaken belief that their designation as government directors placed them in importance ahead of the other twenty directors. "There is a difference in their mode of creation," Ewing noted, "but any privilege claimed on that score is similar to that of being better born than their neighbors, and is entitled to the same respect." Nothing in the charter gave the five government directors any added power than the rest, leading Ewing to conclude sarcastically that he "will be obliged to any one who will tell me exactly what their additional powers and privileges are."[5] Building on

---

[1] *Register of Debates*, 23rd Cong., 1st sess., (Jan. 8, 1834), 166 (Senate).
[2] *Congressional Globe*, 23rd Cong., 1st sess., (Jan. 23, 1834), 123 (Senate).
[3] *Register of Debates*, 23rd Cong., 1st sess., (Jan. 20, 1834), 319 (Senate).
[4] *Register of Debates*, 23rd Cong., 1st sess., (Jan. 13, 1834), 212 (Senate).
[5] *Register of Debates*, 23rd Cong., 1st sess., (Jan. 20, 1834), 320 (Senate).

this point, the report of the Senate Finance Committee contended that the titles of "public directors" and "officers of the government" given by Taney to the five directors nominated by the government was misleading. Webster explained, "[t]he whole twenty-five directors are joint managers of a joint fund, each possessing precisely the same powers, and charged with the same duties as every other." Therefore, the chairman added, the five government appointed directors should "not [be] called public directors, nor officers of the government, nor public agents; nor are they entitled to, so far as the committee can perceive, to either of these appellations, any more than the other directors."[1]

The Jacksonians, predictably, pushed back against these arguments. Grundy sought to discredit the view shared by Ewing and Webster that the government directors stood on equal footing with the others. The Tennessean pointed out that the government held stock in several companies and that in each one, the government voted for directors like any other stockholder. But in the case of the BUS, the government had sole authority to appoint and remove the directors representing them. To Grundy, this implied a unique station for the five appointed in this manner versus the other twenty. Additionally, the charter stated that unlike the other directors who had to be stockholders, should the government sell its stock and dissolve all financial connection with the BUS, the five government directors would continue in their same roles. Grundy wondered, "[w]hat reasons could have produced [such a contingency] unless it were intended that the Government should at all times have its sentinels in this institution to give information whether any thing was transacting detrimental to the public welfare?" Employing this logic, Grundy defended both the government directors' and the president's actions, stating that since "[the government directors] were appointed by the law...to watch over and take care of the public interest, it was [the president's] duty to apply, and theirs to give the information."[2] Wilkins joined Grundy in referring to the government directors as sentinels of the public interest and added that only through them could the president obtain direct information on the conduct of the Bank. The president could not compel a stockholder meeting for the purpose of gathering information. The secretary's power to obtain information as outlined in section fifteen was confined to only a statement on the condition of the Bank, not its conduct. The twenty-third section granted Congress the power to appoint a committee to inspect the books and conduct of the Bank, but for the president to benefit from this section, he would need Congress to be in session and to call for an investiga-

---

[1] *Register of Debates*, 23rd Cong., 1st sess., Appendix, 152.

[2] *Register of Debates*, 23rd Cong., 1st sess., (Jan. 30, 1834), 427, 429 (Senate).

tion on his behalf. Therefore, to obtain information, such as that connected to rumors of rampant misconduct perpetrated by the BUS in 1832, Jackson had nowhere to turn but to the government directors.[1]

These rumors were the impetus behind Jackson's request of the public directors for an investigation and the Jacksonians also rejected the characterization of their final report as some sort of cloak and dagger operation to feed the president information on the Bank and its subscribers. Shepley regretted that the character of the discussion had deteriorated to the point where the government directors were referred to as spies and informers. But the degradation of the debate allowed the senator to make a compelling observation; the labeling of informer upon the public directors implied a crime had been committed. Shepley asked, "[w]here is there an informer unless there is crime known to him, and against which he is to inform?"[2] To Shepley, the designation of the monikers, spies and informers, by the anti-Jacksonians confirmed that the Bank had committed a crime to inform against. Forsyth declared that "[n]o secret investigation was made by the Government directors, nor was a secret investigation required by the President." The Georgian explained, "[t]he President called on those gentlemen for information resting on their personal knowledge of facts whose existence there had been rumor. To comply with this call, the directors made an open investigation, an investigation known to all their brethren on board." He added that they only concealed how their research would be ultimately used out of fear of being shut out from their investigation had their purpose been discovered. Wilkins chimed in that the letter Jackson wrote requesting the investigation has been misconstrued as a directive to maintain secrecy throughout. "The first paragraph," the Pennsylvanian explained, "simply enjoined on the public directors not to pay any attention to rumors, or to newspaper accounts, but to let their information come from their own knowledge." Wilkins added that the public directors performed their task "[n]ot secretly, but openly, in a manly style."[3]

The controversy surrounding the issuance of these reports dated back to the debates over the chartering of the Second Bank of the United States. Some argued, Forsyth among them, that the government directors' role was to operate as a watchdog over the Bank's affairs on behalf of the public and safeguard against any wrongdoing that could bring harm to the public. Jackson, in his mind the ultimate "custodian of the public's interests," believed then that the government directors should report directly

---

[1] *Register of Debates*, 23rd Cong., 1st sess., (Feb. 6, 1834), 488 (Senate).
[2] *Register of Debates*, 23rd Cong., 1st sess., (Jan. 14, 1834), 234 (Senate).
[3] *Register of Debates*, 23rd Cong., 1st sess., (Feb. 6, 1834), 488 (Senate).

to him when they sensed or uncovered dangerous conduct by the BUS.[1] Because the anti-Jacksonians rejected Jackson's characterization of his role as protector of the public, they naturally pushed back against these reports as encroaching onto the territory the president had no right entering.[2] This too explains the anti-Jacksonian description of the government directors as spies and informants, as not only did they divulge information they had no right to divulge, the recipient of that information was someone who had no right to it.

Ewing had chastised the government directors for violating the charter by looking into the accounts of individual investors and disclosing private information in their report. Forsyth shot back at Ewing that his reading of the charter was flawed. The section he had relied on in claiming the charter forbade the examination of private accounts applied to the secretary of the Treasury only. On the contrary, Forsyth lectured, "[d]irectors must examine into the private accounts of all in order to do their duties to the institution." The senator allowed for the general rule of not using any private information for personal injury, but held that that consideration was secondary to the interests of the Bank and the public. Forsyth reasoned, "[i]t would be very strange if the directors of the Government have not the right to state to Congress, when in session, or to the President when Congress is not in session, as the constitutional representatives of the great stockholders, the United States, the general or the particular mismanagement of the funds put under their care."[3] Furthermore, Grundy added, the personal account information contained within the directors' report had already been disseminated for public consumption by a House committee during the previous session, thus exonerating the directors from exposing private information.[4]

The clash between Ewing and duo of Forsyth and Grundy on this matter requires a bit more examination. In making his point, Ewing had quoted section fifteen of the Bank's charter, which gave the secretary authority to require statements from the BUS on its financial condition. The section concluded with a proviso stating that this did not mean individual accounts could be subject to inspection. There is no mention in the section of any Bank personnel besides the secretary of the Treasury, and the section is bookended by two others that speak specifically to the duties and responsibilities of the secretary, so it would seem that Forsyth was correct in his assessment that the section to which Ewing referred did not apply to the

---

[1] Catterall, *Second Bank*, 308.
[2] Jackson's self-appointed role as protector of the people and the anti-Jacksonian push-back is covered in greater detail in Chapter 13.
[3] *Register of Debates*, 23rd Cong., 1st sess., (Jan. 27, 1834), 366 (Senate).
[4] *Register of Debates*, 23rd Cong., 1st sess., (Jan. 30, 1834), 429 (Senate).

Bank directors.[1] However, Rule 9 of the *Rules and Regulations for Conducting the Business of the Bank of the United States* enacted in 1816 stated, "[n]o director, without special authority, shall be permitted to inspect the cash account of any person with this bank."[2] It is unclear why Ewing, whose command of detail in his speech earned him the description from one news organ as "a book worm" and a "black-letter man," would make such a simple yet glaring oversight, but in terms of his overall point — that the directors were not legally able to inspect the accounts of private individuals — the Ohioan stood vindicated by Rule 9.[3]

Although few anti-Jacksonians opted to defend the much maligned committee of exchange, one who did, Samuel Southard, proved characteristically able in his effort. The freshman senator followed Clay's lead and took to precedent — a curious choice given the anti-Jacksonians spirited opposition to their opponents' use of it on other matters. Southard recounted that a plan for an exchange committee had been in the works as early as 1816 and operational by 1820. No secretary had voiced any hostility toward the committee's existence and even when the Bank was under intense scrutiny and nearly lost its charter in its early years, the exchange committee was absent from any list of the Bank's offenses. The New Jerseyan did not stop at merely defending the existence of the exchange committee, he defended its conduct and maintained its transparency as well. The committee of three, plus the Bank president and cashier, met almost daily to purchase bills at rates they themselves set and eventually took to discounting notes, to the chagrin of the public directors.[4] The exchange department, headed by the committee, laid before the directors weekly statements of all transacted business. Any misconduct by the exchange committee, Southard argued, should have been caught by the directors, had they adequately performed their duties and given the weekly statements proper attention. In their reports to Jackson, the government directors admitted that the committee had been forthcoming with these statements, prompting the senator to express his confusion over how the committee could be accused of concealing its actions.[5]

The most robust defense of the exchange committee emanated from the report of Webster's Finance Committee. First, Webster reported that the complaints of the exchange committee discounting bills was simply that — that a committee and not a group of at least seven directors was discounting bills. Nowhere could be found complaints that these discounts brought forth

---

[1] Stat. 266. 14th Congress, 1st Session, Ch. 44, specifically, 273-274.
[2] Catterall, *Second Bank*, Appendix III, 492.
[3] *Baltimore Patriot*, January 21, 1834.
[4] Catterall, *Second Bank*, 280-281.
[5] *Register of Debates*, 23rd Cong., 1st sess., (Jan. 8, 1834), 193 (Senate).

any loss to the government or business community. Webster questioned if the only complaint stemmed from the supposed irregularity of a committee of exchange discounting bills, how was removing the deposites the proper remedy. "What connexion is there between the two things?" the chairman probed. "It is not pretended that this mode of discounting bills endangered the deposits; it is not pretended that it made the bank either less able or less willing to perform every one of its duties to Government." Webster finished his point asking, "[h]ow should the withdrawal of the deposites, then, be suggested by the discovery of such an irregularity, real or supposed?" The Committee also found that the discounting of bills by the exchange committee was common banking practice considering the volume of bills presented every day. Expecting a board of at least seven, who could not meet more than twice a week, to handle the whole business of discounting would be impracticable. None of the exchange committee's actions, in the eyes of the Senate Finance Committee, took away from the "general management and control" of the Bank's affairs by the directors.[1] Just as Clay and Southard had argued before, the Finance Committee viewed the actions of the committee of exchange as consistent with other similar institutions and therefore, had committed no offense.

The strongest denunciation of the exchange committee's conduct and the Senate Finance Committee's excusal of its actions came from the hunchbacked senator from New Hampshire, Isaac Hill. Hill believed that excusing the exchange committee for discounting bills because no pecuniary loss had occurred was a "sorry justification of acts improper and unlawful in themselves." The exchange committee, he protested, was guilty of multiple violations, including but not limited to assuming the duties of the board without its consent, making loans of questionable security contrary to the Bank's by-laws, conducting such business on days when the board had the opportunity to do so itself, and neglecting to report to the board their proceedings in writing. And the Finance Committee's response to all this, Hill announced derisively: "'The bank has been advised that [the exchange committee] might rightfully do this; and if it be not clear that this opinion is right, it is certainly far from clear that it is wrong.'" The friends of the Bank may accept that justification, but the American people certainly did not. The Finance Committee was seemingly unable to turn up evidence that the exchange committee had purposely concealed its business from the public directors. "If the Committee on Finance are really unable to perceive any evidence in this matter," Hill bellowed, "have the president of the bank and the directors ever denied the fact? On the contrary, does not every circumstance that

---

[1] *Register of Debates*, 23rd Cong., 1st sess., Appendix, 152.

has come to the knowledge of the public, show that there have been many transactions involving the deepest public interest, the history of which has never been told?"[1]

To those such as Hill and Benton, the violations of the exchange committee were clear, so much so that the Bank did not even try to conceal its illegal activities. But the other side, specifically Southard, had argued that the exchange committee reported its conduct to the board and its actions were of general benefit to the country, an opinion held by the Finance Committee as well. Was the exchange committee a small handful of Biddle insiders conducting clandestine operations to enrich themselves and their leader, or was it a transparent committee typical of and necessary to any large banking operation that ultimately did well by its stockholders and country at large? Historians have generally leaned toward the latter. Banking historian, Fritz Redlich, spoke to the necessity of an exchange committee, citing the low attendance at board meetings that rendered them useless as administrative bodies. Consequently, committees filling the role of administration among large banks had, by 1820, become "typical." For banks striving to profit from the exchange business, exchange committees were necessary since they met regularly and could keep up with the volume of bills for discount. (This corresponds with the argument put forth by the anti-Jacksonians and the Finance Committee.) Redlich also characterized Biddle's actions, and by extension those of the exchange committee that he oversaw, as cutting edge for his time and foreshadowing the management style that would typify nineteenth century business administration in the coming years. Redlich argued, "[i]t would have been ridiculous for [Biddle], one of the greatest bankers of his time, to poll the members of his board, ignorant in the particular field in comparison to himself, to find the answer to a banking problem...Neither did he wait for a decision of the board...if quick action was needed." Banking had changed considerably between the chartering of the Bank in 1816 and 1833 when these debates began. The national economy was rapidly moving towards global capitalism and the Bank followed suit under Biddle. This forced the Bank, out of necessity, to keep secret certain larger transactions and thus fed into the Jacksonian narrative of the corrupt and underhanded Bank led by its equally corrupt and underhanded president.[2] If the Bank was guilty of anything, it was that it, like other large banks of its day, merely adapted to the evolving economic climate of the country that necessitated changes to how banks were administered, most conspicuously,

---

[1] *Register of Debates*, 23rd Cong., 1st sess., (Mar. 3, 1834), 759-760 (Senate).

[2] Fritz Redlich, *Molding of American Banking: Men and Ideas* (New York: Hafner Publishing Company, 1951), 56-59, 118, 121.

a shift of power from the board of directors to bank presidents and committees. The Jacksonians had applied an outdated economic model when crafting their admonishment of Biddle and the exchange committee when in fact, had the Bank not operated in the manner that they so ridiculed, the BUS likely would have been far less profitable and an unsafe depository for the public funds.

The evidence suggests that the institutional changes in administration as developed by Biddle were beneficial to the Bank and the country's economy in general. Jane Knodell, in her groundbreaking study of the Bank's exchange operations, credited the exchange committee's pursuit of profits through the domestic and foreign exchange markets with "generating positive externalities in the form of lower, more stable internal exchange rates, and lower risk for merchants involved in interregional and international trade."[1] Although she stopped short of calling the committee's actions altruistic and sacrificing profit for public good, she discredits commentators who have argued that the BUS generated greater profits through "monopolistic mark-ups," a charge leveled originally by Jacksonians in the Senate and beyond. That the BUS pursued profits to the fullest extent is not debatable; this is the goal for any business. But the notion that Biddle, through the committee of exchange, sought to work purposely outside the bounds of the charter to profit in ways detrimental to the public interest does not appear supported by the historic record.

***

A smattering of senators chose to speak to the two specific examples of BUS misconduct presented in Taney's report — the payment of 3 percents and the French spoliation bill. Among the anti-Jacksonians, just Southard and Ewing addressed the 3 percents, and only briefly. The issue had been litigated in House during the last session and that body overwhelmingly absolved the Bank of wrongdoing and determined the deposits safe. Neither senator could understand why, in light of the acquittal by the House, Taney would cite this as a reason for removal. "How dare [Taney], by repeating the accusation," Southard thundered, "[t]hus insult a Congress in which the friends of the Executive had control?"[2] Ewing argued that since the issue had been settled by the proper tribunal, there was nothing more to say on the matter, adding in his typical lawyerly style, "[i]n politics, as well as in law, there ought to be some end to litigation."[3]

---

[1] Jane Knodell, "Profit and duty in the Second Bank of the United States' exchange operations," *Financial History Review* 10, (2003): 28.

[2] *Register of Debates*, 23rd Cong., 1st sess., (Jan. 8, 1834), 192 (Senate).

[3] *Register of Debates*, 23rd Cong., 1st sess., (Jan. 20, 1834), 320 (Senate).

Most of the Jacksonians followed Ewing's advice and avoided talk of the 3 percents. William Rives though, thought the subject deserved attention. No senator, Jacksonian or otherwise, spent more time on this matter than Rives. The Virginian explained that the Bank's handling of the 3 percents displayed its inability to promptly disburse public monies when called upon, a duty Rives felt of equal, if not greater importance than the Bank's solvency. Rives recalled that on April 1, 1832, the day the Bank was informed that the government would be redeeming the 3 percents, it held $9,513,000 of public funds. On July 1, when the payment was originally due, that number had increased by nearly $300,000, surpassing the $6,500,000 in public funds requested by the government by over three million. Yet the Bank could not make the payment as obligated? Indeed, on October 1, when the extended payment came due and while Cadawalder was conducting the secret negotiations explained above, the Bank would have held a surplus of $3,222,792 after deducting the amount due. Rives could conceive no reason why the Bank could not pay the requested amount in a timely manner given the amount of public funds in its vaults.[1]

The Virginian also sought to discredit the anti-Jacksonian argument that since Congress had put the issue to rest at the last session, Taney had no right to bring it up now as a reason for removal. The House Committee of Ways and Means considered the matter closed since the Bank had surrendered the certificates to the government, stating, "'[the issue] no longer presents a practical object of inquiry, or to call for or admit any action of Congress upon it.'" The Committee though also condemned the transaction set up by Cadawalder and ruled that the Bank "'had exceeded its legal authority.'" Because the transaction, not the end result, was at the core of Taney's complaints against the Bank, Rives insisted, borrowing the Committee's phrasing, "it necessarily becomes 'a practical object of inquiry,' demanding the serious consideration, if not 'the action of Congress;' and none, in my estimation, could more signally illustrate the delinquency of the bank in its relations of fiscal agent to the Government."[2] In Rives' view, Congress closed the matter because the government had gotten what it demanded of the Bank — the redemption of the 3 percents. But that did not mean that the Bank had not acted illegally and it was for that illegal action that Taney removed the deposits and why Rives believed the issue was relevant to the ongoing discussion.

The French bill, in contrast to the 3 percents, drew more attention from the anti-Jacksonians while most Jacksonians chose to ignore it.

---

[1] *Register of Debates*, 23rd Cong., 1st sess., (Jan. 17, 1834), 268-269 (Senate).
[2] *Register of Debates*, 23rd Cong., 1st sess., (Jan. 17, 1834), 269-270 (Senate).

The protests from the anti-Jacksonians over Taney's citing of the bill as a reason for removing the deposits centered on two main points — the Bank purchased the bill outside of its capacity as an agent of the government, and if the Bank had acted the way Taney believed it should have when the bill went to protest, it would have violated the terms of the charter. The anti-Jacksonians clarified to the rest of the Senate that the Bank had originally offered to *collect* the bill on behalf of the government. Had the government agreed, the Bank, in regards to this bill, would have then been acting as an agent of the government. Instead, the government declined and opted to sell the bill, which it did to the BUS, "for no reason," according to the Finance Committee report, "except that the terms of the bank were more satisfactory."[1] Therefore, as Ewing capably pointed out, the transaction fell outside the bounds of the Bank's duty as a fiscal agent to the government. The transaction was not a transfer of funds within the United States, nor did it involve commissioning or paying loans. Indeed, the Bank was acting as an individual purchaser and thus entitled to exercise the same rights as any other who may have purchased this particular bill. "Suppose the broker who bid the next best price for the bill had got it," Ewing proposed. "[W]ould any man have thought of complaining of him for claiming his damages for the protest?"[2] Sprague added that when bills held by the government went into protest, they acted in the same manner as did the BUS and claimed damages — at times from BUS stockholders. It was both the Bank's right as a purchaser and its duty to protect the interests of its stockholders to claim the appropriate damages on the bill. Failing to do so, Sprague argued, would open the BUS up to charges of intrigue. He asked, "[w]hat if the bank had offered to relinquish this part of the debt [the damages], should we not then have heard that it was attempting to purchase the favor of the Secretary? To bribe him by $150,000 of the money of the stockholders? Would it not have been imputed as a crime of much deeper dye?"[3] The government, through its Treasury secretary, could have employed the BUS as its fiscal agent in the collection of the bill in question. Instead, by its own choice, the government chose to deal with the BUS as a buyer and the anti-Jacksonians argued that by making that choice, the government became liable for any damages should the bill go into protest. That the BUS happened to be the buyer did not change that.

To the anti-Jacksonians, Taney's insistence that the Bank should not have sought damages from the government for the protested bill implic-

---

[1] *Register of Debates*, 23rd Cong., 1st sess., Appendix, 153
[2] *Register of Debates*, 23rd Cong., 1st sess., (Jan. 20, 1834), 320 (Senate).
[3] *Register of Debates*, 23rd Cong., 1st sess., (Jan. 29, 1834), 396 (Senate).

itly meant that the BUS should have instead taken it up on account of the government. As stated above, it would have been impractical for the Bank to simply absorb the losses from the protested bill; if Taney felt the BUS should not seek damages *from* the government, the only alternative would be to seek damages *for* the government, as the original holders of the bill. To take up the bill on the behalf of the government, the BUS would had to have advanced the principal amount of $900,000 to the Treasury, a fact that compelled Clay to question if Taney had read the charter at all. If he had, Clay observed, Taney would have known that section thirteen of the charter specifically forbid the Bank from advancing or lending any sum in excess of $500,000 for government use or on its account under the threat of fine three times the amount of the sum lent or advanced.[1] The Senate Finance Committee agreed with the anti-Jacksonians assessment of the situation and added, as it had in regards to other subjects, that even if the Bank were guilty of wrongdoing, how was removing the deposits the proper response? The BUS felt it was entitled to the damages from the protested bill; the secretary did not. Webster, reading from the report bellowed, "it is quite inconceivable to the committee that the pendency of such a difference of opinion, on such a question, should furnish any reason whatever for withdrawing the deposites." Accepting the Bank's actions surrounding the French bill as a reason for removal, Webster concluded, amounted to "admiss[ion] that the Secretary holds the power of removal as a perfectly arbitrary power, and may exercise it, by way of punishment, whenever, in any particular, the conduct or the opinions of the bank do not conform to his pleasure."[2]

Most Jacksonians, perhaps recognizing the difficulty in refuting their opponents' arguments, chose not to address the French bill. Two though, Forsyth and Hill, took up the issue in support of Taney. Forsyth found it curious that the anti-Jacksonians would reference section thirteen of the charter to explain why the BUS would not take up the protested bill on account of the government. The anti-Jacksonians argued that advancing the $900,000 to the government to take up the bill on their account would be penalized by the issuance of a fine three times the amount loaned, as stipulated by the charter. However, Forsyth pointed out, the Bank had recently advanced $600,000 to the British government to help the crown meet its obligation to the United States outlined in the Treaty of Ghent. The Georgian noted, "[w]e see...that when a foreign Government was concerned, [section thirteen] was not thought of, but when our own is alone concerned, the penalty is referred to as the justification of the conduct of the present admin-

---

[1] *Register of Debates*, 23rd Cong., 1st sess., (Dec. 30, 1833), 87-88 (Senate).
[2] *Register of Debates*, 23rd Cong., 1st sess., Appendix, 154.

istrators of the bank."[1] Hill briefly touched on the subject as well, stating that all the money the Bank was out due to the bill going into protest was money belonging to the United States. Therefore, the senator concluded, by seeking damages from the government, the BUS attempted "to grasp what cannot in equity be said to belong to the bank."[2]

These minor ventures into the subject that took up just seconds of the Senate's time were but obligatory gestures of solidarity to Taney and did little to advance the Jacksonians' case that the Bank's behavior had shown a pattern of impropriety. But to the transgression over which Taney saved his strongest contempt, the Jacksonians would react with equal fire.

---

[1] *Register of Debates*, 23rd Cong., 1st sess., (Jan. 27, 1834), 369 (Senate).
[2] *Register of Debates*, 23rd Cong., 1st sess., (Mar. 3, 1834), 760 (Senate).

CHAPTER 9: WE ARE ALL POLITICAL ELECTIONEERS

Taney spent considerable time outlining the financial and managerial misconduct exhibited by the Bank but those indiscretions paled in comparison to what he believed to be its most offensive transgression — the Bank's flagrant attempts to insert itself into the country's politics. Taney presented statistical evidence to show how the BUS used its enormous financial resources and influence to force its recharter upon Congress. Between the December 31, 1830, and May 1, 1832, a span of sixteen months, the bank extended its loans by a whopping $28,025,766.48. The sixty-six percent increase over that span of time was unprecedented in the history of banking.

The reason for such expansion was obvious to Taney. The Bank had petitioned for recharter at the start of the December 1831 congressional session after having increased its loans by staggering amounts over the previous year to convince Congress that due to "the great extent of its business," allowing the charter to expire would create much economic distress across the country.[1] The recharter effort and rapid expansion of business also occurred ahead of a looming presidential election where the BUS had a vested interest in its outcome. The timing of all this not lost on Taney, he condemned the Bank as a "great moneyed corporation determined to enter the political arena, and to influence the measures of the Government, by causing its weight to be felt in the election of its officers."[2]

As if this was not evidence enough of the Bank's efforts to sway the country's politics, Taney submitted before Congress an audit of the Bank's

---

[1] *Register of Debates*, 23rd Cong., 1st sess., Appendix, 66.
[2] *Register of Debates*, 23rd Cong., 1st sess., Appendix, 66.

expenditures, completed and signed by four of the government directors in August, 1833. This report showed the Bank's capital and revealed that how it was spent was governed entirely by Biddle. Specifically, he spent as much as he saw fit to circulate various communications to inform the people as to the nature of the Bank's operations. As innocuous as this may sound, the reality painted by the government directors' report was far more dangerous. In fact, much of the thousands of dollars spent by the Bank for purpose of "communicating to the people information in regard to the nature and opera-tions of the bank" were instead devoted to attacks on those who wished to see the Bank's charter expire.[1] The directors' report listed in great detail the amount of money spent on various anti-Jackson publications, a sum Taney described as "shockingly startling."[2] That vouchers showing the purpose for these expenditures were not included (only the recipient of the money was provided) only lent more credence to the argument that the Bank was oper-ating in secrecy. Doing nothing, Taney concluded, would make him and the Treasury department a party to the Bank's flagrant violation of the sanctity of the nation's institutions and thereby threaten the liberties of the people.

The Bank had contended that the increase in printing expenditures was solely to defend itself from attacks by the Jacksonians. Taney expressed harsh skepticism of this argument. In reference to the 1832 presidential and congressional elections, he asked, "[c]an it be permitted to a great moneyed corporation to enter unto such a controversy, and then justify its conduct on the ground that it is defending its own interests? The right of such an institu-tion to interfere in the political concerns of the country, for any cause what-ever, can never be recognised."[3] The public owned one-fifth of the stock in the bank and therefore, one-fifth of the money squandered for electioneering purposes was that belonging to the people. The resolution above granting Biddle sole power to spend the public's money on printing communications to the people as he saw fit was in direct violation of the aforementioned section of the charter requiring all business to be conducted by a board of no fewer than seven directors. Under such circumstances, Taney felt the public's money unsafe in the Bank's hands. It is worth analyzing further Taney's concern that since the government owned one fifth of the BUS stock it followed that one fifth of electioneering expenses came from the govern-ment funds. Examination of the Bank's balance sheets reveals that govern-

---

[1] *Register of Debates*, 23rd Cong., 1st sess., Appendix, 66; Taney is sarcastically quoting the minutes from the Bank's November 30th, 1830, board of directors meeting from which the quoted is part of a resolution created by Biddle and approved by the board of direc-tors.

[2] *Register of Debates*, 23rd Cong., 1st sess., Appendix, 66.

[3] *Register of Debates*, 23rd Cong., 1st sess., Appendix, 67.

ment funds were set aside for government expenditures and were not used for other BUS expenses, such as printing. Understanding this distinction would require a knowledge of finance that few at the time possessed, and the time and ability to pore over pages of balance sheets. For Taney and the Jacksonians, a much easier and more effective move was to accuse the BUS of using government funds for electioneering purposes.[1]

The charge of electioneering leveled by Taney revolved around two issues — the large expansion of its business in the months leading up the election and the increase in money the BUS spent on printing and distributing material for the purposes of influencing both local and national elections. A daunting charge to counter given the evidence, the anti-Jacksonians, nonetheless, attempted boldly to refute it. Clay shrugged off the charge as a common one leveled by those in power. "Those in the actual possession of power," Clay explained, "are perpetually dreading its loss...Their suspicions are always active and on alert...A thousand spectres glide before their affrighted imaginations, and they see in every attempt to enlighten those who have placed them in office a sinister design to snatch from them their authority." Clay reasoned, as many of his colleagues would echo later, that the Bank had every right to defend itself considering it had "been assailed in every form of bitterness and malignity." The Kentuckian blasted Taney for assuming the power to judge who can and cannot use the strong arm of the free press. "Who invested the Secretary of Treasury with power to interpose himself between the people, and light and intelligence?" Clay thundered. "Who gave him the right to dictate what information shall be communicated to the people and by whom...[w]ho made him the censor of the public press?" He concluded his point with a final dig at Taney and the administration, advising that if the secretary felt it his "Herculean duty" to purify the press, "he had better begin with the Augean stable, the press nearest to him — his organ — as most needing purification."[2] Clay's refutation of electioneering charges showcased fully his supreme talents as a debater and performer. His use of consecutive questions to crescendo towards the final jab at Taney and the Jacksonian press was Senate theater at its most entertaining and to some, most persuasive. It mattered little that Clay offered no hard facts in making his rebuttal — he would leave the details to his allies. The force of delivery and the weight of two decades of statesmanship behind his words counted for more than financial records taken from dusty ledgers.[3]

---

[1] Campbell, *The Bank War and the Partisan Press*, 95.

[2] *Register of Debates*, 23rd Cong., 1st sess., (Dec. 30, 1833), 88-89 (Senate).

[3] Schlesinger has pointed out that by this point, dramatic oratory such as exhibited by Clay and Webster made for effective political theater but its effectiveness "was highly vulnerable" to the arm wringing floor tactics and backroom dealings perfected by Van

Most of the anti-Jacksonians who defended the Bank against election-eering charges followed Clay's blueprint and avoided the hard facts in favor of deflection and general lines of defense. Calhoun agreed with Taney that any attempt on the part of the BUS to interfere with the country's politics would constitute "a most heinous offence." The Bank, after all, was "a great public trust," replete with considerable authority and the application of that power towards political ends would be a great perversion of that power. The South Carolinian, without providing any explanation outside of its duty to defend itself against attacks, dismissed Taney's charge against the Bank and offered a curious observation instead. Calhoun pointed out that like the BUS, the government too was a great trust vested with enormous power and any attempt on its part to influence the outcome of elections would be met with the same reproof as the Bank. Having established the comparison, he then asked, "[c]an it be unknown to [Taney] that the Fourth Auditor of the Trea-sury, (an officer in his own department,) the man who has made so promi-nent a figure in this transaction, was daily and hourly meddling in politics, and that he is one of the principal political managers of the administration?" Calhoun was referring to Amos Kendall, the agent Taney sent to coordinate with the state banks on the new deposit banking system. Kendall was also a key cog in the Jacksonian press machine that existed to bolster support for the Old General's policies and aid in his bid for reelection. It was the government, not the Bank that had clearly meddled in the nation's politics. The Jackson administration had turned the government into a giant political machine, consolidating power through the distribution of patronage as a reward for loyalty at the expense of competent officials. The Bank's offense, Calhoun sardonically charged, was not that it interfered with nation's poli-tics but that it would not interfere in favor of the administration. Calhoun could think of nothing "more odious, more hateful" to the imagination than when "the guilty reprove, and the criminal punish."[1]

Sprague joined Calhoun and added to his point. To the Mainer, the government's response to the Bank flexing political muscle was exceedingly duplicitous. To punish the Bank for exercising influence over politics, the administration moved to withdraw the deposits. To effect this change, the government sent Kendall out "to select [banks] to be under the sole control of the officers of the Treasury; whose very existence is political; who live, move, and have their being in politics! nay, when it is avowed by [Kendall] himself, that political considerations enter into these new selections!" Poli-

---

Buren that had come to characterize politics in the Jacksonian Era. See, Schlesinger, *The Age of Jackson*, 51-52.

[1] *Register of Debates*, 23rd Cong., 1st sess., (Jan. 13, 1834), 212 (Senate).

tics weighed heavily on the government's choosing of appropriate depositories for the public deposits. The hypocrisy of the situation infuriated Sprague. The senator roared, "this removal of the public moneys — a movement, political in its conception and consummation, not merely tinctured, but saturated, with politics — is to be justified on the ground that the bank had become political!"[1]

Others, notably Ewing and Frelinghuysen carried on Clay's point that the Bank had every right to defend itself against what the Ohioan called "accusations false in fact or false in argument." Not conceding the right to defend itself, Ewing called the response to such defense an "attempt to exaggerate a very trifling pecuniary transaction into one of vast magnitude and danger."[2] Frelinghuysen detailed the "trifling pecuniary transaction" in his remarks. "Here have been expended twenty or thirty thousand dollars," the New Jerseyan explained, "in the publication of speeches and reports on the bank question — expended with the knowledge and wish of the private stockholders; and the Secretary removes eight millions of dollars of public money from an institution that still had ten millions of specie, thirty-five millions of capital, and in the full tide of business — and this to cripple its ability to print pamphlets!" Why should the Bank not print materials to set the record straight? Frelinghuysen prayed that the nation had not reached "that point of humiliation, when the right of self-defence is considered audacious — when to repel injurious aspersions is denounced as deserving frowns of power!" In this regard, Frelinghuysen had assumed the argument made by the anti-Jacksonians who spoke before him; the BUS had been assaulted and it was its right to strike out in its own defense.[3]

Frelinghuysen followed with an observation no one else dared to make, but surely some concurred. What crime was there in engaging in political electioneering? "We are all political electioneers," he pointed out. "Who is exempt from the charge of desiring a continuance of political favor and confidence?" The attacks on the Bank and their requisite responses were both "free and animated" and therefore, in the opinion of Frelinghuysen, welcome to a functioning democracy. The senator explained, "[t]his excitement of public debate — this collision of mind with mind — this entire freedom of the press, is the healthful action of our institutions." These public debates, Frelinghuysen concluded, should be "cherished and firmly maintained" as signifying the vigor of American democracy and politics.[4]

---

[1] *Register of Debates*, 23rd Cong., 1st sess., (Jan. 29, 1834), 396 (Senate).
[2] *Register of Debates*, 23rd Cong., 1st sess., (Jan. 20, 1834), 321 (Senate).
[3] *Register of Debates*, 23rd Cong., 1st sess., (Feb. 3, 1834), 459 (Senate).
[4] *Register of Debates*, 23rd Cong., 1st sess., (Feb. 3, 1834), 459 (Senate).

The Senate Finance Committee joined the anti-Jacksonians in ridiculing the charges of electioneering aimed at the Bank, charges they felt too general to either prove or disprove. Since a charge of that nature "must always rest mainly on mere opinion," Webster reported, it served as "a convenient cloak under which to disguise the true motives of official conduct." In other words, an unverifiable electioneering charge could be conjured up to justify an action such as removing the public deposits. This served as further proof that the secretary of the Treasury was never meant to possess such sweeping power over the deposits. If the secretary could dole out a punishment so damaging to the continued existence of the Bank stemming from an indefinable charge based solely on opinion, he could conceivably remove the deposits at any time.[1]

Despite rejecting the charges of electioneering as unprovable, the Committee felt it important to examine the causes Taney assigned for the charges. Taney cited the extension of business during election season as proof of the Bank's attempt to inject itself into the nation's politics. If the extension of business was so blatantly for nefarious purposes, Webster asked, "[h]ow should it have escaped the vigilance of the Secretary of that day, at the time it took place?" The information on the Bank's dealings was readily available throughout 1831 and 1832. Yet, no complaints emerged from the Treasury secretary at that time. Why was the BUS only now being punished for "this great mischief"?[2]

The Committee wrapped up this point by joining the anti-Jacksonians in denouncing Taney for judging the manner in which the Bank went about defending itself. The Bank had been charged with misconduct and with violating its charter. If Congress had been the accusing party, the Bank would have had to defend itself before that body. If the charges had come judicially, the Bank would have had its day in court. The charges though came from the administration and were disseminated to the public through the press. The Bank, therefore, took to defending itself in that same forum. Webster allowed for the possibility that the Bank, in exercising its right to defend itself, could "carr[y] their measures beyond this fair object of defence," but this was not what Taney (and as will be evident below, the Jacksonians) argued. The secretary reproved the Bank merely for answering to the charges through the press, casting a judgement upon the institution well outside his duties as head of the Treasury.[3]

---

[1] *Register of Debates*, 23rd Cong., 1st sess., Appendix, 154.
[2] *Register of Debates*, 23rd Cong., 1st sess., Appendix, 154.
[3] *Register of Debates*, 23rd Cong., 1st sess., Appendix, 155.

Although the anti-Jacksonians largely steered away from an analysis of the Bank's spending during the years of the Jackson administration, one brought the specifics before the Senate. Samuel Southard recalled that Taney had ridiculed Biddle and the Bank for passing a series of resolutions giving the Bank president sole authority to order the printing of materials communicating to the people the operations of the Bank. In Taney's view, these resolutions handed to Biddle control over the whole capital of the Bank. The resolutions, however, were for the specific object of disseminating information to the public, and every expenditure towards that end was reported in the Bank's expense account. How then, Southard wondered, could Taney claim that the resolutions put the Bank's capital at Biddle's mercy? An analysis of the expense account seemed to prove otherwise. Since November, 1830, when the resolutions in question were created, by Southard's calculations, the Bank spent roughly $50,000 on printing materials for self-defense ($30,000 less than Taney had indicated over the same period).[1] Approximately half of that was for the printing and distributing of congressional reports while just $2,000 was devoted to the printing of essays by banking and economics authorities such as Gallatin and Josiah Tucker. The New Jerseyan wondered aloud what crime there was in printing reports that Congress deemed appropriate to print by the thousands. Taney's assault on the Bank for defending itself against the charges of the administration sent a clear message to Congress and the people; freedom of the press only extended to those who advocated the present administration.[2]

Southard also dove into the numbers in refuting Taney's assertion that the Bank expanded its business around election time to influence its outcome. The senator argued that for the "arbitrary period" between January, 1831 and May, 1832 that Taney chose for his analysis of the Bank's business, the secretary had made significant errors.[3] Taney had calculated an unprecedented $28,000,000 extension over that period, explainable only by the Bank's desire to force recharter on the people before the upcoming presidential election. Southard, however, accused the secretary of miscalculating. According

---

[1] The discrepancy was due to the source each referenced for their information. The lower figure cited by Southard came from the Bank directors' report submitted to Congress. The higher figure cited by Taney came from the report of the public directors, a report Taney referenced often when making his case against the Bank. William Wilkins would also cite the higher figure in his remarks later in the session.

[2] *Register of Debates*, 23rd Cong., 1st sess., (Jan .8, 1834), 195-196 (Senate).

[3] Southard's speech as recorded in the *Register of Debates* shows the timeframe under consideration as between January 1830 and May 1831. It is clear though from the statistics provided and context of the statement that Southard was referring to the period cited in Taney's report (January 1831 through May 1832). It is unclear whether the mistake was made by Southard or due to a recording error. See, *Register of Debates*, 23rd Cong., 1st sess., (Jan. 8, 1834), 193 (Senate).

to Southard, in January 1831 the Bank had not $42,000,000 in debts due but $52,000,000 and likewise, at the end of the sixteen month period, the Bank's debts had increased to just under $62,000,000, not $70,400,000 as Taney indicated. Using Southard's numbers, the BUS extended its business by less than $10,000,000 rather than $28,000,000 reported by Taney. To justify the extension over the time period, the senator cited an increase of $1,400,000 in specie, $2,828,000 in deposits, $1,762,000 in debts due from state banks, as well as a decrease of $211,000 in expenses from real property. Common banking practice revealed that given the increase in funds over the sixteen months, the corresponding extension of business was normal or perhaps slightly higher than normal. Southard called the charge of electioneering "the sleeping and waking dream in some minds," and attributed the uptick in business to fulfilling "the commercial wants of the community." Had the Bank not extended its business accordingly, Southard concluded, the nation would have experienced financial distress.[1]

The Jacksonians hit hard on the electioneering charge and none with greater force than Benton. To the Missourian, the Bank's interference with the nation's politics was its gravest offense and he consequently devoted considerable time on explaining why. Indeed, Benton's coverage of the matter consumed just over a quarter of his whole speech that spanned three days. He began by reading from a report of the Bank directors in defense of electioneering charges submitted to Congress at the outset of the session. The report detailed how after Jackson expressed hostility to the BUS in his first annual address, it adopted the often referred to resolutions granting Biddle authority over the printing of materials in its defense. By its own calculations, between the years 1829 and 1833, the BUS spent $105,057.73 on printing expenses. Of that, $58,265.05 was devoted to "defence of the bank" while the remaining $46,792.69 covered "miscellaneous expenses of books and stationary." (Southard omitted any mention of this latter amount in his remarks.) The piece concluded by advising that the stockholders could judge whether the expenses incurred were too high but that the decision of the Bank to defend itself in light of the attacks upon it was beyond reproach.[2]

Benton was near giddy at the Bank having submitted in its own words the ammunition he needed to uphold Taney's charge against it. The senator examined the Bank's defense of its actions from three angles; the Bank's right to defend itself, the truth of the defense, and the manner in which the Bank went about defending itself. Benton argued the Bank had no right to defend itself and certainly no right to spend the government's money in doing so. The

---

[1] *Register of Debates*, 23rd Cong., 1st sess., (Jan. 8, 1834), 193-194 (Senate).
[2] *Register of Debates*, 23rd Cong., 1st sess., (Jan. 2, 1834), 113-115 (Senate).

Bank's defense amounted to a push for recharter, a decision over which the government had sole authority. "The bank was created for the convenience of Government, as a thing necessary to the Government, and not for the benefit of itself," Benton observed. Therefore, the government, not the Bank, was to judge whether the convenience and necessity that brought about its creation still existed to warrant recharter. The Bank "had been chartered for twenty years," the Missourian continued, "has enjoyed eighteen years of its exclusive privileges, and would enjoy the remainder unless it died under the sentence of the law for a violation of its charter." The BUS would have its twenty years as contracted and it had no right to "refuse to be discontinued." Benton likened the Bank's behavior to a band of dragoons who, upon the termination of their enlistment took up their arms and stormed Congress to force their reenlistment. In this imagined scenario, the dragoons would have no right to force their reenlistment just like the Bank had no right to force its recharter. The only difference between the two, the senator intimated, was the choice of weapons — the dragoons wielded the sword, the BUS the purse, the purse being the far more dangerous of the two.[1]

Benton continued with his analogy. The Bank was created during a time of economic crisis much like an army raised during times of war. When peace returned, the army would disband. The same should be said for the BUS. "Every reason urged at that time for the creation of the bank has passed away," he asserted; "all necessity for it, if any ever existed, has passed away...but, like an army that refuses to be disbanded in time of peace, she revolts against the Government, sets up her will above that of the Government, and uses her appropriate weapon, money, to prolong and perpetuate her existence." Benton's analogy was driven by a specific comment Clay made during his speech. Clay had remarked in that Jackson endangered the country's liberties by joining the sword with purse by seizing control of the public funds. Benton warned that corrupt wielding of the purse was far more dangerous than the sword. In his view, the spending of public money to force its recharter was an overt "attempt to upset the Government — the popular elective Government — secured to the by the constitution, and to substitute for it a bank government, representing, not the people, but the bloated oligarchy of a moneyed power," and thus, the Bank had no right to defend itself. If Clay wanted to talk of dangerous wielding of the power of the purse, he needed not look any further than the BUS.[2]

Benton next moved onto an examination of the second aspect of the defense offered by the Bank directors, its truthfulness. The Missourian

---

[1] *Register of Debates*, 23rd Cong., 1st sess., (Jan. 2, 1834), 115-116 (Senate).
[2] *Register of Debates*, 23rd Cong., 1st sess., (Jan. 2, 1834), 117 (Senate).

shrewdly dismantled the truthfulness of the Bank's defense by underscoring a discrepancy between the date cited for when the assault upon it began and when the BUS actually began defending itself. The directors' report identified Jackson's first message to Congress, delivered in December 1829, as the opening salvo against the BUS. However, in the next line, the Bank totaled its expenses spent on defense for the years 1829 through 1833. The inclusion of all of 1829 as part of the total expenditures on defense amounted, to Benton at least, as admission by the Bank that it began "defending" itself *before* the first assault upon it. The Bank's own words served as substantial proof that the actions it took during Jackson's presidency were not merely out of self-defense, but to ensure that the statement he referred to had not been in error, Benton supplied another form of proof. The senator examined attorney fees incurred over different periods to challenge further the claim that the Bank acted purely in self-defense. Throughout the five years spanning between 1817 and 1821, at a time when "there was a great mass of business to be done by lawyers," the BUS paid out roughly $35,000 in attorney fees. During the shorter three-year span between 1829 and 1831, a comparatively quiet period for lawyers — the Bank was prosperous, few suits were brought upon it, debts were being paid off without incident — the Bank's attorney fees totaled upwards of $34,000. A closer look revealed that in 1829, roughly one year before the first attacks upon the Bank commenced, the BUS paid $16,298 to attorneys. In 1821, the single busiest year for lawyers during the Bank's existence, the attorney bill was only slightly higher, to the sum of $17,618. Benton felt an explanation was in order. What accounted for the comparably high lawyer fees over the two years when one year witnessed "the greatest law business the bank ever had" while the during the other, "it had little or nothing to do"? And if these expenditures were in some way connected with defending itself after attacks by Jackson, why were fees higher in 1829, the year preceding the first attacks on the Bank, then any other subsequent year after the attacks commenced?[1]

Benton refused to allow the matter of the truthfulness of the Bank's defense to rest there. For a defense to be necessary, an assault had to take place and the Missourian could find nothing in the president's first annual message, which by the Bank's own admission served as the source prompting its defense, to indicate that an attack had been made. Benton asked for the most conspicuous paragraph to be read aloud.[2] Upon its reading, the senator remarked that from these words, the BUS justifies its rampant misconduct. Benton could not hide his disdain; "[i]s it true? Is it, in point of fact, an assault

---

[1] *Register of Debates*, 23rd Cong., 1st sess., (Jan. 2, 1834), 117-118 (Senate).
[2] For the content of this paragraph, see Chapter 1.

upon that institution? Certainly none." Jackson complained of the constitutionality and expediency of the law creating the Bank itself. If Jackson meant
to assail anyone, it was the Congress that created the Bank in the first place.
The president did not call for the repeal of the law, yet the Bank reported
a scheme was afoot to destroy it. "What he says of the present bank refers
to its future application for a charter, not to its present existence," Benton
observed, "and however opposed he might be to grant the new charter, that
opposition cannot be charged as a design to destroy the present charter."
Even the assertion that the BUS had not adequately furnished a sound
currency could not be taken as a signal that the present Bank was in danger
of dissolution. Rather, it merely served as evidence convincing the president
that the charter should not be renewed. Therefore, the defense employed by
the BUS was more accurately an attempt to extend its survival by forcing its
recharter, a result Benton had already established the Bank had no right to
seek.[1]

Benton continued his three-pronged attack by denouncing the manner
in which the BUS went about defending itself. Despite an abundance of
damning evidence of electioneering found in publications put out on the
Bank's dime, Benton chose to let those words speak for themselves as a
matter of public record. Instead, he would focus solely on the words and
actions directly ascribed to the BUS found within the report he read earlier,
so no doubt could arise as to the Bank's intentions. Benton first brought up
a resolution passed by the Bank that dealt with punishing counterfeiters, a
subject it referred to as "kindred...to the President's first assault." Placing
in the report the resolution for dealing with counterfeiters alongside the
resolution driven by Jackson's first annual address revealed their simili-
tude and proved "that the bank placed the President of the United States
and the counterfeiters of its notes on a level with each other, and actually
affirmed a relationship, or kindred, between their respective conducts."
Such a comparison horrified the loyal Jacksonian, compelling him to reread
the offending resolution aloud multiple times either for effect, out of pure
outrage, or perhaps a little of both. The brazen comparison was an affront to
not only the president, but to the people who elected him and the government that he oversaw. The directors' report contained other remarks aimed
at the president — "'injurious calumnies...calumniated down...misrepresen-
tations...sacrificed by falsehoods'" — that Benton found "revolting and atro-
cious." The senator read off the names of the directors who sanctioned the
report, not to disparage them, but to put before the American people all the

---

[1] *Register of Debates*, 23rd Cong., 1st sess., (Jan. 2, 1834), 118-119 (Senate).

facts and appeal to their intelligence to judge if self-defense or electioneering propelled their actions.

Benton concluded his lengthy remarks on electioneering by revisiting the Bank's printing expenses and behavior, as well as the allocation of dividends over the five year period under examination. Clay and later others would argue that the materials printed, such as Gallatin's essay and the McDuffie report, simply informed the public as to the conduct of the Bank and its benefits. Benton countered that these publications were but a small fraction of the Bank's printing expenditures. For example, the BUS ordered the printing of the seventy thousand copies of a paper entitled, *Address to State Legislatures*, to be delivered throughout the country ahead of senatorial elections advocating the election of anti-Jacksonians. Benton was familiar with the paper since it was circulated widely in Missouri to impede his own election chances. The move backfired and "[t]he Legislature of Missouri rebuked the insolence which would dictate to them, by instantly electing the man they were intended to defeat." However, Benton pointed out, others targeted by the Bank may not have enjoyed the same good fortune.[1]

The identities of individual payees from the Bank's printing expenses coupled with its refusal to distribute gains in net profits to shareholders in the form of increased dividends also underscored its electioneering designs. While printers and editors comprised a large portion of the money doled out, some of the funds landed in the pockets of treasurers of election committees opposed to Jackson's reelection. Two well-known anti-Jacksonians who fit this description were Philadelphians, Edward Olmstead and John S. Riddle; they were paid $1,371.04 and $2,583.50 respectively. These small amounts paled in comparison to the money the BUS inexplicably held onto as profits rose during Jackson's presidency. In July, 1829, the BUS netted $1,682,575 and paid out $1,225,000 in dividends; in July, 1831 gross profits rose to $1,943,533 while dividends paid to the stockholders remained the same. The United States government, as the Bank's largest stockholder, had a right to know why it did not share in the increased profits and for what purpose that money was spent. The Bank refused, prompting Benton to ask, "would the Senate go on to acquit the bank without examination, and to convict the President and the Secretary of the Treasury with having falsely accused it of applying the moneys of the institution to political and electioneering objects?"[2] The Missourian sought to force an answer to his question by introducing an amendment to Clay's second resolution, essentially striking it out and instead calling upon Nicholas Biddle to testify before the

---

[1] *Register of Debates*, 23rd Cong., 1st sess., (Jan. 2, 1834), 123 (Senate).
[2] *Register of Debates*, 23rd Cong., 1st sess., (Jan. 2, 1834), 123-124 (Senate).

Senate to explain the curious allocation of the Bank's funds over the past five years. The amendment was defeated 34–12 with even some Jacksonians, notably Forsyth, Rives, and Wilkins, contributing to its defeat.[1]

Perhaps no senator poured more into a singular topic of this extensive debate than did Benton in condemning the Bank's electioneering. The senator's distrust and general hatred for banks was rooted in his western upbringing. First elected to the Senate in 1821, he became known as the most rabid anti-Bank member of the upper chamber and, after the Bank War, earned for himself the nickname, "Old Bullion" due to his preference for hard money. It is therefore unsurprising that Benton spoke immediately after Clay and established the template for his fellow Jacksonians to follow. Benton felt a certain responsibility to uphold the administration's position vis-à-vis the BUS, knowing full well the anti-Jacksonian majority would most likely win the day. And while his speech, and specifically his excoriation of the Bank's involvement in the country's politics, drew rave reviews from his political allies, Old Bullion's most significant impact on the session and the Bank War itself would come later.

So thorough was Benton's dismantling of the Bank's claim to self-defense that the rest of the Jacksonians who spoke on the matter had little to add. The one exception, however, was Nathaniel Tallmadge. He broke down by year the often referenced printing expense of $58,265.05 incurred by the Bank between 1830 and 1833 to show that its highest spending came during the peak of election season. In 1830 when the election was still far off and 1833 after the election was decided, the Bank's printing expenses stood at $7,375 and $2,607 respectively. However, in 1831, as the presidential contest drew closer, printing expenses exploded to $21,708 and during the election year that followed, jumped to $26,579. Upon disclosing these figures, Tallmadge challenged anyone to sustain "that these sums were not expended to influence the Presidential election." The senator continued by speaking to the absurdity of the situation. The government owned one-fifth of the stock of the BUS and the duly elected president and the administration he created deemed the institution dangerous and therefore should expire upon the termination of its charter. How ridiculous, the New Yorker groused, that "the bank is employing funds of the Government to put down the administration of the Government, in order to thereby secure a re-charter, which that administration think it unconstitutional and inexpedient to grant." To remove any doubt that the Bank's use of the press went well beyond self-defense, as the anti-Jacksonians had argued for months, Tallmadge read from a publication released by the Bank entitled, "Important facts for the people:"

---

[1] *Register of Debates*, 23rd Cong., 1st sess., (Jan. 3, 1834, Jan. 8, 1834), 139,143 (Senate).

The solemn truth is as clear to the eye of every intelligent man as the sun at noon day, that the existence of this Union depends on the defeat of Andrew Jackson, and on the election of Henry Clay as President. No future event can be more certain, than the breaking to pieces of this Union, if the pernicious doctrines of General Jackson, and the evil counsellors by whom he is surrounded, are to prevail for another Presidential term.

The paragraph provided no information regarding the Bank's conduct or operations; it was a purely partisan statement promoting Jackson's defeat. "What stronger evidence is wanting to support the charge of the Secretary," Tallmadge wondered, "that the bank was striving to obtain political power and using its means for electioneering purposes?"[1]

As the last to comment on the subject of electioneering, Tallmadge concluded the debate on what the Jacksonians viewed as the Bank's most egregious offense. Senators from both sides tossed around spending figures, often times in conflict with each other. But, ultimately, the Bank's guilt to the charges of electioneering were largely in the eye of the beholder. A neutral observer could certainly argue that electioneering and self-defense were one in the same. Biddle's correspondence and behavior between 1829 and 1833 makes clear that he actively sought to promote to the public the positive effects of the BUS on the country as a way to ward off unscrupulous attacks from the Jacksonians while simultaneously building support for recharter. As Bank antagonists, Jackson and his allies would naturally become targets for pro-BUS publications. Jacksonians, in turn could cherry pick publications of a viler, non-economic tone to argue that the Bank had gone beyond merely defending itself and was instead trying to unduly influence the electorate. Conversely, the anti-Jacksonians could point to the more benign, information-based articles in building their case for the Bank's use of self-defense. One thing is clear: as a profit-seeking business with shareholder interests to protect, the BUS was fully within its rights to shape public opinion in its favor in the face of harsh attacks from the Jacksonians. As Bank War historian Stephen W. Campbell points out, "[i]n an era in which customers' bank deposits were not protected by insurance, psychological and political factors alone could lead to devastation. A damaging headline in a partisan newspaper, might, under the right circumstances, trigger a bank run where customers withdrew their deposits en masse."[2] Biddle did the right thing by his Bank and its shareholders; whether he and the news-

---

[1] *Register of Debates*, 23rd Cong., 1st sess., (Mar. 12, 1834), 939-941 (Senate).
[2] Campbell, *The Bank War and the Partisan Press*, 56.

paper editors who sided with him went too far and inserted the BUS into a political milieu where it did not belong is altogether subjective.

***

Much like the debate over the timing of the removal, the debate over the Bank's conduct detailed in this and the previous chapter went in circles. Even instances when the anti-Jacksonians conceded to their opponents that the BUS may have acted imprudently, they universally agreed that removing the deposits was not a fitting punishment. In their view, calling upon the United States government to pay damages on a spoiled bill or circulating publications that could be viewed as electioneering material had nothing to do with the safety of the deposits, so therefore, removing them was unjustifiable. Besides, there were other more appropriate remedies, specifically the ordering of a *scire facias* by the president, if it were believed the BUS had violated its charter. The Jacksonians felt differently; the Bank's corrupt and secretive dealings were proof that it could not be trusted with a cent of the public's money. That its transgressions did not involve the deposits or weaken their safety was irrelevant. The Bank's greatest privilege was serving as the repository for the public funds. Divesting the Bank of its greatest privilege was the most fitting punishment for violating its charter. Because the two sides had different views on the appropriateness of certain punishments, neither side could truly take the upper hand in the argument. Each side could be correct, depending on one's view on how the Bank should be punished and the role of the Treasury secretary in doling out that punishment.

The Jacksonians, of course, took the initiative and followed the president's lead in handing down the punishment of their choice. In doing so, the onus fell upon them to replace what had served as the country's central financial instrument for nearly two decades. And although Clay's resolutions did not speak specifically to the replacement decided upon by the administration, the Senate nonetheless devoted significant time both attacking and defending it.

Chapter 10: An Army of Retainers

The removal of the public deposits made up just one part of Jackson's and Taney's bold plan; the selection of replacement depositories made up the other part. Although Clay's censorial resolutions made no specific mention of the decision to deposit the public funds in various state banks — a move many of its supporters (Jackson included) optimistically referred to as "an experiment" — the subject naturally worked its way into the Senate's larger debate. The anti-Jacksonians held the general position that Taney had no authority to choose a new depository for the public money while the Jacksonians predictably staked the ground that he did. The noteworthy discussion generated by this topic revolved around the efficacy of the contracts Taney entered into with the state banks chosen to house the public money and if those banks could adequately replace the BUS.

Taney did not provide to Congress many of the contracts entered into with the state banks, but the two or three that he did submit became a source of dispute between the two sides. As stipulated by the first section of the contract with the Girard Bank of Philadelphia, the bank agreed "to receive and enter to the credit of the Treasurer of the United States all sums of money offered to be deposited on account of the United States, whether offered in gold or silver coin, in notes of any bank which are convertible into coin in its immediate vicinity, or in notes of any bank which it is, for the time being, in the habit of receiving."[1] The anti-Jacksonians pounced on this first section. Clay explained that under this system, the Girard Bank would

---

[1] "Contract Between the Girard Bank & the United States [September 28, 1833]," https://www.historycentral.com/documents/Girard.html.

not be required to accept the notes of the Louisville Bank (as one possible example), despite the latter's designation as a deposit bank. The BUS, on the other hand, "receives every where, and credits the Government with the notes, whether issued by the branches or the principal bank."[1] Southard added that because the state banks were not obligated to receive notes from distant branches, they would likely refuse those notes for their own protection. The only way to remedy this would require either the federal government to be responsible for the state banks or the state banks themselves to be responsible for each other. This prompted the New Jerseyan to question, "[a]re we prepared to pass a law, taking upon ourselves the solvency of these banks, and agreeing to receive [their notes] at par from our debtors? Will the banks become responsible for each other? The misconduct of a single one might prostrate the whole...neither by contract nor by law can the Secretary render these notes receivable every where, much less can he make them payable in specie every where." The only outcome under this new system would be a depreciation of the currency, such as occurred during the War of 1812 when no central bank existed. Southard did not wish to demean state banks entirely. "I admit...their entire competency to accomplish the objects of their creation within the limits of action and agency which were contemplated by those who formed them," he remarked. "But they were intended to be local: their nature and capital do not fit them for the purposes of the Secretary."[2] Webster proved his Mid-Atlantic colleague prophetic when he observed while speaking on January 20 (roughly four months after the removal) that the exchange rates of notes between distant cities had already worsened and cited the state banks' inability to "act with the same concert, the same identity of purpose" as the reason.[3]

Senator Frelinghuysen offered a most stinging rebuke of Taney, calling the secretary's insistence that the deposit bank system could furnish a uniform and sound currency matching or even exceeding the stability of that created by the BUS, "one of the boldest financial propositions ever put forth." The New Jerseyan recounted that when the First Bank of the United States closed its doors and its functions replaced by the state banks, the results were disastrous and specie payments were suspended. Frelinghuysen quoted then Secretary of the Treasury, Alexander J. Dallas, who in his report on the nation's finances following the Bank's closure wrote, "[t]he circulating medium of the country, which has consisted principally of bank notes, is placed upon a new and uncertain footing; and those difficulties and

---

[1] *Register of Debates*, 23rd Cong., 1st sess., (Dec. 30, 1833), 91 (Senate).
[2] *Register of Debates*, 23rd Cong., 1st sess., (Jan. 8, 1834), 144, 183 (Senate).
[3] *Register of Debates*, 23rd Cong., 1st sess., (Jan. 20, 1834), 293 (Senate).

embarrassments will extend, in a greater or less degree, into the pecuniary operations of the citizens in general.'" After a year of observing the shortcomings of the state bank system, Dallas wrote to Congress, "'[t]he authority of the States, individually, or the agency of the State institutions, cannot afford a remedy commensurate with the evil, and a recurrence of the national authority is indispensable for the restoration of a national currency.'" The former secretary concluded that only the chartering of a new national bank would cure the economic ills as it would "'possess the means and the opportunity of supplying a circulating medium, of equal use and value in every State, an in every district of every State.'" Borrowing Clay's phrasing from the opening lines of his speech, Frelinghuysen followed with the bold claim that "we are indeed in the midst of a revolution, when the lessons of experience and wisdom are to be unlearned, and the prosperity of this country subjected to the sad consequences of rash experiment."[1] Recounting the financial hardship that befell the country after state banks replaced the first BUS and calling upon the words of the Treasury secretary at the time to do so effectively bolstered the anti-Jacksonians' overall argument that a sound, stable currency could not be achieved under the new deposit banking system.

To argue that the stable currency under the BUS could continue to remain so under the state banks was no simple feat. Despite its flaws, both perceived and real, the greatest advantage of the BUS, according an 1831 observation by Albert Gallatin, was its uniform currency that it "secur[ed] with certainty."[2] Nevertheless, some Jacksonians did attempt to defend this challenging position. Wilkins, speaking in February, denied the existence of any problems with the currency since the removal, arguing, "[a]t this moment, there is not a single note in circulation of any bank in the United States which is not as good, at this moment, as it was before, or at the time of the removal of the deposites." As long as the state banks continued to pay specie, the nation's currency would remain stable. (Wilkins conceded though that if any of the state banks suspended specie payments, the stability of the currency would be in question.) The Pennsylvanian then took issue with Webster's use of exchange rate tables to argue that the currency had already been disrupted. The developers of these tables, Wilkins complained, are "interested persons, who live and fatten upon the very inequality and confusion which they themselves represent to prevail in bank-note circulation." Any fluctuations in currency exchange rates were explainable by differences in the cost of transmitting notes and specie across large distances. To blame any perceived

---

[1] *Register of Debates*, 23rd Cong., 1st sess., (Feb. 3, 1834), 457-458 (Senate).
[2] Albert Gallatin quoted in, Hammond, *Banks and Politics*, 304-305.

currency disruption among the state banks on the removal of the deposits made little sense, as the removal meant to the strengthen the state banks at the expense of the BUS which had held sway over them for nearly two decades.[1]

Wilkins based his argument on the notion that the state banks could continue furnishing the sound currency established by the BUS, a difficult but not impossible position to advance especially when argued using hypotheticals such as he did. Isaac Hill took a more audacious position that only the most steadfast anti-Bank Jacksonians would take, arguing that the BUS had not created a sound currency and that the state banks were more capable of creating one. The sound currency enjoyed by the country over the last fifteen years, Hill argued, was due to good management of state banks, not the BUS. The BUS had created a façade currency, heavily reliant on bank drafts that, within his legal right to do so, the Treasury secretary could at any time disallow as acceptable payment for debts to the United States.[2] Hill claimed instead that there were multiple times during the existence of both national banks when currency was not sound and general bank management around the country was corrupt. For example, between the years 1808 and 1811, when the charter of the first BUS was winding down, the stability of currency in the eastern states was worse than any time since the Bank opened its doors. Over the same period state banks engaged in "defalcations and swindling...as we may hope never to witness again" and the BUS was powerless or worse, unwilling to regulate the wrongdoings. Alternatively, Hill remarked, during the interlude between the First and Second Banks, despite the economic hardships brought on by war, state banks were managed more efficiently than during the existence of the First BUS or since the creation of the Second. A national bank, Hill concluded, was not needed to promote a strong currency and overall economic well-being. "Both currency and the exchange will be in as favorable a position when the national bank is dead as when it is alive," the senator confidently proclaimed. "So long as the vast products of the South and West are vendible either in New York or Boston, or in Europe, so long may exchange be had in abundance at those marts; and so long as those places furnish every species of imported goods that the West consumes, will the balance of trade between the North and the South, the East and the West, be kept up." Hill believed trade itself would serve as the regulator of a stable economy rendering useless the need for a national bank;

---

[1] *Register of Debates*, 23rd Cong., 1st sess., (Feb 17, 1834), 598 (Senate).
[2] See Chapter 1 for a description of how the bank drafts functioned.

the confident senator predicted that within a year, the rest of the country would share his belief.[1]

***

The second section of the Girard Bank charter covered the details for the security of the public deposits. Once the amount of public money exceeded half of the total capital stock of the bank, the secretary of the Treasury would determine a satisfactory amount of collateral to ensure the deposits' safety. The section too stated that the secretary could require collateral prior to the public money accruing to half the bank's capital stock if he deemed it necessary. Clay and his allies ripped into Taney for agreeing to terms they argued would effectively remove all security for the public money once in the hands of the chosen state banks. The anti-Jacksonian leader admonished the secretary with stinging condescension, commenting that "a freshman, a schoolboy, would not have thus dealt with his father's or guardian's money." Clay could barely contain his disgust as he laid out how security would look under this section: "Instead of security *preceding*, it is to *follow* the deposite of the people's money! That is, the local bank gets an amount of their money, equal to one-half of its capital, and then condescends to give security! Does not the Secretary know that, when he goes for the security, the money may be gone, and that he may be entirely unable to get one or the other? We have a law...which forbids the advancing of any public money...without previous security. Yet, in violation of the spirit of that law, or, at least, of all common sense and common prudence, the Secretary disperses upwards of twenty-five millions of public revenue among a countless number of unknown banks, and stipulates that, when the amount of the deposite exceeds one-half of their respective capitals, security is to be given!"[2] Realistically then, Southard pointed out, the only security afforded to the public money under this system depended on the solvency of the chosen banks and even given their solvency, security was "commensurate with the powers of their charters." Without examining the chosen banks' individual charters, it would be impossible to know if certain clauses placed restrictions precluding them from serving as proper depositories for the public money according to the contracts Taney drew up. Southard questioned if Taney himself had even taken the time to fully examine each banks' charter. It appeared that he had not, as one of the chosen banks rejected the public money, citing limitations in their charter that prevented them from fulfilling the terms of the agreement.[3]

---

[1] *Register of Debates*, 23rd Cong., 1st sess., (Mar. 3, 1834, Mar. 4, 1834), 775, 789-790 (Senate).
[2] *Register of Debates*, 23rd Cong., 1st sess., (Dec. 30, 1833), 91-92 (Senate).
[3] *Register of Debates*, 23rd Cong., 1st sess., (Jan. 8, 1834), 144-145 (Senate).

With the exception of Nathaniel Tallmadge, the Jacksonians largely avoided directly defending this aspect of the contract (likely due to the shakiness of any ground a true defense could rest upon). The New Yorker argued that although banks were required to provide security after the above mentioned thresholds had been reached, the secretary could, at any time, demand security if he saw fit. Clay, understanding this provision of the contract could void his inadequate security argument, claimed in his initial speech that the secretary lacked the requisite power to examine adequately the banks' affairs to determine if early security was necessary. However, Tallmadge pointed out, resolutions introduced in the Virginia legislature regarding a local bank chosen by Taney stated that the scrutiny under which the bank has agreed to subject itself to under the terms of the contract was harmful to the state, its citizens, and other Virginia banks. In addition, the resolutions complained that security required gave the secretary too much sway over the state banks. Tallmadge could not help but point out the irony between the anti-Jacksonians' position and that of the Virginia legislature. "With one, security is insufficient; with another, it is not only sufficient, but it gives too much power. With one, there is not ample power to examine into all the affairs of the banks; with another, the power is not only ample for that purpose, but the examination too critical!" The situation brought to the senator's mind a story told by N.P. Willis in his "First Impressions of Europe" that appeared in newspapers in early 1832. While in Vienna, Willis witnessed an exhibition in which sand was placed on a pane of glass and manipulated into different shapes by a fiddle-bow drawn across the glass at different angles. The showman would ask the audience what shape they wanted to see and he would create it for them in the sand. Tallmadge saw an affinity between the showman and the anti-Jacksonians' treatment of the state bank contracts. "Let the great fiddle-bow of opposition be applied to it," he announced, "and it is made to assume any shape or form which best suits the purposes of the exhibiter, or which best tends to excite the admiration and gratify the curiosity of those who may have assembled to witness the performance."[1]

Tallmadge, having spoken last on the matter, brought full circle the debate over the safety or lack thereof of the public money under the new banking system. And, such as was the case so often throughout the three month spectacle, each side viewed the same phenomenon as having starkly different implications. Tallmadge, in arguing that the deposits were secure, cited the secretary's control over them as his main reason for believing so. Anti-Jacksonians, on the other hand, were aghast at the prospect of the

---

[1] *Register of Debates*, 23rd Cong., 1st sess., (Mar. 12, 1834), 938 (Senate).

Treasury secretary having increased authority over the deposits. To them, it was further confirmation that Jackson, through his Treasury secretary, intended to seize total control over the public purse. "Where is the money of the people of the United States?" an incensed Henry Clay asked. In response to his own question, Clay answered, "[f]loating about on treasury drafts or checks, to the amount of millions...scattered to the winds by the Secretary of the Treasury...put into a bank here, and a bank there, in regard to the solvency of which we have no satisfactory knowledge."[1] Webster described the new financial system as "left completely at the pleasure of the Secretary of the Treasury, who may change the public moneys from place to place, as often as he pleases."[2]

Calhoun, more apt to criticize his antagonist, Andrew Jackson, than defend the BUS called out the new banking system for what it was — a total surrendering of the nation's finances to the chief executive under the guise of an association of state banks. The states' rights champion again found a way to weave his cause into the debate, struggling to decide between "audacity and hypocrisy" to describe the suggestion that the administration created the new banking system to protect the states from the encroachment of federal power. "The authors of the war message against a member of this confederacy — the authors of the 'bloody bill' — the guardians and defenders of the rights of the States!" the bitter South Carolinian seethed.[3] The "association of banks, created by the Executive, bound together by its influence" was nothing more than another Bank of the United States but under the thumb of the executive rather than that of Congress. Not trusting of banking in general by this point in his life, Calhoun believed the new system dangerously susceptible to corruption. "Not only the selected banks, but the whole banking institutions of the country, and with them the entire money power, for the purpose of speculation, peculation, and corruption, would be placed under the control of the Executive," the senator warned. A system not unlike Jackson's spoils system to dole out patronage would emerge among the local banks of the nation, exchanging political loyalty for public money with the threat of removal if those loyalties should ever waver. This would allow the president to raise and lower stock prices at his will. "Nothing more will be required than to give or withhold deposites; to draw or abstain from drawing warrants; to pamper [state banks] at one time, starve them at another," Calhoun explained, and then detailed an even

---

[1] *Register of Debates*, 23rd Cong., 1st sess., (Dec. 26, 1833), 74 (Senate).

[2] *Register of Debates*, 23rd Cong., 1st sess., (Jan. 30, 1834), 406 (Senate).

[3] Calhoun is referencing the Force Bill enacted at Jackson's urging in 1832 which granted the president expanded authority over the states, including the power to send the federal troops into states to enforce federal laws.

more nefarious scenario. "Those who would be in the secret, and who would know when to buy and when to sell, would have the means of realizing, by dealing in the stocks, whatever fortunes they might please."[1] The reference to what 21st century observers would describe as insider trading demonstrated the corrupt possibilities of the new financial scheme, all under the thumb of the chief executive. That the state banks initially chosen as depositories for the public funds were run by those friendly to the president, among them the Union Bank of Maryland in which Taney held roughly $5,000 in stock, reinforced Calhoun's and the anti-Jacksonians' charges that the new system was just another tentacle of Jackson's vast spoils system.[2]

Like his Deep South colleague, John Tyler was more inclined to attack the administration and its leader for the new financial scheme than defend the BUS. Unafraid to call out the Old General by name, Tyler remarked, "I speak of the President, not Andrew Jackson, when I ask if it be true, that he has used none of the money for the advancement of Presidential power." He used the national revenue to create "an army of retainers" more dangerous to liberty than an armed force. "So long as the spirit of liberty exists," Tyler explained, "there is no danger from [an armed force]...But what can brave men do to guard against the effects of money and patronage?" The president and secretary have laid these chosen state banks prostrate "in order to obtain a small pittance" of the public treasure. Now, the money men of the nation, whom Tyler described as being the most powerful individuals in their respective cities, "look up to [Jackson] for salvation from bankruptcy and ruin." For Tyler, the new system posed an incredible threat to the people and their freedoms as it combined two great dangers — central banking and Jackson's corrupt administration. Like Calhoun, Tyler saw the amalgamation of state banks as nothing more than a new national bank with Jackson at its head.[3]

The Jacksonians, by contrast, downplayed their counterparts' concern that the new system was nothing more than a way for the administration to seize control over the public treasure. Rives found the argument that the state banks would be reliant upon and therefore subservient to the executive absurd. The Virginian explained that once the public moneys were doled out among thirty or forty state banks, the amount received by each bank would be too small "to affect the independent exercise of the feelings or the judgements of the State banks." But to quell any ill-conceived concerns, Rives recommended that Congress devise a set of fixed rules for the new depos-

---

[1] *Register of Debates*, 23rd Cong., 1st sess., (Jan 13, 1834), 217-219 (Senate).
[2] Kahan, *The Bank War*, 123.
[3] *Register of Debates*, 23rd Cong., 1st sess., (Feb. 24, 1834), 672 (Senate).

itories.[1] Forsyth added that even if the allure of the public deposits could tempt weaker souls, it was reprehensible to assume, as the anti-Jacksonians did, that the state bank directors would unquestionably succumb to temptation. "The sweeping denunciation of the respectable and irreproachable directors of all the State institutions trusted by the Secretary of the Treasury, is without the shadow of foundation," the Georgian scolded. Furthermore, the characterization of "favorite partisan banks" thrown around by the anti-Jacksonians to connect the administration to the receivers of the public money was misleading, as "the great mass" were managed by supporters of the recharter effort who voted for Clay.[2] Hill argued that corruption and intrigue were far more likely under a central bank acting as the sole fiscal agent for the government as opposed to several state banks performing that same function. The "want of concert between them," Hill explained, "will be a great security against abuse, both to the government and the people." The state banks would be bolstered by the infusion of public moneys, but still act within their own local sphere of interest. With no possibility of obtaining a monopoly over public funds, there would be little incentive to join forces to manipulate the exchange market to increase their own power.[3]

***

In addition to debating the merits of the new banking system installed by Jackson and Taney, a handful of senators took an opportunity during their speeches to lay out for their colleagues their thoughts on banking in general and what direction the country should follow vis-à-vis banking and the currency. More than once, Jacksonian senators called on the nation to return to a purely hard currency, with the most forceful argument coming not from Old Bullion, Thomas Benton, but from William Rives. The Virginian called a return to hard money the "most urgently demanded" reform of all towards the promotion of public good while voicing his frustration for why a paper money system still afflicted the nation:

> We are too much in the habit...of regarding the evils of the paper money system as necessary and incurable, and of being content with the delusive palliation of those evils supposed to be derived from the controlling supremacy of a National Bank. Nothing, in my opinion, is more demonstrable than the great evil of that system, its ruinous fluctuations arising from alternate expansions and contractions of bank issues, making a lottery, in effect, of private fortunes, and converting all prospective contracts and transactions into a species of gambling — nothing can be more certain than that these ruinous fluctuations...

[1] *Register of Debates*, 23rd Cong., 1st sess., (Jan. 17, 1834), 263-264 (Senate).
[2] *Register of Debates*, 23rd Cong., 1st sess., (Jan. 27, 1834), 364 (Senate).
[3] *Register of Debates*, 23rd Cong., 1st sess., (Mar. 4, 1834), 790 (Senate).

are increased, instead of being diminished, by the existence of an institution of such absolute ascendancy, that when it expands the State Banks expand with it; when it contracts, those banks are forced in self-defence to contract also. Whatever influence such an institution may be supposed to exert, in preserving the soundness of currency, that object would be much more effectually promoted by a return, as far as practicable, to a metallic currency.

Rives laid out a roadmap to restore the country to a hard money system, the first step being the destruction of the BUS. With the BUS gone and its notes withdrawn, gold coins would fill the gap, thus restoring their value, diminished during the BUS years. Additionally, steps to suppress small denomination notes would further bolster the need for metallic currency. With gold and silver flooding the country, the government would then be able to demand payments in specie and the country would be safely returned to a hard money system.[1]

Hill too promoted a return to hard money, arguing "that any system of currency that has not hard money for its basis, must fail." Paper money lacked "intrinsic value" and therefore could never serve as a viable, long-term currency whereas gold and silver possessed a "common and universal equivalent." The fluctuations and panics that bedeviled the country brought on by the mercurial paper-driven currency would be eliminated by a return to hard money.[2] It was for these reasons that Forsyth, a month before Hill spoke, expressed "[sincere] hope...that the hard money days may indeed come, and speedily come, and always continue."[3]

Thomas Ewing articulated the most able rejection of the Jacksonians' desire for a return to a hard money currency. He described this desire as "a strange one to be uttered at this day in a deliberative assembly in a populous country, and an enterprising, especially a commercial community." The Ohioan conjured up images of merchants travelling accompanied by an escort of armed guards to protect wagons packed with gold coins, of graziers lugging horse-loads of coins back from markets after selling off their livestock, of laborers receiving half a week's worth of pay in metal rather than the full amount in paper, redeemable in specie. "[T]he merchant, the mechanic, the laborer, would laugh at the idea [of a return to a hard currency]," Ewing remarked; "they know as well as we know, that it could never be effected, and, if it could, that it were only distressing the community for the purpose of substituting a currency which would be inconvenient, and would not

---

[1] *Register of Debates*, 23rd Cong., 1st sess., (Jan. 17, 1834), 264-265 (Senate).
[2] *Register of Debates*, 23rd Cong., 1st sess., (Mar. 4, 1834), 786 (Senate).
[3] *Register of Debates*, 23rd Cong., 1st sess., (Jan. 27, 1834), 345 (Senate).

answer the necessities of business, for one that is every way convenient and does fully answer those necessities."[1]

For the overwhelming majority of the three month debate, the members of the upper chamber argued with their toes affixed firmly to their respective partisan lines. Discussion of the future of banking served as the notable exception when a slight blurring of those lines occurred among Jacksonians and the anti-Jacksonian alliance visibly cracked. On the Jacksonian side, just Senator Forsyth broke party ranks, and only slightly. As described earlier, the Georgian indicated that he would have waited for Congress to reconvene before issuing the order to remove the deposits, a remark that drew surprise from the anti-Jacksonian press. Another source of surprise came from his support of Daniel Webster's bill to recharter a national bank with proper modifications in place to restrict its power.[2] These modifications included a reduction of interest rates to five percent, the ability of state governments to tax BUS funds used for in-state purposes, and the clear settlement of the question over the federal government's authority over the Bank.[3] Although personally in favor of a hard money system, he predicted that given the political realities of the time, a new bank would be chartered at some point and so it would be expedient to do it now before the country's financial situation became critical. Forsyth added that despite his difference of opinion with Jackson and many of his colleagues, he would stand behind the administration, which he believed had the popular mandate do act as it pleased.[4] This final assertion that he would stand behind Jackson despite differences of opinion on the BUS showcased his reliability as a "democratic soldier" that made up the bulk of Old Hickory's support. Even when at odds with administration policy, party loyalty trumped all.[5] Jacksonians who were unable to separate their loyalty to their visions from their loyalty to Jackson, when those loyalties were at odds with one another, soon found themselves looking elsewhere for a political home.

The anti-Jacksonians, in contrast, endured sharper breaks over banking and its future. John Tyler at one point stated directly, "I am against the bank...I oppose it because it is unconstitutional, and that is reason enough." Regardless of the benefits to the country, and Tyler believed the Bank's benefits to be numerous, no amount of benefit justified "mak[ing] an inroad

[1] *Register of Debates*, 23rd Cong., 1st sess., (Jan. 20, 1834), 325 (Senate).
[2] See Chapter 11.
[3] *Register of Debates*, 23rd Cong., 1st sess., (March 10, 1834), 841 (Senate).
[4] Alvin Laroy Duckett, *John Forsyth, Political Tactician* (Athens, GA; University of Georgia Press, 1962), 143.
[5] Perry M. Goldman, "Political Virtue in the Age of Jackson," *Political Science Quarterly* 87, no. 1 (1972): 60-61.

on the constitution." Therefore, the Virginian suggested a constitutional amendment allowing for the creation of national bank, to put to rest forever the question that had agitated the country since its inception.[1] Given that the Senate lacked a three quarter majority of pro-Bank men and the House could not muster even half in its support, the bold suggestion enjoyed little chance of success. Tyler, of course, understood an amendment authorizing a national bank would never pass, so it must be assumed he had no real intention of seeing the Bank rechartered, something his two famous vetoes as president would appear to confirm.

Calhoun too made very clear that while he accepted the BUS as necessary due to the economic path the country had taken, he would much rather see the whole central banking system done away with, although for different reasons than Tyler. Whereas Tyler's misgivings about the Bank were constitutional, Calhoun's were systemic to banking itself. The former champion of national banking remarked, "I have great doubts (if doubts they may be called) as to the soundness and tendency of the whole [banking] system, in all its modifications." He continued, "I have great fears that it will be found hostile to the liberty and the advance of civilization — fatally hostile to liberty in our country, where the system exists in its worst and most dangerous form." Because the government received notes as payment — as money — it had the constitutional obligation to regulate those notes. In Calhoun's estimation, a national bank best served that function. Unless the government completely divorced itself from the banking system and returned to a purely metallic currency, banking would be necessary and a central bank overseen by Congress was far safer than the state bank system implemented by the administration.[2]

Calhoun's and Tyler's comments revealed the tenuous nature of the anti-Jacksonian alliance when the discussion shifted away from Jackson's usurpation of power and to the BUS. The BUS fractured the ground upon which the anti-Jacksonian alliance stood; when one of their own presented his plan for a national bank moving forward, the ground crumbled out from beneath it.

---

[1] *Register of Debates*, 23rd Cong., 1st sess., (Feb. 24, 1834), 673-674 (Senate).
[2] *Register of Debates*, 23rd Cong., 1st sess., (Jan. 13. 1834), 217-219 (Senate).

CHAPTER 11: EFFICIENT AND IMMEDIATE RELIEF

On March 10, Daniel Webster announced to the Senate that he would present a bill to renew the charter of the BUS the following Monday. He indicated that the bill would be conciliatory in nature to unite the differing factions and offered a glimpse into what would comprise its final form. The senator expressed confidence in a letter to Nicholas Biddle that the bill might succeed, confidence that was bolstered when Georgia's John Pendleton King, an anti-Bank Jacksonian, expressed support for the bill although his ultimate goal was to see the central banking system, "dispens[ed] with... altogether."[1]

On March 18, Webster stood before the chamber to present the bill. Before outlining the details of the new bank, however, he reiterated the importance of central banking and, in direct opposition to his hard money opponents, promoted the credit system driven by paper money, describing it as "the creation of modern times, and belongs, in the highest perfection, only to the most enlightened and best governed nations." He also spoke to the hypocrisy of those who expressed concern over a national bank but condoned and even welcomed the new state bank system. "I confess I find it difficult to respect the intelligence, and, at the same time, the motives of those who alarm the people with the cry of danger to their liberties from the bank," Webster began. "Do they see the same danger from other banks? I think not." The master orator then borrowed from the master playwright when drawing an analogy between banking and a lion whose danger to others depended on its

---

[1] Catterall, *Second Bank*, 337; *Register of Debates*, 23rd Cong., 1st sess., (Mar. 10, 1834), 849 (Senate).

keeper. "Under the control of this Government, it is fearful and dangerous," he wryly observed, "but under state authority, it 'roars as gently as a sucking dove; it roars as it were a nightingale.'"[1]

Not content with issuing a blanket condemnation to the Jacksonians for their hypocrisy, Webster took aim specifically New York senators Silas Wright and Nathanial Tallmadge. The latter had addressed the Senate just days earlier and spent considerable time defending his state's banking system, which had come under fire at various points throughout the session. Both Wright and Tallmadge spoke of the "imminent danger" posed by the BUS and its thirty-five millions in capital. "And yet," Webster countered, "they feel no fears for the liberty of the people of their own State, with a banking capital of twenty-three millions, and a proposed addition of ten millions... but their anxiety is intense, lest a bank of thirty-five millions should enslave all the people of the twenty-four states." To Webster, these "false cries of danger to liberty" were nothing more than attempts to promote the Jackson agenda at the expense of "fair discussion on the real merits of public questions" and even a cursory examination of the debate proved as much.[2]

Upon finishing his attacks on the Jacksonians and the reiteration of the benefits of central banking that the anti-Jacksonians had been espousing for months, Webster presented his main reason for addressing the Senate — a proposal for the rechartering the Bank of the United States with the possibility to create a new national bank. To make any progress, Webster repeated the indispensable need to unite what he divided up as the country's three banking factions — those who supported the current BUS and believed in its constitutionality, those who thought the BUS useful but questioned its constitutionality, and those who believed a national bank constitutional but opposed the current BUS. (Webster conspicuously did not mention those who believed a national bank to be unconstitutional and denied the need for one, perhaps understanding those who held those views would view any proposal for a new central bank anathema.) To unite these three disparate groups, the New Englander adopted a tactic generally associated with his western colleague — compromise.

Like most of his pro-Bank colleagues, Webster preferred to see the recharter of current BUS or the creation of a new one for the duration of another twenty years. The state of Congress, however, specifically the House that tipped, if not heavily, against the BUS, rendered any long-term charter renewal hopeless. This reality compelled Webster to "sacrifice my opinions

---

[1] *Register of Debates*, 23rd Cong., 1st sess., (Mar. 18, 1834), 991 (Senate). Webster here quoted from Shakespeare's, *A Midsummer Night's Dream.*
[2] *Register of Debates*, 23rd Cong., 1st sess., (Mar. 18, 1834), 991 (Senate).

to that necessity which I feel to be imposed upon me by the condition of the country." Of sole importance to the senator was "efficient" and "immediate relief." With these contingencies and personal desires in mind, Webster offered his proposal. Because Congress could not legally create a new national bank until the termination of the old one in 1836, and unwilling to watch the country suffer over the next two years in anticipation of that moment, Webster suggested a stopgap measure of extending the current Bank for six years (although he was willing to shorten the extension to four or five years if a majority felt six too long). Along with that extension, though, came the provision that upon the original termination of the charter in 1836, Congress could at that point establish a new bank as it saw fit. Webster viewed this as "the great feature of the bill. Congress is thus left at perfect liberty to make another bank whenever it chooses. When the present agitation shall have subsided, when a day of calm consideration comes, and the people have had time for deliberation, then Congress may make a permanent provision, satisfactory to itself and the country."[1] This overly optimistic view of the situation indicated Webster's belief that common ground existed between the factions and that fundamental disputes over central banking were not the cause of the present turmoil. Instead, the turmoil was driven by inflammatory partisan rabblerousing — rabblerousing that would ease over time once cooler heads prevailed and not coincidentally when Jackson would likely be out of office.

The second section of Webster's proposed bill would restore the deposits to the BUS and its branches as of July 1, 1834 with removal of the deposits occurring thereafter only by the order of Congress. This clause would allow Congress to move the deposits to a new national bank, should one be created after the expiration of the original charter in 1836. Equally important, the clause would "give to Congress, at all times, what rightfully belongs to them — a full control over the public purse. It separates the purse from the sword, and re-establishes the just authority of the legislature."[2] The parallel effect of the clause, although Webster did not state it directly, was to remove any authority over the public deposits from the executive branch, to which the anti-Jacksonians believed no authority was vested.

Another section of the bill aimed at placating hard money advocates. This section stipulated that Congress could compel the BUS to cease the issuing of notes less than twenty dollars at any time it saw fit after March, 1836. Webster envisioned this protocol aligning with states issuing the same decree to their own local banks, but for notes under five dollars. This

---

[1] *Register of Debates*, 23rd Cong., 1st sess., (Mar. 18, 1834), 993-994 (Senate).
[2] *Register of Debates*, 23rd Cong., 1st sess., (Mar. 18, 1834), 994 (Senate).

would create a currency where the use of gold and silver would fulfill all transactions up to five dollars, gold and silver and state notes for all transactions between five and twenty dollars, and gold and silver, state notes, and BUS notes for all transactions exceeding twenty dollars. Webster believed the clause would garner some hard money support as it would "extend the specie basis of our circulation."[1]

Other sections of the bill included a bonus paid by the BUS for the continuance of the charter and a mechanism for the Bank directors to divide unused capital among the stockholders. Webster concluded his remarks with a direct challenge to the people to support the bill. "I would say to them," he began, "that the constitution and the laws, their own rights and their own happiness, all depend on themselves; and if they esteem these of any value; if they were not too dearly bought by the blood of their fathers; if they be an inheritance fit to be transmitted to their posterity, I would beseech them — I would beseech them — to come now to their salvation."[2] With that final appeal to the will of the people and their overwhelming desire to be rescued from the financial embarrassment that had befallen them, Webster ceded the floor.

The overly optimistic senator received a further boost when the first to speak on the bill, Virginia's Benjamin Watkins Leigh, expressed his lukewarm support. Leigh had assumed the seat vacated by William Rives earlier in the session and like his Virginia counterpart, John Tyler, was a Jackson detractor but harbored misgivings about the BUS. Support from men like Leigh would be crucial to the bill's ultimate success. The newest senator conveyed the consensus within his state that Congress had no constitutional authority to create a national bank, a belief he himself shared. Despite his own thoughts on the Bank's constitutionality though, Leigh recognized that because so many have come out in favor of the BUS, he "cannot say that the incorporation of a national bank, on the principles on which the present bank has been framed, is palpably unconstitutional." Holding such an opinion would require "a degree of presumption; a want of respect for the opinion of others; a pretension to infallibility" he was incapable of. Indeed, the people of Virginia's opposition to the BUS notwithstanding, Leigh felt the recent developments under examination in the Senate "may serve to convince them that the renewal of the charter of the present bank," as dictated by Webster, "may be the only means which human wisdom can devise, to avert or to correct measures far more unconstitutional, more abhorrent in principle from their opinions, and more dangerous and baleful

---

[1] *Register of Debates*, 23rd Cong., 1st sess., (Mar. 18, 1834), 995 (Senate).
[2] *Register of Debates*, 23rd Cong., 1st sess., (Mar. 18, 1834), 995 (Senate).

in consequences. The alternatives but too likely to be presented to us are, indeed, awful." The awful alternative to which Leigh spoke, of course, was the creation of a league of state banks to act as a new national bank under "the absolute control and dominion of the President of the United States." Leigh feared such power, power he would not even trust with his own father, would allow Jackson to purchase a crown and rule over the country as a king. Like Webster before him, the Virginian was baffled by the hypocrisy of the Jacksonians. How could anyone who shared his constitutional objec-tions to the BUS, Leigh pondered, "[p]ossibly think that the President has the constitutional authority to frame a league of State banks, and make them fiscal agents?"[1] Leigh ended his remarks without committing full support to Webster's scheme, but he made clear his preference for the bill over the new banking system under the control of the president.

The sanguinity Webster felt for the success of his bill, however, was short lived. Silas Wright took the floor next and was unequivocal in his position that the bank bill should not pass. It was certainly a longshot to expect Wright to support the bill, but Webster hoped the concessions he made would soften the Jacksonian's resolve. That Wright voiced such stri-dent opposition did not bode well for the prospect of garnering support for the compromise from other hard money Jacksonians. The New Yorker spent considerable time defending both Jackson and Taney as his colleagues had done over the last few months. He also reiterated a defense of his own state's banking system and repudiated, as he had done nearly two months prior, any talk of the new system serving as a mechanism to enrich the state in exchange for political loyalty to Jackson (a conspiracy Leigh rekindled during his remarks and Wright felt obliged to respond). It was towards the end of the speech that Wright directly addressed Webster's bill. The finances of the country were strong, Wright argued, and if the country could not rid itself of a national bank now, "in vain shall we try in future to shake it from us." Webster had tried to convince the Senate of the perpetual need for a national bank to ensure the economic stability of the nation. To quell concerns, Webster proposed revoking the monopolizing character of the current bank by allowing Congress to create a new one in its stead. To Wright, this simply would not do. "My object is the entire discontinuance and eradication of this or any similar institution," he explained. "When will the time come," Wright questioned, "that this odious institution can finally be closed with less distress than now?"[2]

---

[1] *Register of Debates*, 23rd Cong., 1st sess., (Mar. 18, 1834), 999-1000 (Senate).
[2] *Register of Debates*, 23rd Cong., 1st sess., (Mar. 20, 1834), 1036 (Senate).

Wright's forceful denunciation was a blow to the bill's chances, although, coming from someone with such strong Jacksonian credentials, not terribly unexpected. The death knell for the bill came when the strongest voices from his own side, John C. Calhoun and Henry Clay, withheld support as well. Three days after Webster presented the bill, Calhoun shared his thoughts. Within the first few moments of his speech, the senator stated he could not support Webster's measure because "[i]n every view which I have been able to take, it is objectionable." Calhoun felt the bill's ultimate object unclear. Was the bill meant to extend the Bank's life or to provide it time to wind down its affairs? If the former, six years was too short a time, if the latter, six years was too long. More objectionable though was that in Calhoun's view, the bill did nothing but prolong the Bank question for another two presidential elections. He saw the measure as one "to palliate and temporize in order to gain time, with a view to apply a more effectual remedy." But the question at hand required a permanent solution and in Calhoun's mind, Webster was not even addressing the correct question. The financial concerns of the nation did not revolve solely around the continuance of the BUS but also around the future of currency and by focusing solely on the continuance of the BUS, Webster "has given an undue prominence to that which has by far the least relative importance." For the purpose of creating a currency characterized by "uniformity, permanency, and safety," Calhoun explained, "the bank is a mere subordinate agent, to be used or not to be used, and to be modified as to its duration and other provisions wholly in reference to the higher question of the currency." And the currency, Calhoun intimated, "is the disease which afflicts the system...It consists of great and growing disproportion between metallic and paper circulation of the country, effected through the instrumentality of the banks."

To fix the currency problem, the South Carolinian reluctantly saw no other solution but to continue with central banking for a time with the goal to slowly wean off it, to "use a bank to unbank the banks," as he put it. Calhoun then offered his own vision; a renewal of the national bank with a twelve-year charter, time "long enough to permit the agitation and distraction which now disturbs the country to subside, while it is sufficiently short to enable us to be derived from the operation of the system under its new provisions." These provisions included a suspension of the issuance of notes under ten dollars upon termination of the charter, a prohibition on the government from receiving payment in notes under ten dollars, and a prohibition on the government from receiving payment in notes from any bank that issues notes under five dollars. The BUS would also be barred from receiving in payment or on deposit, notes from banks whose notes were not receivable by the government. Lastly, six years into the new charter, the BUS would be banned from issuing notes less than twenty dollars and all payments to the government under twenty dollars must be in specie. While some of Calhoun's plan aligned with Webster's, their ultimate goals diverged.[1] Whereas Webster hoped to buy time with his plan to devise a national banking scheme digestible to all (or to buy time until a more bank-friendly administration took power), Calhoun's plan aimed to provide a slow weaning off of national banking and ultimately restore a currency based on metal, a plan more akin to the hard money Jacksonians. One hoped to resuscitate the Bank, the other hoped to bring about its painless death.

Clay's preference was to forego all debate on the Bank's future knowing full well it would strain the nascent opposition party he hoped to build. As discussed earlier, Clay had met with Biddle prior to the session to express concern over introducing a recharter bill, a concern Biddle too shared. By February, Clay remained steadfast that the issue of recharter should be left for a later time. Clay wrote to Biddle, "[i]f we take up the Bank, we play into the adversarys hands...It is the usurpation which has convulsed the Country. If we put it by and take up the Bank, we may & probably would divide about the terms of the charter, and finally do nothing leaving things as they are." Biddle agreed, writing back to Clay, "a force would be rallied upon [usurpation] which might not continue united on the [recharter of the BUS]."[2] Clay's meeting before the session and his correspondence with Biddle months later explains his cold reaction to Webster's bill. Not only did Clay want to delay any action on the BUS until May, he viewed Webster's bill as too friendly to Jackson and preferred a long term recharter. In fact, the plan was so offensive to Clay that he insisted Webster move to lay it on the table or he would do it himself.[3] A week after presenting the bill, Webster did as Clay asked and tabled the measure, likely realizing that without united support, its chances for success were slim. Two months later, Webster assured the Senate he was still bullish on the bill's chance for passage, expressing supreme confidence "that when all the passing ephemeral projects had had their little day, they would disappear, and a national bank would be the final result in Congress."[4] The senator's confidence, though, was misplaced and the recharter bill was not heard from again.

Jackson's usurpation of power unified those of varying political sensibilities into a common political force in a way that the BUS could not.

---

[1] *Register of Debates*, 23rd Cong., 1st sess., (Mar. 21, 1834), 1057-1069 (Senate).

[2] Clay to Biddle, February 2, 1834, *Papers of Henry Clay*, 694; Biddle to Clay, February 4, 1834, *Papers of Henry Clay*, 694-695.

[3] Catterall, *Second Bank*, 337.

[4] *Register of Debates*, 23rd Cong., 1st sess., (May 21, 1834), 1791 (Senate).

Former National Republicans, states' rights Southerners, and radical nullifiers found common ground in their disgust over, in their view, the appalling
way Jackson ruled over the country. The BUS, on the other hand, provided
little common ground as exemplified by how the leading anti-Jacksonians
differed in their tactics towards it. Webster, like many New England
National Republicans, had close ties to the Bank and hoped strongly for its
recharter. Calhoun shared the view of many states' rights Southerners that
the country would be better off without a national bank. Calhoun at least
recognized that the realities of the day required a gradual severing between
the government and central banking and his plan moving forward revealed
as much. For Clay, like others who hoped to form a cohesive, national party
to challenge Jackson, the BUS became a necessary casualty. By this point,
Clay's sights were set firmly on taking down Jackson and ascending to the
presidency. Although he pushed to charter the Bank two decades ago and
it formed a piece of his American System, he certainly did not care enough
about it at this point to let it interfere with his larger goals. Achieving those
goals required a unified party and Clay knew well enough from his experience as a candidate in 1832 that the BUS was not a unifying issue. The BUS
burned Clay once; he was not about to let that happen again.

Chapter 12: The Vote and the Aftermath

After three months of continuous debate spanning "the longest period which had been occupied in a single debate in either house of Congress since the organization of the Government," Henry Clay took the Senate floor for the final time in defense of his resolutions.[1] Over the previous three months, the Kentuckian bore witness to both impassioned defenses and inflammatory assaults on his resolutions and personal integrity. Already a legendary figure in the lower house, Clay's work during the first session of the 23rd Congress elevated him to a similar station in the Senate. Clay's two day speech largely recounted much of what he and his allies had been arguing throughout the session. Towards the end of his remarks, Clay tried again to frame the debate as being a question of executive tyranny and not just a comparatively unimportant one as bank or no bank. "Give us back the authority of the laws," Clay declared, "and [I] would be willing to see every stone in that splendid building in Chestnut Street pulled down and returned to its native quarry." With that final declaration leaving no doubt as to his ultimate purpose for instigating this whole turmoil, Clay yielded the floor.[2]

After a handful of senators provided some short remarks indicating their final decisions, the Senate finally voted on Clay's resolutions on March 28, 1834. The second resolution calling Taney's reasons for removal unsatisfactory and insufficient came up for vote first and passed by a comfortable 28–18 margin. The first resolution (and the one of greater importance to Clay) came next, but not before a change of wording initiated by its author.

[1] *Register of Debates*, 23rd Cong., 1st sess., (Mar. 27, 1834), 1172 (Senate).
[2] *Register of Debates*, 23rd Cong., 1st sess., (Mar. 27, 1834), 1176 (Senate).

Clay, at the insistence of some allies, truncated the original resolution into a far less specific form to read, "*Resolved*, that the President, in the late executive proceedings in relation to the public revenue, has assumed upon himself authority and power not conferred by the constitution and laws, but in derogation of both." The newly worded resolution passed by a 26-20 vote. Senator John Pendleton King from Georgia, who had voiced tepid support for Webster's recharter measure, and William Hendricks from Indiana were the only two who voted for the second resolution but not the first. With the vote officially recorded, Andrew Jackson had been censured.

The Old General certainly was not going to let the censure pass unchallenged and Jackson wasted little time voicing his disgust. The president's response (written with the aid of Taney, Kendall, and Benjamin Butler), titled simply, "Protest," arrived in the Senate on April 17. Jackson touched on many of the same themes as did his supporters but also included some unique and revelatory ideas of his own. The president railed against the censure as "not only unauthorized by the constitution, but in many respects repugnant to its provisions and subversive of the rights secured by it to other co-ordinate departments." Repeating charges leveled by Thomas Benton, Jackson characterized Clay's resolution as entirely judicial, and therefore beyond the Senate's constitutionally granted powers that limit their judicial capacity to trials of impeachment. By passing the resolution, the Senate had effectively judged the president guilty of the charge of assuming unconstitutional powers. But, the wily Jackson pointed out, even had the proceedings been a formal impeachment hearing and therefore, within the Senate's power to rule upon, the 26-20 vote did not reach the two-thirds majority required for a conviction. So not only had the Senate violated the Constitution by conducting a de facto trial of the president outside of an impeachment hearing, its guilty verdict fell short of the threshold needed for a conviction had an actual impeachment trial occurred.[1]

Jackson too addressed the last minute change to the wording of the resolution, citing it as evidence that the specific charges levied against Jackson were flimsy. The president wrote that the resolution was stripped of its specificity only after "perhaps, it was apprehended that a majority might not sustain the specific accusation contained in it." The modified, stripped down resolution served as a most "striking illustration of the soundness and necessity of the rules which forbid vague and indefinite generalities, and require a reasonable certainty in all judicial allegations." For Jackson, a former

---

[1] *Register of Debates*, 23rd Cong., 1st sess., (Apr. 17, 1834), 1318-1320 (Senate).

attorney and therefore intimately familiar with law, "a more glaring instance of the violation of those rules, has seldom been exhibited."[1]

The Old General introduced a few new points beyond those raised by his defenders in the Senate. Jackson presented the resolutions of several state legislatures whose senators ignored instructions to vote against the censure and lectured, "I disclaim and repudiate all authority or design to interfere with the responsibility due from members of the Senate to their own consciences, their constituents, and their country." Simple math and past experience can at least partially account for Jackson's stern rebuke. Had the four senators who spurned their states' instructions not done so, the censure resolution would not have passed; a development bearing a striking resemblance to state delegations who ignored their legislature's instructions to vote for Jackson and instead cast their vote for John Quincy Adams to settle the disputed election of 1824. Of greater significance though, the rebuke stemmed from Jackson's novel vision for the role of the president. Serving as president, Jackson matter-of-factly referred to himself as "the direct representative of the American people." As the only official elected by the people of the entire nation (outside of the vice president), Jackson viewed the president as the sole representative for *all* people, unlike congressmen who served their localities and unelected senators who served their states. While Jackson certainly aimed to and succeeded at bolstering his own power within the office of the presidency, his design to increase that power in order to protect the American people from the caprices of unelected figures like bank officials and stuffy senators coincided with his broader political ideology and cannot be overlooked. Even before his questionable defeat to John Quincy Adams in 1824, Jackson had made very clear his desire to see the government operate through the will of the people. Upon ascending to the presidency, Old Hickory took it upon himself to ascertain the will of the people (and often mold that will himself) and put it into action. In believing himself to be "the direct representative of the American people," Jackson took the presidency to a place none who held the office before him, even Thomas Jefferson, could have imagined; that of protector and executor of the people's will.[2]

Jackson ended with a grand proclamation of the importance of the contents of his message to the furtherance of American liberties and a request that the Senate officially log his protest into the *Senate Journal*. The protest led to another showdown between the Jacksonians and anti-Jacksonians just as intense, if not as long, as the one over Clay's resolutions. George Poindexter set the tone for the anti-Jacksonians, urging the Senate to not even receive

---

[1] *Register of Debates*, 23rd Cong., 1st sess., (Apr. 17, 1834), 1323-1324 (Senate).
[2] *Register of Debates*, 23rd Cong., 1st sess., (Apr. 17, 1834), 1333-1334 (Senate).

the paper, claiming it a direct appeal to the people and therefore wholly inappropriate as an official communication. "I will not dignify this paper by considering it in the light of an executive message; it is no such thing," the Mississippian scoffed. "I regard it simply as a paper with the signature of Andrew Jackson, and, should the Senate refuse to receive it, it will not be the first paper with the same signature which has been refused a hearing in this body, on the ground of the abusive and vituperative language which it contained."[1]

Other anti-Jacksonians responded with similar outrage. The indignant Theodore Frelinghuysen could not believe that instead of working to alleviate the distress gripping the country, the Senate was subjected to "[a] lecture of an hour and a half...for daring to question the authority under which this blow at our prosperity has been inflicted!"[2] Peleg Sprague expressed disgust at Jackson's reference to Taney as "his secretary" rather than as the secretary of the law. Even more shocking, Jackson claimed power "never before... heard in this country...that, under the constitution, the President must have possession of all the public property, and all the public money!" Even Jackson's most ardent supporters, Sprague observed, had not ventured to suggest anything so audacious.[3] Samuel Southard chided the Old General for ordering senators to vote in alignment with the perceived will of their state's citizens, and insinuating that those who did not were violating their duties. He called the suggestion an "attack as a gross and impertinent interference between me and my constituents." The New Jerseyan continued, "[w]hat has the President of the United States to do with the obedience or disobedience of a Senator to the instructions which he may receive from the people. Who constituted him judge of the one, or guardian of the other?"[4]

Attacks of this nature upon the president's protest flowed from the anti-Jacksonians over the next couple weeks with Jacksonians meeting those attacks with the requisite opposition. Thomas Benton was first to defend Jackson, and did so using such specific details that Benjamin Leigh later surmised that the Missourian must have received an advance copy of the protest to prepare such a pointed response.[5] On May 7, the Senate voted on four resolutions drafted by Senator Poindexter condemning the president's protest, refusing to enter it into the *Senate Journal*, and denying the president had the right to send protests against its proceedings. The resolutions, taken up separately, each passed by the identical 27–16 vote with one

[1] *Register of Debates*, 23rd Cong., 1st sess., (Apr. 17, 1834), 1336 (Senate).
[2] *Register of Debates*, 23rd Cong., 1st sess., (Apr. 17, 1834), 1345 (Senate).
[3] *Register of Debates*, 23rd Cong., 1st sess., (Apr. 17, 1834), 1341 (Senate).
[4] *Register of Debates*, 23rd Cong., 1st sess., (Apr. 17, 1834), 1359 (Senate).
[5] *Register of Debates*, 23rd Cong., 1st sess., (Apr. 18, 1834), 1374 (Senate).

senator, Alabama's Gabriel Moore, joining the majority after voting previously against Clay's first resolution. As the session mercifully neared its end, the anti-Jacksonians, by now united under the banner of the Whigs, dealt the administration another blow when the new party used its majority in the Senate to reject Taney's nomination as secretary of the Treasury, the first time in history that the Senate rejected a president's cabinet nomination.

***

Any victories the nascent senate Whigs may have won during the "Panic Session," however, were short-lived, and in many ways, non-existent. Throughout the session, as the Whig-controlled Senate hammered away at Jackson and his Treasury secretary, the president worked both overtly and behind the scenes to shore up his defenses elsewhere while continuing his attack on the BUS to steer public opinion against it. When worried businessmen seeking relief called upon Jackson at the White House, the wily president directed them to "[g]o to Nicholas Biddle...Biddle has all the money."[1] The tactic of redirecting people's hostility to Biddle worked and as winter gave way to spring in 1834, blame for the struggling economy began shifting away from Jackson and onto BUS president. The situation became dire for the BUS when the pro-Bank governors of two crucial states, George Wolf of Pennsylvania and William L. Marcy of New York, broke with Biddle, with Wolf even admitting that restoring the deposits was not necessary to relieve the public distress.[2] Biddle certainly did not help himself by contracting business far beyond what was needed following the removal, but the stubborn Bank president wanted to make a point — his Bank kept the country's economy functioning and it would not be trifled with. It is worth noting, in hindsight, that while the economic downturn did hit hard in certain parts of the country, the impact of the "panic," did not create the long-term national economic distress that the level of concern at the time would suggest. Foreign investment still poured in to offset rising interest rates, prices fell but not disastrously so, bank runs occurred but in small numbers, and the state banks held the currency relatively stable.[3] Areas of the country were certainly hit harder than others by the Bank War, but it did not seem to trigger widespread national economic hardship. The perception of such hardship, however, was real and as the blame came to fall on Biddle and the BUS as the session wore on, the Bank's position in the eyes of the public rapidly declined and as a result, support from some Whigs declined

---

[1] Howe, *What Hath God Wrought*, 391.
[2] Campbell, *The Bank War and the Partisan Press*, 108.
[3] Wilentz, *The Rise of American Democracy*, 400.

as well.[1] Under pressure from those who had been hit hard by Biddle's policies and Whig politicians concerned the Bank would hurt them politically, the beleaguered president caved and the BUS resumed normal lending by the fall of 1834. By that point, however, the Bank's public image was likely beyond repair.

Additionally, Jackson manipulated a scenario with pension payments to war veterans to injure the Bank's image. The BUS had been responsible for the issuing of pension payments for some time but in January, 1834, Jackson, to chip away at some of its power by relieving the Bank of this particular duty, ordered Biddle to surrender all pension funds to the War Department. Biddle, of course, refused and in response, Secretary of War Lewis Cass issued an order to suspend all pension payments. Veterans were outraged by the news and demanded answers. The Jacksonian press roared into action and blamed the whole mess on Biddle's truculence. It was impossible, the Jacksonians argued, that the hero of the New Orleans would do anything to jeopardize the well-being of war veterans. The public relations maneuver worked, so well in fact that even some Whigs, Daniel Webster most prominent among them, warned Biddle that standing firm on such a touchy subject could backfire. Biddle, stubborn as ever, did not listen and the Bank's image continued to deteriorate.[2]

Sensing the tide turning against the BUS, Jackson's allies in the House passed a series of anti-Bank resolutions in April, among them a call for a full investigation of the Bank to determine the cause of the panic. This final measure passed by a more comfortable margin than any of the others and drew support from Jacksonians and anti-Jacksonians alike, revealing the desire among those of all political persuasions to get answers on the Bank's conduct. Biddle stonewalled the investigation at every turn, drawing the ire of Congress and prompting them to consider bringing up charges of contempt. The House ultimately decided against taking such action, but Biddle's obstinacy fed into the Jacksonian portrayal of the Bank as putting itself above the law and answerable to no one but itself. Jackson may have dug the Bank's grave, but Biddle rolled it in.

When it became clear to Biddle that the BUS would not be rechartered — upon the start of the 24th Congress began Biddle put out feelers to gauge support for recharter but drew little interest — the Bank prepared to close up quietly in advance of its inglorious termination in March, 1836. Biddle, grasping at straws, was able to keep the Philadelphia branch open under a Pennsylvania state charter, but the heavy price to incorporate, roughly six

---

[1] Campbell, *The Bank War and the Partisan Press*, 110.
[2] Remini, *Jackson and the Bank War*, 160-161.

million dollars, forced the Bank to start in a weakened position. The Bank put much of its resources into the cotton market, but when prices crashed in 1837, the Bank had no choice but to draw on its credit until none remained. The Bank closed in 1841, two years after Biddle resigned as its president. Biddle would live just another few years before dying in February, 1844.[1]

The Whigs could not even revel in their censuring of Jackson for very long. In his defense of Jackson's protest, Thomas Benton immediately planted the seed of having the censure expunged from the *Senate Journal*. The Missourian brought up an offensive resolution passed by the English House of Commons in 1768 that was expunged after fourteen years of wrangling and cited it as his own motivation to act. Such perseverance "was a sufficient encouragement for [Benton] to begin, and doubtless would encourage others to continue, until the good work should be crowned with success, and the only atonement made, which it was in the Senate's power to make" to remedy the offensive censure — expungement.[2] The senator would not have to wait fourteen years to realize his goal. Less than three years after pledging to erase the censure from the record, the Senate, now in the firm grasp of the Jacksonians, voted by a 24-19 margin to expunge the resolution from its official journal despite the Whigs employing the first filibuster in United State history to prevent it.[3] As many Whigs walked out in protest, Senate secretary, Ashbury Dickens scrawled across the now defunct resolution in black pen, "Expunged by the order of the Senate, this 16th day of January, 1837." The censure of Jackson that his opponents fought for months to effect, officially, no longer existed.[4]

***

Despite vanquishing the Second Bank of the United States and having his actions, at least officially, vindicated by the Senate, the Bank War cannot be viewed as a total victory for Jackson either. Having taken the action he did to destroy the Bank and employing such harsh rhetoric opposing central banking in general, Jackson and his allies had wedded themselves to deposit banking and a push towards a hard currency. The early returns on this "experiment," as it was often called, were shaky due to several contributing factors. For one, some of the pet banks acted irresponsibly and engaged in wild speculation without the regulating authority of the BUS hovering over their heads. But that explanation does not go far enough to explain the economic troubles that bedeviled Jackson's banking system, especially when factoring

---

[1] Remini, *Jackson and the Bank War*, 174-175.

[2] *Register of Debates*, 23rd Cong., 1st sess., (Apr. 17, 1834), 1347 (Senate).

[3] Kahan, *The Bank War*, 140.

[4] Benjamin Perley Poore, *Perley's Reminiscences of Sixty Years in the National Metropolis, Volume I* (Philadelphia: Hubbard Brothers, Publishers, 1886), 142.

in the efforts of new Treasury Secretary, Levi Woodbury, to curb the reckless behavior. Additionally, the extinguishing of the national debt in 1835 added to a growing federal surplus that, coupled with a boom in western land sales fueled by an influx of foreign silver, created the makings of a very dangerous speculative bubble. Furthermore, an abundance of these land sales were paid for in paper which not only flooded the Treasury with notes but also carved out for the government the role as chief creditor to speculators and banks hoping to turn the west into their own cash cow. Finally, although Woodbury's reforms helped scale down the amount of small denomination notes issued by the deposit banks, private local banks still issued their own small notes which further diminished currency values.[1]

To ease the looming trouble, Jackson pushed Congress to pass a series of reform measures angling towards hard currency in 1834 and again the following year when the original proposal went nowhere. By this point though, Jackson's hard money stance and the level of constitutionally questionable executive regulation required to put it into action had pushed away more allies, including some, such as Nathaniel Tallmadge, who had stood by the president's decision to remove the deposits. These Jackson defectors, known as Conservative Democrats, joined with Whigs in Congress to pass a currency reform bill far short of the changes Jackson sought. The Deposit Act of 1836 did help curtail the issuance of small denomination notes, to the delight of hard money advocates, but also included a plan dear to Clay to distribute the surplus funds from land sales to states for improvement projects. The Jacksonians had long opposed this scheme and were no more amenable to it now. In addition, the Deposit Act reduced the amount of public funds each pet bank could hold, thereby creating the need to greatly expand the number of banks holding government deposits. The drastic increase of banks holding public money from roughly twenty to ninety made regulating their actions impossible and only increased the level of speculation.[2]

Jackson largely disproved of the Deposit Act but had little choice but to sign it. Vetoing the measure could have led to accusations that Jackson simply wanted to keep the number of deposit banks small to more easily control them for his own purposes. Additionally, vetoing a measure supported by many Democrats could have negatively impacted Martin Van Buren's chances of succeeding him to the presidency. So Jackson signed the bill, speculation continued, and state banks flooded the market with its paper creating an economic climate in direct opposition to the one he hoped

[1] Wilentz, *The Rise of Jacksonian Democracy*, 441; Schlesinger, *The Age of Jackson*, 128.
[2] For more on the passage of the Deposit Act, see, Wilentz, *The Rise of Jacksonian Democracy*, 442-443, and Remini, *Jackson and the Bank War*, 169-170.

to foster. These developments ironically increased the nation's attachment to paper money, much to the chagrin of his more rabid hard money allies.[1] The Old General did have one more trick up his sleeve though. In July, 1836, just months before leaving office and while Congress was out of session, Jackson issued his Specie Circular, an executive order of sorts that ordered all land sales to be paid in specie in an attempt to reduce the flow of paper across the country. Land sales decreased (although perhaps not as much as Jackson had expected) but by this point the course towards a crash could not be reversed. The bubble burst in 1837 and plunged the country into a panic followed by a depression worse than it had experienced in 1819.[2]

The blame for the crash has divided historians of the era. Those generally friendly to Jackson tend to blame the Whigs for obstructing the administration's reforms aimed at stemming the torrent of paper that inundated the country and fueled the speculative bubble. A particularly friendly interpretation suggests that had the hard money policies advocated by Jackson been applied fully, evenly, and quickly, the economic disaster could have been averted. On the other end of the spectrum, one Jackson critic calls his failure to implement a hard money scheme "no bad thing," citing modern economists who believe that had metallism been fully adopted, it would have restricted economic growth through the remainder of the antebellum period. Another interpretation argues that due to his own naivety regarding the benefits of hard money, Jackson unwittingly set the stage for unprecedented industrial growth and speculation. Perhaps the most renowned Jacksonian historian of all, Arthur Schlesinger Jr., takes a measured approach, blaming Jackson for killing the BUS which served as a check on rampant speculation but also crediting the hard money advocates for trying to reel in the speculative mania only to be stymied by the Whigs and their business-class supporters. Finally, economic historian, Peter Temin has largely downplayed the role of the Bank War in creating the bubble that plunged the country into financial disaster. He instead emphasizes external factors mentioned above, specifically the silver boom from Mexico, as the major contributing factor.[3]

Regardless of how historians and economists have judged the impact of Jackson's hard money policies and the Bank War more generally, the fact remains that Jackson and his allies did not escape unscathed. For all its

---

[1] Kahan, *The Bank War*, 127.

[2] The discussion of the state of the economy under the deposit banking system was drawn from several sources. See; Wilentz, *The Rise of American Democracy*, 436-446; Howe, *What Hath God Wrought*, 393-395; Remini, *Jackson and the Bank War*, 168-173; Schlesinger, *The Age of Jackson*, 126-128, 217-218.

[3] Peter Temin, *The Jacksonian Economy* (New York: W.W. Norton & Company, 1969), 11-17. Wilentz expresses a more favorable view of Jackson's economic policies while Howe is more critical. Remini and Schlesinger take a more balanced view.

victories, the Bank War inflicted on Jacksonism a deep and lasting wound. The president's inconsistent handling of different issues, such as promoting federal supremacy in his battle with nullifiers but supporting states' rights in his handling of Native Americans, created challenges to forming a cohesive bloc of opposition to resist his administration during his first term. The fight with the BUS, though, finally gave his opponents — former National Republicans, southern States' Righters, wayward Democrats, strict constructionists, and Anti-Masons — an issue around which they could coalesce and served as the foundation for the creation of the anti-Jackson, Whig party. And although they would ultimately fail to recharter a new national bank, without the Bank War the Whig party may never have come into existence.[1] It was not saving the BUS as much their shared desire to resist the blatant executive usurpation of unconstitutional authority exhibited by Jackson's actions towards the Bank that joined them together. From that shared desire, the Whigs found enough common ground on other issues, such as advocating moral reform bolstered by government intervention, and suppressed issues where common ground did not exist, mainly on slavery, to form a cohesive national party strong enough to wrest the presidency away from the Jacksonians in 1840 and had it not been for a stroke of bad luck, perhaps held that power throughout the decade.

***

It is this final point that reveals the most lasting outcome of the Bank War. For after all the debate over national bank versus state banks and hard money versus paper, the greatest impacts of the Bank War were not economic, but political. The war corralled a meandering group of anti-Jacksonians into cohesive national party that although riven by sectional and policy differences, maintained enough unity to win two presidential elections in the 1840s. At the same time, the war weeded out reluctant members of the president's camp, leaving behind a devoted collection of Jackson followers that only the slavery question could rip asunder. These hardened groups formed the Second Party System around which American politics would revolve for the next two decades. But perhaps the most long-lasting legacy of the Bank War was its revolutionary recasting of the American presidency. The power Jackson seized and wielded in his fight against the

---

[1] Despite serving as the Whig's *raison d'être*, working a new national bank into the party's main platform was a struggle. Whig presidential candidate William Henry Harrison pronounced during a stump speech ahead of the 1840 election that he was not a bank man but that he would agree to one if Congress demanded it. When John Tyler became president upon Harrison's untimely death, he proved unwilling to follow his predecessor's pledge. The new president would veto two bills chartering a new national bank, demonstrating the varying levels of support within the party to see one created. See, Wilentz, *The Rise of American Democracy*, 504; Watson, *Liberty and Power*, 218.

BUS set new standards of executive authority for future presidents. His willingness to veto a major piece of legislation such as the Bank recharter bill would force Congress to forever consider presidential will when crafting laws. His use of his reelection as a mandate from the people to move forward in crushing the Bank established a direct connection between the people's vote and executive action. By removing Secretary Duane for not acceding to his wishes and replacing him with someone who would, Jackson, despite the occasional legal challenge since, cemented the supremacy of the president over the executive branch and the power of removal as the mechanism to maintain that supremacy. Lastly, by claiming to be the direct representative of the people in his protest message to the Senate, Jackson descended the presidency from its lofty perch as distant ruler of the people and instead became their voice, defender, and champion. Jackson had been accused of expanding presidential power beyond its limits before the Bank War and would continue to draw criticism for the same after. What changed is that before the Bank War, the possibility existed to reel in the chief executive's rapidly growing authority; after Jackson's victory, that possibility all but disappeared.

With a few exceptions, over the next sixty-five years, the White House would be occupied by a series of weaker presidents, unable and or unwilling to take hold of the power Jackson had left for them. But this was not due to a systemic shift backwards to diminish the authority and role of the president; it was due to the individual choices, will, and political views of the men who took the oath of office. Indeed, the power was there for the taking, and those who have had the ability and desire to seize it since have Andrew Jackson and his Bank War to thank.

Final Thoughts

The Senate debates during the "Panic Session," inspired largely by Henry Clay's resolutions, became a final battlefield of the Bank War. While the Bank and its allies suffered defeat after defeat in other theaters, a handful of senators, including some of that body's greatest figures and others who are largely forgotten, stood firmly on its behalf and against the executive power that sought to destroy it. For their efforts, the anti-Jacksonians were rewarded with a new party that would in time, reign supreme, if only briefly, over the country.

Much credit for this seismic change has deservedly been heaped upon the new party's leader, Henry Clay. After all, it was Clay who proposed the resolutions that prompted the debate that produced these momentous results. But while Clay made the proposal, in many ways Samuel Southard articulated the finer points more effectively. Clay and Daniel Webster drew accolades for their captivating orations, but it was Peleg Sprague whose words carried the most vitriolic disgust aimed at the president. Clay and Calhoun both put forth a constitutional argument in refuting Jackson's measures against the Bank, but Thomas Ewing and Theodore Frelinghuysen showcased a stronger command of the details of the Constitution. On the Jacksonian side, Thomas Benton is often, and rightfully, credited with being the president's staunchest ally in the Senate. Yet much of his opening speech was a thrashing of the Bank and it only briefly defended Jackson's actions, as he felt the Senate was not the venue for such discussion. The most articulate defenses of Jackson came from William Rives (who would ironically later join the Whigs), Felix Grundy, and Ether Shepley.

Historic events are rarely driven by the will or actions of one person. History is made by the piecing together of the wills and actions of many, working in concert with and in opposition to the will and actions of others. The Bank War changed the course of American history and the "Panic Session" deserves a significant place in the telling of the war's story. But that story is merely an incomplete fragment, a snapshot, without the words and contributions from all who were involved in what might still be the most tumultuous session ever to take place in the United States Senate.

ACKNOWLEDGEMENTS

As with any book, its realization would not have been possible without the help and support of so many. Those who have cultivated a passion for history within me are numerous, but I would like to take a moment to recognize those whose influence has been most significant.

First, the since deceased Robert McTague from my days as an undergraduate at Fairleigh Dickinson University showed me how gripping history can be when told with the right combination of passion and knowledge. I still remember his lectures starting with handwritten chalk notes in two foot columns from the top left corner of the board and finishing once he ran out of room, without the need to consult notes. It was the most interesting hour and fifteen minutes of my day and instilled in me an understanding that history can be just as compelling as a mystery novel if told the correct way.

While my passion for history was cultivated during my undergraduate years, the honing of my craft as a historian came later as a graduate student at Arizona State University's online program. I would like to thank Calvin Schermerhorn and Peter Van Cleave for their unwavering devotion to their students in general and me specifically. Through their guidance, I was able to develop my raw abilities as a researcher and writer into a more polished form, guidance without which this book would never have been possible. Their advice to bring my work from manuscript to publication has also been invaluable.

Furthermore, I would also like to acknowledge and thank Stephen W. Campbell, a man whom I have never physically met, but who always offered a listening ear to parse through the nuances of banking lingo. His own book, *The Bank War and the Partisan Press*, served not only as a source of information for my work, but as an affirmation that the Bank War is a relevant and important topic to today's readers. He is likely unaware of the impact he has had on my book so I would be remiss if I did not thank him here.

I must also offer my utmost gratitude to the wonderful people at Algora Publishing. I was drawn to the company's reputation for friendliness to first-time authors and I have not been disappointed. The professionalism and care with which they have transformed this work from a computer file into a printed book is commendable and only reinforces that I made the right choice in seeking them out to make my dream of publishing a book come true. My thanks go out to Martin DeMers, Andrea Secara, and all the other kind people at Algora who made this possible.

I feel it is also important to acknowledge the countless people who have spent hours on the too often thankless work of digitizing so many historic documents for the world to access. As much of this book was researched and written during the Covid pandemic, the ability to research extensively from the comfort of my home was critical. I do not envy their work, but I could not have done without it.

That brings me to my family. I always took for granted when people would thank their parents after accomplishing something in life. I believed it was an obvious, almost obligatory thing to say. But as I have aged and have become a parent myself, I have come to appreciate my own, Debbie and Andrew, all the more. They have proven time and again that there is no limit to what they would do for me. I wish I could forever hold onto the moment I told them my book was being published; the joy and proudness they felt was overwhelming. They have made parenting as easy as possible for me, as I simply have to model the example they have worked tirelessly to provide over the last forty years.

I did not grow up in the house alone; my older brother Brian was a fixture in my upbringing as well. I have never met a more humble person than my brother. For someone who has worked so hard to accomplish what he has in life, he refuses to draw attention to himself and only seeks to praise others. Brian has a way of making every one of my accomplishments bigger than they are through the genuine joy he gets in seeing his little brother succeed. In that way, this book is as much his accomplishment as mine and I thank him for his unshakable love and support.

Lastly, and most importantly, I must thank my wife, Kelly, and my two little girls, Addison and Everly. Without them, there would be no acknowledgements to write as there would be no book in which to write them. My girls are far too young to read this book, let alone understand it, but without knowing it, they have inspired me to complete this project so that at some point they may appreciate that their Daddy wrote a book. That leaves my wife. Kelly is the most supportive partner a husband could ask for. Whether it be packing up the girls for the day to give me a quiet space to write or spending her first childless minutes of the night reading over my work, Kelly has been a constant pillar of love and support throughout this process. She is the foundation upon which this book and, our more importantly, our lives are built. I love her with everything I have.

BIBLIOGRAPHY

Government Documents

American State Papers, "An Act to Establish the Treasury Department." 1st Congress, 1st Session: 65.

American State Papers, "An Act to Incorporate the Subscribers to the Bank of the United States." 14th Congress, 1st Session: 266.

American State Papers, "Correspondence Related to Public Deposits." 18th Congress, 1st Session: 501.

Humphrey's Executor v. United States, 295 U.S. 602 (1935).

"Contract Between the Girard Bank & the United States [September 28, 1833]." https://www.historycentral.com/documents/Girard.html.

U.S. Congress. *Annals of Congress.* 1st Congress, 1st Session.

U.S. Congress. *Congressional Globe.* 23rd Congress, 1st Session.

U.S. Congress. *Register of Debates.* 23rd Congress, 1st Session.

U.S. Congress. *Register of Debates.* 23rd Congress, 2nd Session.

U.S. Congress. *Senate Journal.* 23rd Congress, 1st Session.

Books, Articles, and Dissertations

Ayton, Mel. *Plotting to Kill the President: Assassination Attempts from Washington to Hoover.* Potomac Books: Sterling, VA, 2017.

Campbell, Stephen W. *The Bank War and the Partisan Press: Newspapers, Financial Institutions, and the Post Office in Jacksonian America.* Lawrence, KS: University of Kansas Press, 2019.

Catterall, Ralph C. "The Charges Against the Bank," in *Jackson Versus Biddle: The Struggle Over the Second Bank of the United States*, ed. by George Rogers Taylor. Boston: DC Heath and Company, 1949, 36-53.

Catterall, Ralph C. *The Second Bank of the United States*. Chicago: University of Chicago Press, 1902.

Chitwood, Oliver Perry. *John Tyler: Champion of the Old South*. Newtown, CT: American Political Biography Press, 1939.

Claiborne, John Francis Hamtramck. *Mississippi as a Province, Territory, and State: With Biographical Notices of Eminent Citizens* Volume I. Jackson, Mississippi: Power & Barksdale, 1880.

Duckett Alvin Leroy, *John Forsyth, Political Tactician*. Athens, GA; University of Georgia Press, 1962.

Goldman, Perry M. "Political Virtue in the Age of Jackson." *Political Science Quarterly*, 87, no. 1 (March, 1972), 46-62.

Hammond, Bray. *Banks and Politics in America: From the Revolution to the Civil War*. Princeton, NJ: Princeton University Press, 1957.

Howe, Daniel Walker. *What Hath God Wrought: The Transformation of America, 1815–1848*. New York: Oxford University Press, 2007.

Kahan, Paul. *The Bank War: Andrew Jackson, Nicholas Biddle, and the Fight for American Finance*. Yardley, PA: Westholme Publishing, 2016.

Klotter, James. *The Man Who Would Be President*. New York: Oxford University Press, 2016.

Knodell, Jane. "Profit and duty in the Second Bank of the United States' exchange operations." *Financial History Review*, 10, (2003), 5-30.

Loizeau, Pierre-Marie. *Martin Van Buren: The Little Magician*. New York: Nova Science Publishers, Inc., 2008.

Matson, Cathy. "Matthew Carey's Learning Experience: Commerce, Manufacturing, and the Panic of 1819." *Early American Studies: An Interdisciplinary Journal*, 11, no. 3 (Fall 2013), 455-485.

Meacham, Jon. *American Lion: Andrew Jackson in the White House*. New York: Random House, 2009.

Montgomery, William Meigs. *The Life of Thomas Hart Benton*. J.B Lippincott Company: Philadelphia, 1904.

Moore, John L. ed. *Congressional Quarterly's Guide to U.S. Elections*: Third Edition. Washington D.C.: Congressional Quarterly Inc., 1994.

Owen, Thomas M. *History of Alabama and Dictionary of Alabama Biography*, Volume IV. Chicago: S.J. Clarke Publishing Company, 1921.

Peterson, Merrill D. *The Great Triumvirate: Webster, Clay, and Calhoun*. New York: Oxford University Press, 1988.

Redlich, Fritz. *Molding of American Banking: Men and Ideas*. New York: Hafner Publishing Company, 1951.

Remini, Robert V. *Andrew Jackson and the Bank War*. New York: W.W Norton & Company Inc., 1967.

Schlesinger, Jr., Arthur. *The Age of Jackson*. Boston: Little, Brown and Company, 1953.

Simon, James F. *Lincoln and Chief Justice Taney: Slavery, Secession, and the President's War Powers*. New York: Simon & Schuster, 2006.

Swearingen, Mack Buckley. "The Early Life of George Poindexter: A Story of the First Southwest." PhD diss., University of Chicago, 1932.

Temin, Peter. *The Jacksonian Economy*. New York: W.W. Norton & Company, 1969.

Towers, Frank. "The Rise of the Whig Party," in *A Companion to the Era of Andrew Jackson*, ed. Sean Patrick Adams. Somerset: John Wiley & Sons, Inc., 2013, 328-347.

Watson, Harry L. *Liberty and Power: The Politics of Jacksonian America*. New York: Hill and Wang, 2006.

Wilentz, Sean. *The Rise of American Democracy: Jefferson to Lincoln*. New York: W.W. Norton & Company, 2005.

Willis, William. *A History of the Law, the Courts, and the Lawyers of Maine, From its First Colonization to the Early Part of the Present Century*. Portland: Bailey & Noiles, 1863.

Wood, Kirsten E. " 'One Woman So Dangerous to Public Morals,' Gender and Power in the Eaton Affair." *Journal of the Early Republic*, vol. 17 no. 2 (Summer 1997), 237-275.

Published Correspondence, Public Papers, Letters and Memoirs

Bassett, John Spencer and David Maydole Matteson, eds. *Correspondence of Andrew Jackson*: Volume V 1833–1838. Washington D.C.: Carnegie Institution of Washington, 1931, Hathitrust.org.

Duane, William J. *Narrative and Correspondence Concerning the Removal of the Deposites and Occurrences Connected Therewith*. Philadelphia, 1838.

Perley Poore, Benjamin. *Perley's Reminiscences of Sixty Years in the National Metropolis*, Volume I. Philadelphia: Hubbard Brothers, Publishers, 1886.

Seager, Robert II and Melba Porter Hay, eds. *Papers of Henry Clay Volume 8: Candidate, Compromiser, Whig, March 5, 1829 – December 31, 1836.* Lexington, KY: University of Kentucky Press, 1984.

Shanks, Henry Thomas ed. *The Papers of Willie Person Mangum.* Raleigh: NC State Department of Archives and History, 1950.

Shanks, Henry Thomas ed., *The Papers of Willie Person Mangum: Volume II.* Raleigh: NC State Department of Archives and History, 1952.

Thomas Jefferson to John Holmes, April 22, 1820. founders.archives.gov/.

Tyler, Samuel. *Memoir of Roger Brooke Taney, L.L.D.: Chief Justice of the Supreme Court of the United States.* Baltimore: John Murphy & Co., 1872.

Washburn Jr., Israel. "Memoir of Hon. Ether Shepley, LL.D." in *Collections of the Maine Historical Society Volume VIII*, Portland, Hoyt, Fogg, & Donham, 1881.

Newspapers

Alexandria *Gazette.*

Baltimore *Patriot.*

Boston *Post.*

Charleston *Mercury.*

Commercial Advertiser (New York).

The Lancaster Examiner.

National Gazette (Philadelphia).

New Hampshire Patriot and State Gazette.

Philadelphia Gazette.

Portland *Advertiser.*

Richmond *Enquirer.*

Salem *Gazette.*

United States Gazette (Philadelphia).

Index

Figures

3 percents, 124-126, 137, 138

A

Adams, John Quincy, 8, 11, 18, 181
Articles of Confederation, 62

B

bank drafts, 10, 162
Bank War, 2-4, 9-16, 19, 63, 90, 91, 115, 125, 126, 145, 155, 156, 166, 183-189, 191-194
Barings Brothers, 125
Benton, Jesse, 22
Benton, Thomas Hart, 3, 20, 22
Biddle, Nicholas, 8-14, 82, 83, 86, 90, 102, 114, 115, 125, 126, 128-130, 136, 137, 144, 149, 150, 154, 156, 171, 177, 183-185
   as BUS president, 12, 82, 183, 185
   and curtailing loans, 114
Black, John, 19
Blair, Francis P., 40
Board of Directors, 55, 99, 102, 124, 125, 128, 129, 137, 144
Butler, Benjamin, 180

C

Cadwalader, Thomas, 125
Caesar, Julius, 39, 68
Calhoun, John C., 3, 8, 17, 19, 37, 48, 52, 68, 95, 176
   and Bank recharter, 19, 78, 86, 177, 178
   and nullification, 19, 48, 50, 68, 97
censure of Andrew Jackson, 180, 181, 185
   censure expunged, 185
central banking, 2, 3, 9, 19, 28, 166, 170-173, 176, 178, 185
charter of the Second Bank of the United States, 8, 9, 14, 45, 52, 53, 57, 67, 78, 92-94, 97, 100, 102, 108-110, 112, 114, 115, 118, 120-127, 129, 131, 133, 137, 139, 140, 143, 144, 148, 151, 153, 155, 157, 162, 171-174, 176-178, 184
   section sixteen, 43, 45, 48, 57, 78, 92-96, 98, 99, 107
   section fifteen, 53, 131, 133
   section four, 123, 124
   section fourteen, 99
   section thirteen, 140
   section twenty-three, 131
Cheves, Langdon, 10
Clay, Henry, 1, 3, 4, 8, 9, 13, 14, 17, 22, 28, 29, 51, 83, 84, 89, 156, 165, 176, 177, 179, 191

and Bank recharter, 13, 14, 19, 86, 112, 118, 151, 156, 167, 177, 178, 180

and removal of officers, 8, 14, 19, 21, 22, 25-29, 32, 35-37, 40, 43, 51, 54, 57, 59, 62, 71, 72, 81, 83-85, 89-92, 94, 97, 101, 104, 111, 112, 128, 140, 147, 157, 159, 161, 165, 179, 183

and resolutions, 3, 4, 26-28, 44, 83-86, 90-92, 101, 112, 157, 159, 164, 179, 181, 191

Clinton, George, 9

Committee of Finance, 89-92, 115

Congress, authority over the Treasury, 22, 25, 43, 46, 48, 52, 54, 55, 57, 67, 72, 92-94, 98, 100, 102, 103, 105, 120, 133, 161, 165

Congress, role regarding the deposits, 14-17, 21, 22, 25, 27, 43, 45, 48, 49, 52, 54-57, 60, 67, 72, 78, 82, 91-103, 105, 108, 110-115, 120-122, 124, 137, 138, 148, 150, 159, 165, 169, 173, 186

Constitution, the, 3, 16, 18, 20, 21, 24, 27-33, 37, 40, 41, 45, 47, 48, 51, 53, 54, 57, 58, 60, 62, 66, 67, 69, 71-76, 79, 81, 83, 84, 86, 93, 99, 116, 117, 127, 151, 169, 170, 174, 180, 182, 191

Coffee, John, 22

Crawford, William, 26, 94, 100

currency, hard, 122, 167, 168, 185, 186

currency, paper, 2, 10, 14, 167, 168, 171, 187

curtailment, 9, 110, 111, 114, 115

D

Dallas, Alexander J., 160

Deposit Act of 1836, 186

deposit banking (see also pet banks), 146, 161, 185, 187

Dickens, Ashbury, 185

distress, public, 90, 122, 183

Duane, William J., 7, 14, 15

and removal of, 14-16, 21, 25, 27, 35, 36, 71, 76, 77, 79, 82-84, 189

E

electioneering, 11, 128, 144-148, 150, 153-157

election of 1828, 11, 13, 14

election of 1832, 13, 14, 117, 128, 143, 148, 149

as a mandate, 108, 115-117

election of 1836, 14, 19

Ellis, Powhatan, 19

Ewing, Thomas, 3, 20, 36, 45, 55, 65, 66, 73, 89, 113, 168, 191

exchange committee, 125-128, 134-137

F

First Bank of the United States (BUS), 8, 9, 56, 160

First Congress, 60, 75, 82

Force Bill, 18, 49, 105, 165

Forsyth, John, 21, 23, 55, 85, 112, 169

Frelinghuysen, Theodore, 3, 20, 32, 36, 67, 69, 76, 77, 79, 85, 113, 114, 121, 147, 160, 161, 182, 191

French spoliation bill, 126, 137

G

Gallatin, Albert, 56, 61, 120, 161

Gerry, Elbridge, 74

Girard Bank of Philadelphia, 159

government directors (see also public directors), 57, 126-134, 144

exclusion of, 128-130

reports of, 127, 128, 130, 132-134

Grundy, Felix, 3, 21, 39, 46, 47, 55, 191

Gwinn, Samuel, 79

H

Hamilton, Alexander, 8, 11, 47, 56, 74, 75

Harrison, William Henry, 188

Hendricks, William, 180

Hill, Isaac, 21, 63, 89, 114, 119, 135, 162

Holmes, John, 37

House of Representatives, 13, 29, 112

Humphrey's Executor v. The United States, 76

I

impeachment, 24, 29-33, 46, 180

Ingham, Samuel, 102

J

Jackson, Andrew (see also Censure of Andrew Jackson), 1-4, 7-33, 35-40, 43, 45, 47-49, 51, 56-69, 71, 72, 76-80, 82-87, 89, 91, 92, 97-99, 102, 105, 108, 109, 112, 115-120, 122, 124-126, 129, 132-134, 145, 146, 149-154, 156, 159, 165-167, 169, 170, 172-175, 177, 178, 180-189, 191

    cabinet paper, 23, 25, 29, 35, 39

    control over executive officers, 45, 78, 82

    protest message, 22, 85, 126, 180-182, 185, 189

    and usurpation of power, 28-30, 40, 45, 49, 51, 57, 64, 65, 86, 99, 126, 170, 177, 188

Jefferson, Thomas, 8, 15, 37, 63, 181

K

Kant, Immanuel, 75

Kendall, Amos, 26, 40, 109, 146

King, John Pendleton, 171, 180

King, William Rufus, 92

Kitchen Cabinet, 7, 63, 114

L

Lawrence, Richard, 20

Leigh, Benjamin W., 17

Lewis, William, 12

M

McDuffie, George, 103

McLane, Louis, 13, 126

Madison, James, 57, 60, 73-75, 85

Mangum, Willie P., 19, 86

Marbury v. Madison, 57

Marcy, William L., 183

Marshall, John (Chief Justice), 8, 57

Mechanics Bank of New York, 26, 94, 100

Moore, Gabriel, 18, 183

Myers v. The United States, 76

N

National Republican Party, 13, 14, 50, 86, 178, 188

Necker, Jacques, 66

Nichol, Josiah, 12

Nullification Crisis, 18, 19, 48, 68, 97

O

Olmstead, Edward, 154

P

Panic of 1819, 10, 15

Panic Session, 2-4, 21, 183, 191, 192

Peggy Eaton affair, 12, 68, 102

pension payments, suspension of, 99

Poindexter, George, 20, 24, 91, 181

Poindexter, George and break with Jackson, 20

Poindexter, George and Finance Committee resolutions, 92

Preston, William, 20, 130

public deposits, removal of, 8, 14-17, 19, 21, 22, 25, 26, 28, 29, 35, 36, 39, 40, 43, 51, 54, 56, 57, 59, 62, 67, 71, 81, 82, 87, 89-94, 96, 99, 101-105, 107-115, 120, 122, 123, 138-140, 148, 157, 159, 162, 169, 173, 186

public deposits, safety of, 56, 93, 94, 97, 102, 107, 122, 157, 163

R

recharter of the Second Bank of the United States, 11-14, 16, 19, 78, 86, 108, 109, 112-115, 118, 143, 149-151, 153, 156, 167, 169, 172, 177, 178, 180, 184, 188, 189

    recharter in 1832, 13, 14, 19, 109, 112, 118, 143, 149, 178

    recharter by Daniel Webster, 13, 86, 115, 169, 172, 177, 178, 180, 184

removal of officers, 71, 77

Riddle, John S., 154

Rives, William, 41, 44, 49, 52, 69, 72, 138, 167, 174, 191

Robbins, Asher (Judge and Senator), 30

Rules and Regulations for Conducting the Business of the Bank of the United States, 134

S

Second Party System, 188

Senate, 1, 3, 4, 9, 11, 13, 15, 17-33, 35-69, 71-86, 89-92, 96, 98-105, 111-122, 124, 128-141, 145-157, 159-175, 177, 179-183, 185, 189, 191, 192

Senate Finance Committee, 11, 131, 135, 140, 147, 148

Shepley, Ether, 3, 21, 37, 38, 41, 82, 191

Smith, Samuel, 11

Smith, William Loughton, 74

Southard, Samuel, 3, 20, 30, 54, 77, 111, 134, 149, 182, 191

specie, 10, 100-102, 110, 147, 150, 160, 161, 168, 174, 177, 187

Specie Circular, 187

speculation, 9, 82, 165, 185-187

spoils system, 18, 69, 165, 166

Sprague, Peleg, 3, 20, 47, 65, 75, 103, 182, 191

state banks, 9, 10, 14, 21, 26, 27, 51-56, 67, 78, 94, 100, 101, 108-110, 113, 146, 150, 159-168, 175, 183, 186, 188

Story, Joseph, 31

T

Tallmadge, Nathaniel, 3, 20, 31, 32, 39, 42, 47, 61, 62, 75, 76, 99, 102, 112, 119, 155, 156, 163, 164, 172, 186

Taney, Roger B., 7

    reasons for removing deposits, 107, 108, 114, 138

    report to Congress, 21-23, 26, 89-92, 100, 104, 126, 137, 149

tariffs, 9, 19, 48, 49

Tariff of Abominations, 48

Treasurer of the United States, 55, 56, 159

Treasurer duties of, 42, 54, 55

Treasury of the United States and who controls it, 62, 77, 79, 146, 165

Treasury Department, 12, 14, 16, 40-43, 45, 51, 52, 54, 55, 71, 98, 144

Treasury, executive versus legislative in function, 28, 30, 40, 43-45, 56, 61, 68, 107

Treasury and naming controversy, 41-43, 132, 144

Tucker, Josiah, 149

Tyler, John, 16, 18, 19, 36, 46, 67, 68, 77, 89, 103-105, 166, 169, 170, 174, 188

    on precedent, 103-105

    and usurpation of power, 46, 170, 188

    and usurpation by Andrew Jackson, 170

    and usurpation by Roger Taney, 16, 46, 103, 105

V

Van Buren, Martin, 1, 2, 18, 19, 21, 28, 91, 92, 145, 186

veto of Bank recharter bill, 13, 14, 16, 40, 65, 66, 69, 78, 109, 111, 114, 115, 118, 119, 188, 189

W

Walker, Robert J., 19

War of 1812, 2, 9, 22, 61, 160

Washington, George, 2, 5, 7, 8, 20, 28, 30, 63, 69, 83, 86, 126

Webster, Daniel, 3, 13, 17, 25, 28, 89, 92, 96, 119, 169, 171, 184, 191

Webster and his bill to recharter the BUS, 140, 169, 171, 173, 175-177

Whig Party, 14, 19, 32, 49, 50, 86, 105, 183-188, 191

Wilkins, William, 3, 21, 28, 29, 39, 41, 42, 55, 56, 60, 62, 63, 69, 82, 83, 89, 99, 113, 117, 131, 132, 149, 155, 161, 162

Willis, N.P., 164

Wolf, George, 183

Woodbury, Levi, 80, 186

Wright, Silas, 20, 31, 62, 90, 172, 175

Printed in the United States
by Baker & Taylor Publisher Services